The Oregon Literature Series

General Editor: George Venn
Managing Editor: Ulrich H. Hardt

Volume 6: Oregon Letters and Diaries

A project of the Oregon Council of Teachers of English

The Oregon Literature Series

The World Begins Here: An Anthology of Oregon Short Fiction
        Glen A. Love
Many Faces: An Anthology of Oregon Autobiography
        Stephen Dow Beckham
Varieties of Hope: An Anthology of Oregon Prose
        Gordon B. Dodds
From Here We Speak: An Anthology of Oregon Poetry
        Primus St. John & Ingrid Wendt
The Stories We Tell: An Anthology of Oregon Folk Literature
        Suzi Jones & Jarold Ramsey
Talking on Paper: An Anthology of Oregon Letters & Diaries
        Shannon Applegate & Terence O'Donnell

Talking on Paper
An Anthology of Oregon Letters and Diaries

Shannon Applegate & Terence O'Donnell

Oregon State University Press
Corvallis, Oregon

Cover art: Detail of Quilt, ca. 1876. More information on page xvi.
Cover design: John Bennett
Text design: Jo Alexander
Permissions: Susanne Shotola
Art photographer: Susan Seubert

Library of Congress Cataloging-in-Publication Data
Talking on paper : an anthology of Oregon letters and diaries / [edited by]
Shannon Applegate & Terence O'Donnell
    p. cm. — (Oregon literature series ; v. 6)
    Includes bibliographical references (p.) and index.
    ISBN 0-87071-377-9. — ISBN 0-87071-378-7 (paper)
    1. American letters—Oregon. 2. American diaries—Oregon. 3. Oregon—
Biography. I. Applegate, Shannon. II. O'Donnell, Terence. III. Series.
CT256.T35 1994
920.0795—dc20   94-27826
                                                         CIP

Acknowledgments

Without steady collaboration by many individuals, agencies, and institutions, the *Oregon Literature Series* would never have appeared in print. We wish to recognize those who contributed support, time, and resources here—more or less in the order in which their contributions were received—and knowing even now that the real evidence of our gratitude lies open before all of them.

In 1986, the Executive Committee of the Oregon Council of Teachers of English (OCTE) began to discuss the idea of publishing a collection of Oregon literature. We wish to identify the members of that Executive Committee and thank them for their pioneering role: Lauri Crocker, Joe Fitzgibbon, Robert Hamm, Ulrich Hardt, Michelann Ortloff, and Ed Silling. Under then-OCTE President Ulrich Hardt, the Publications Committee was given the goal to further develop the idea of a state-based literary collection.

In 1988-89, the Executive Board of OCTE approved the pilot study by George Venn which became the *Oregon Literature Series.* We would like to recognize the members of that distinguished professional group of teachers by listing them here: Brian Borton, Sister Helena Brand, Suzanne Clark, Darlene Clarridge, Elaine Cockrell, Edna De Haven, Joe Fitzgibbon, Robert Boyt Foster, David Freitag, Debra Gaffney, Tim Gillespie, Irene Golden, Robert Hamm, Ulrich H. Hardt, Martha House, Ilene Kemper, Debbie LaCroix, Bill Mull, Thomas Nash, Debby Norman, Michelann Ortloff, Phyllis Reynolds, Eldene Ridinger, Mei-Ling Shiroishi, Andy Sommer, Daune Spritzer, Kim Stafford, Lana Stanley, Kathy Steward, Paul Suter, Nathaniel Teich, Linda Vanderford, George Venn, Michael Wendt, and Barbara Wolfe. Many members of that board gave many extra hours to reviewing the design, editorial guidelines, rationale, and budgets for that pilot project and other documents.

We would also like to acknowledge the following individuals from Oregon's literary and humanities community who reviewed the pilot proposal, made valuable suggestions, and gave their endorsement in 1988 to the idea of a collection of the best Oregon writing: Richard Lewis, Oregon Council for the Humanities; Brian Booth, Oregon Institute of Literary Arts; Peter Sears, Oregon Arts Commission; Jo Alexander, Oregon State University Press; Bruce Hamilton, Oregon Historical Society. OCTE President in 1988, Tim Gillespie, and Joe Fitzgibbon, OCTE President Elect, also reviewed the pilot proposal and made important contributions not only in these early stages but throughout the project.

When we presented the completed proposal for the *Oregon Literature Series* to the Editorial Board of Oregon State University Press in 1989, they broke with all precedent by signing a guaranteed publication contract and by agreeing to turn over editorial control of the content of the *Oregon Literature Series* to OCTE editors and appointees. We want to thank both press editors, Jeff Grass and Jo Alexander, and the members of that board who voted unanimously in favor of this project: Pat Brandt, Larry Boersma, Richard Maxwell Brown, Bill Denison, Gordon Dodds, Mike Strelow, Dave Perry, Sandy Ridlington, and the late Marilyn Guin. Without their vote for collaboration and its implicit vote of confidence in us, we would have found it difficult to continue this project.

Our first financial support beyond OCTE was provided by a pilot grant from Eastern Oregon State College, School of Education. Specifically, we wish to thank Deans Jens Robinson, Gerald Young, and James Hottois for their willingness to grant a sabbatical and three years of part-time appointments to George Venn so that this project could be undertaken. At Portland State University, we want to thank Dean Robert

Everhart, School of Education, for his steadfast support. He granted Ulrich Hardt a sabbatical to help launch the project, and he continued that support throughout the four years of the project. At Portland State University, we also want to acknowledge Interim Provost Robert Frank and Provost Michael Reardon for the faith they showed in the project by assigning graduate assistant Susanne Shotola to help us.

When we drafted our "Call for Editors" in 1989, we received helpful critiques from Kim Stafford, Edwin Bingham, Paul Suter, Sister Helena Brand, Edna DeHaven, Daune Spritzer, Lana Stanley, Michelann Ortloff, as well as other members of the OCTE Executive Board. When it was time to mail that "Call for Editors" to all Oregon libraries, newspapers, and other regional and national media, Lana Stanley assisted us. When it was time to select Volume Editors, these Publications Committee members assisted us: Robert Hamm, Marti House, Ilene Kemper, Debbie LaCroix, Mei-Ling Shiroishi, Michael Wendt, and Linda Vanderford. We'd like to thank them for the many hours they gave to evaluating the applications of 130 highly qualified individuals from Oregon and across the U.S. who applied for or were nominated for editorships.

When we needed to verify that these anthologies would, indeed, be both needed and used in the public schools, Portland State University School of Business Administration faculty member Bruce Stern gave us important assistance in designing a survey instrument which demonstrated a clear demand for the *Oregon Literature Series* in Oregon schools and homes. When we needed public relations expertise during editorial appointments, Pat Scott in the Portland State University Public Relations Office provided it.

When we needed legal advice, Leonard DuBoff and his firm of Warren, Allan, King, and O'Hara were more than helpful in contributing their contractual expertise.

As the project began to take a clear and definite shape in 1989, we received formal endorsements from these individuals whose confidence in the project made it possible to continue in spite of meager funding: Wes Doak, Oregon State Librarian, and Director, Center for the Book; Brian Booth, Director of Oregon Institute of Literary Arts; Kim Stafford, Director of the Northwest Writing Institute at Lewis and Clark College; Jennifer Hagloch, President of the Oregon Museums Association; Richard Lewis, Executive Director, Oregon Council for the Humanities; Joanne Cowling, President of the Eastern Oregon Library Association; Leslie Tuomi, Executive Director of the Oregon Arts Commission; Peter Sears, Oregon Arts Commission; Michael K. Gaston, President, Oregon Library Association; John Erickson, State Superintendent of Public Instruction; Carolyn Meeker, Chair, Oregon Arts Commission; Carolyn Lott, Chair, National Council of Teachers of English (NCTE) Committee on Affiliates; Shirley Haley-James, president-elect of NCTE; William Stafford, Oregon's past poet laureate; and Terry Melton, Director of the Western States Arts Foundation.

Essential financial support after 1989 came first from a generous allocation by the OCTE Executive Board. Later, we received modest one-time contributions from the Oregon Center for the Book and the Jackson Foundation. We would also like to state that this project was made possible—in part—by two minor grants from the Oregon Arts Commission.

Our sustaining patrons in the final three years (1990-93) of the project have been five; each of them contributed amounts in five figures so that the *Oregon Literature Series* could be completed in a timely and professional manner: (1) the OCTE Executive Board, who sustained and underwrote us when regional foundations failed us; (2) the Oregon Council for the Humanities, an affiliate of the National Endowment for the Humanities, which made and honored an exemplary three-year commitment ably administered by Robert Keeler; however, no funds from NEH or OCH were used to support volume 5, Oregon Folk Literature; (3) the National Endowment for the Arts, Literature Program, which assisted us at a time when we had been sent begging by all but one of the private foundations in Oregon; (4) Portland State University, which granted multi-year support for graduate assistant Susanne Shotola to help with the many details of the publication of this six-volume series; (5) Oregon State University Press, where Jo Alexander and Jeff Grass contributed the vital tasks agreed to in 1989—designing, printing, and distributing these volumes. OSU Press set a national precedent by becoming the first university press in the United States to publish a multi-volume, comprehensive collection of a state's literature in the same state as the university press.

When we came to recommending graphics and cover designs for the *Oregon Literature Series* in 1992, we welcomed the generous and expert advice of three of Oregon's most knowledgeable art historians: Ron Crosier, Portland Public Schools; Gordon Gilkey, Curator, Portland Art Museum; and Nancy Lindburg, arts consultant and former staff member of the Oregon Arts Commission. Some of the works they recommended were selected by them from the slide inventory in Oregon's Percent for Art in Public Places Program. Other works were chosen from the Gordon and Vivian Gilkey Collection of Prints and Drawings at the Oregon Art Institute, and from the Institute's collection of photographs. Petroglyph images were provided by James L. Hansen from sites flooded by The Dalles dam. In addition to those three individuals, we were also fortunate to attract the services of John Bennett, book designer and publisher at Gardyloo Press in Corvallis, who collaborated on all features of the graphic design, and created covers for these volumes.

No literary project of this magnitude can be accomplished without skillful and reliable staff. We would like to express our profound appreciation to Susanne Shotola and Barbara Wiegele—both of Portland State University—for their patient, professional, and timely attention to thousands of pages of details during the past four years: keeping accurate records, handling all permissions and finances, doing all the copying, typing, and mailing. Thanks also to Gayle Stevenson of the OSU Press for all her hard work. We thanked them during the project and here we want to thank them again.

Unfortunately, this naming of our benefactors will be incomplete. We cannot list here all of those writers, families, and institutions who waived permissions fees, those innumerable librarians, archivists, storytellers, and historians who have safeguarded many of these pieces of writing for more than 100 years, those many who sent us notes of encouragement, those members of the public press who considered this project worthy of coverage. What we can say, however, is that every contribution moved us one page closer to the volume you now hold in your hands. Those others who failed us when we needed them most—they may eat—well?—cake?

Finally, George Venn would like to thank his wife, Elizabeth, who has tolerated great financial sacrifice for four years and who has begun to wonder about this tough, miserly Oregon muse her husband seems to have been serving at the expense of his art and her budget. Also, Ulrich Hardt would like to thank his wife, Eleanor, for her insights and interest in this project as Social Studies Specialist for Portland Public Schools, and for being more patient than could have been expected and tolerant of being alone many evenings and weekends while he was occupied with editorial responsibilities.

Ulrich Hardt, Managing Editor *George Venn, General Editor*
Portland State University *Grande Ronde Valley, Oregon*
Portland and Stuttgart
September 1992

Editors' Acknowledgments

Talking on Paper has been a collaborative venture from the beginning. George Venn, General Editor, and Ulrich Hardt, Managing Editor, gave direction, concrete advice, and steady support that has brought this volume safely into port. We also thank Susanne Shotola and Barbara Wiegele for their attention to detail, patience, and good humor throughout a sometimes exasperating process.

One of the most edifying and satisfying aspects of this project has been the stimulating exchange among nine volume editors—named elsewhere—through a cycle of meetings. We listened, then acted upon their specific suggestions. We gratefully acknowledge their assistance. Our advisory committee—Linda Danielson, Nathan Douthit, Jodi Varon, Kathy Steward, Robert Tuttle, and Kim Stafford—offered numerous suggestions and provided invaluable perspectives as they waded through thick manuscript drafts at various stages. Jodi Varon and her student, Ying-Ju Chen, provided excellent translations of several letters in the Kam Wah Chung collection.

Several individuals made important recommendations regarding the volume. James Maguire of Boise State University tendered much useful advice inspired by his own experiences editing an Idaho literary anthology. Brian Booth, expert on regional literature, was especially helpful. Advisory board member Nathan Douthit provided an excellent overview at a critical juncture in the project.

Alerted to our special interest in unpublished letters and diaries, librarians assisted us in myriad ways. We wish to thank the following librarians, their staffs, and their indefatigable volunteers: Aletha Bonebrake and Pearl Jones, Baker County Library; Fred Reenstjerna, Douglas County Museum Library; David Hutchinson, Douglas County Library. Fraser Cox, former curator of Special Collections, University of Oregon Library, provided enthusiastic early support. Vicki Jones and Will Harmon of the University of Oregon Library patiently helped during all phases of the project and should be commended. Recently retired librarians Marty West, Lane County Museum, and Irene Helms, Crook County Museum, provided numerous sources. Theresa Bragg, Malheur County Library, Peg Sitz, Harney County Library, Peg Bermel, Deschutes County Library, and Bonnie Wagner, Port Orford Library brought many local letters and diaries to our attention. Other institutions to which we are indebted include public libraries in Albany, Astoria, and Brownsville, county libraries in Hood River County and Multnomah County, university libraries at Willamette, Oregon State, Portland State, and Pacific, and the official public libraries—the Oregon State Library, Oregon State Archives, and the Oregon Historical Society Library and Museum, where we were assisted by Kris White and Patricia Koehler. We would also like to thank Richard Engeman at the University of Washington, and Guila Ford, Elizabeth Jaycox, and Linda Morton-Keithley at the Idaho Historical Society.

The extraordinary cooperation of numerous museum and county historical society (HS) directors and their staffs, members, and volunteers greatly expedited all phases of our work. While space prevents our giving full names of organizations and institutions, we wish to acknowledge the zeal and concientiousness of the following individuals: Carol Harbison and Steve Wyant, Southern Oregon HS; Carol Micnhimer, Kam Wah Chung Museum; Bob Boyd, High Desert Museum; Patricia McMillan, Klamath County Museum; Ellen Stull and Grace Williams, Oliver Museum; Ann Deering, Union County Museum; Sharon Jones, Harney County Museum; Anne Witty, Columbia River Maritime Museum; Ilea Jones, Malheur County HS; James Beer, Wasco County HS; Karen

Broenneke, Clatsop County HS; Margaret S. Carey, Linn County HS; Patricia Cornett, Hood River County HS; Fred Detering, Polk County HS; Wayne Jensen, Tillamook County HS; Sherry Kaseberg, Sherman County HS; Bill Lewis, Benton County HS; Bob Monaghan, Clackamas County HS; Eric Olsen, Marion County HS; Marilyn Poole, Lincoln County HS; Lucy Skjelstad, Horner Museum; Joan Smith, Washington County HS; Ruth Stoller, Yamhill County HS; Marsha Sweek, Morrow County HS; Rob Wilson, Columbia County HS. Charlotte Pendleton, former curator of Schminck House, Lakeview, provided sources and transcription for a collection of letters represented in this volume.

Authors Mike Hanley, Eugene Luckey, Keith and Donna Clark, Jerry Gildermeister, Jack Evans, Helen Parks, Kathryn Hall Bogle, Helen Fretwell-Johnson, and Judith Austin of *Idaho Yesterdays* were helpful and informative. Professors Thomas Edwards, Edwin Bingham, Michael Arthur Weiss, and Michael Kowalewski generously shared their own research.

Numerous individuals were consulted on specific topics. Among those who pinpointed sources and provided crucial historical context and/or materials concerning various public agencies, policies, organizations, and regions are the following: Stephen R. Mark, Crater Lake National Park; Gerald Williams, U.S. Forest Service; Forrest Cameron, Malheur National Wildlife Refuge; Jeff Thomas, Mazama Club; Sue Waldron, southern Oregon; Grace Bartlett, northeast Oregon. We wish to thank Brian Johnson of the Waldo family for access to his family's unpublished letters and diaries, particularly those of Judge John Waldo. Special thanks to the late Robert Beebe, Portland, and to Jack Steiwer, Fossil. Also, during the research phase of this project, many people offered guidance and identified little-known sources. We are grateful for suggestions from Robert Tuttle, Frances Van Landrum, the late Eddy Fisher, William Kaatz, the late Marcus Haines, Br. Daniel of St. Benedict's Lodge, Philip Lothian, Nellie Zook, Georgia Gallagher, Joan Maiers, and Eleanor Hardt.

Dozens of Oregon families opened their doors and revealed their treasures to us. Some of their names appear in our headnotes or bibliography. In addition, we want to thank the following for their generosity: Diane and Bob Elder, Harold and Aranka Trenkel, Pat Quast, Anthony and Renie Yturri, Mildred Jones, Bob Skinner and family, Barbara Haines, Jeanne Macbeth, Alice and Dan Warnock, Dale and Lu Johnson, Mike and Tom Carstensen.

Shannon Applegate wishes to express her gratitude to her friend, Penny Anderson, who for three long years provided office space, typing, transcriptions, and proof-reading coupled with critical judgment and empathy without limit. Lorraine Stockton, Rebecca Holmes, Rose Mabel, Mildred Karlin, and Rosemary Spires also volunteered their services as tireless transcribers of difficult-to-read texts. Charlotte Applegate and Susan Applegate were patient proof-readers. Daniel Robertson, Shannon's husband, encouraged her throughout her efforts, understood the need for a series of journeys to gather letters and diaries, and graciously took in stride all manner of disruptions to the rhythms of family life associated with her work on this project. Terence O'Donnell wishes to thank Gabriele Sperling, Vancouver, for her research assistance. Both editors also are grateful for the work of Thomas Gerard McNamee, Enterprise, who compiled the joint bibliography and for the excellent work of indexer Jean Brownell.

Finally, Jo Alexander of Oregon State University Press deserves six resounding cheers—one for each volume in the *Oregon Literature Series*! Long may she wave.

Shannon Applegate, Yoncalla
Terence O'Donnell, Portland

Contents

List of Art

Quilt, ca. 1876? (detail on front cover of paperback edition)

Cotton, muslin, red and blue calico, black sateen. 76 x 99 inches. Hand sewn and quilted. Design in squares is an eight-pointed star with a larger star around it. Binding is pale red or pink (faded). Backing is muslin.

The quilt was donated to the Benton County Historical Museum by John Lawrence (formerly Longbottom), great-grandson of Kezia Belknap and Chatman Hawley, who crossed the plains to Oregon in 1848, when their daughter, Sarah, was eight years old. When Sarah Hawley was eighteen, she married Squire Rycraft, whose family had arrived in the Northwest in 1852 and who was considerably older.

There is no clear indication as to who made the quilt. John Lawrence's mother, Mildred, told him that her parents—Sarah and Squire Rycraft—had brought it across the plains, but this is not supported by the family history noted above. Perhaps Sarah's parents brought the quilt and gave it to her on the occasion of her marriage. However, quilt historian Mary Cross has suggested that it was made around the Centennial of the U.S. in 1876, in which case it is likely that Sarah Hawley herself made it. A granddaughter, Hazel McNeill, said, "Grandma always had a quilt on the frame."

General Introduction

The idea for the *Oregon Literature Series*, six anthologies of the best Oregon writing, was first proposed to the Oregon Council of Teachers of English (OCTE) in 1988. At that time, OCTE decided to depart from the conventional state literary anthology—a monolithic tome put together by a few academic volunteers and generally intended for libraries and adult readers. Instead, OCTE decided to create six shorter, genre-based anthologies: prose, poetry, autobiography, folk literature, letters and diaries, and short fiction. OCTE would publish a public "Call for Editors," and the most qualified individuals would be hired for their expertise and treated professionally—honoraria, expenses, research assistance, travel, etc. The anthologies would be intended as classroom/reference texts for students and teachers, and as introductory readers for the general public. Books would be designed to be easily held, carried, and read.

Numerous arguments were raised against this innovative proposal—most of them signaling Oregon's 150-year status as a literary colony. *No one had ever done this before. Oregon's literature was non-existent. There wasn't much writing of merit. Most scholars and critics have ignored Oregon literature—even in the best histories of Western literature. There's no literary history of Oregon. It will take years to find this work. In Oregon, literature has the least financial support of all the major arts. We had no publisher. It might rain.*

Nevertheless, in 1989, Ulrich Hardt and I were appointed by OCTE to complete the *Oregon Literature Series*. The work began when we signed a publication contract with Oregon State University Press, our first and most important professional collaborator. Next, from a pool of 130 applicants, OCTE chose these editors to discover Oregon's literary heritage: Shannon Applegate, Stephen Dow Beckham, Gordon B. Dodds, Primus St. John, Suzi Jones, Glen A. Love, Terence O'Donnell, Jarold Ramsey, and Ingrid Wendt. Appointed in August 1990, those individuals began the search for Oregon writing that eventually spread beyond every corner of the state—from ranch houses to university archives, from oral storytellers in longhouses to Chinese miners in museums, from Desdemona Sands to Burns. Some editors traveled thousands of miles. Others corresponded with hundreds of authors. Most read thousands of pages. Poets, historians, folklorists, critics, scholars, teachers, and editors—they all benefited from and shared their research expertise. Even though honoraria were small, editors gave generously of their time. While the editors looked for Oregon writing, Ulrich Hardt and I sought out and received endorsements from many major cultural and arts organizations. Financial support was like rain in the time of drought, but we attracted a few wise, faithful, and generous patrons, as the Acknowledgments record.

Once the editors had discovered this vast, unstudied, and unknown body of writing, they assembled their manuscripts by using the following guidelines—guidelines that required them to choose writing—in its broadest sense—that might reveal the Oregon experience to both students and the public:

1. The volume must include a representative sample of the best Oregon writing from all periods, regions, occupations, genders, genres and sub-genres, ethnic, religious, political, and cultural backgrounds.

2. Oregon birth should not be used as a single criterion for inclusion. Oregon residence is important, but no arbitrary length of stay is required for a writer to be included.

3. Works about experience in Oregon are preferred, but editors are not limited to that criterion alone.

4. "Oregon" will be defined by its changing historical boundaries—Native American tribal territories, Spanish, Russian, British, U.S. Territory, statehood.

5. One or more translations and original from non-English languages should be included when appropriate to show that linguistic multiplicity has always been a part of Oregon.

6. Controversial subjects such as sexism and racism should not be avoided. Multiple versions of events, people, and places should be included when available.

7. Length of works must vary; limit the number of snippets when possible. Meet the need for diversity in reading, from complex to simple.

8. New, unknown, or unpublished work should be included.

9. Works will be edited for clarity but not necessarily for correctness. Editors may invent titles, delete text, and select text as appropriate and with appropriate notation.

Once assembled in draft, most of these manuscripts were two to three times longer than could be published by Oregon State University Press, therefore much fine writing had to be omitted, which all editors and our publisher regret. After being reduced to the requisite size, the manuscripts passed through two separate reviews: first, a different Advisory Board for each volume read and rated all selections; second, the Editorial Board composed of all fellow editors read, responded, and eventually voted to adopt the manuscript for publication. At all stages, both Ulrich Hardt and I worked closely with editors in many ways: readers, critics, fundraisers, administrators, arbitrators, secretaries, grant writers, researchers, coordinators, pollsters.

Now, we hope that these books will create for Oregon literature a legitimate place in Oregon schools and communities, where the best texts that celebrate, invent, evaluate, and illuminate the Oregon condition have been invisible for too long. Here, for the first time, students will have books that actually include writing by Oregonians; teachers can find original, whole, local, and authentic texts from all regions, periods, and peoples in the state; librarians will be able to recommend the best reading to their patrons; the new reader and the general reader can find answers to the question that has haunted this project like a colonial ghost: "Who are Oregon's writers, anyway?"

Let it be known that an Oregon literary canon is forming—rich, diverse, compelling. Here we give this sample of it to you. Let your love of reading and writing endure.

George Venn, General Editor
Grande Ronde Valley, Oregon
September 1992

Editors' Introduction

I. Preface

In 1990, Terence O'Donnell and I faced a huge task: we had to find and evaluate the millions of Oregon letters and thousands of Oregon diaries written between 1830 and 1990. This would be no small or simple task. As a first step, we divided Oregon into two unequal geographic but equal demographic areas: I would investigate the large archive of the Special Collections at the University of Oregon, and I would also search in smaller archives, museums, ranches, homes, and libraries in remote, rural Oregon. So, with a small copy machine, a hundred feet of extension cord, and a miniature office in my Dodge van, I visited the southeastern corner, the green craggy northeast, the vast basin and range, the luminous lake country, the tilting high desert plateaus. In two years I logged about 8,000 Oregon miles. While I was on the road, Terence O'Donnell would research the northwest quadrant with half of Oregon's present population and more than half of the population in the nineteenth century— Willamette Valley, Columbia River corridor, north coast. He also searched in the Oregon Historical Society archives and publications—a major source.

What did we find? My research uncovered a surprising number of letters and diaries among remote ranches, homes, and small institutions. In fact, about half of the thirty-three diaries published herein have seen only limited, local audiences, or have been read only by the families or individuals who preserved them in shoe boxes or paper-lined drawers. Also, letters and diaries found by both of us in this collection came—as they should—from published works by William Clark (1814), Sarah Winnemucca Hopkins (1883), Alice Day Pratt (1922), Judge Matthew Deady (1975), William Sullivan (1985), and others. Finally, we both found immense quantities of material in the two institutions named earlier, whose archives contain thousands of letters and diaries, and in the county historical societies and museums. In all, there was just too much to publish. However, the full scope of our research is presented in the bibliography.

Once we discovered and selected these texts, Terence O'Donnell and I agreed to publish excerpts from newly discovered texts without correcting or editing. We made this decision because it is good scholarship, and because diarists have the right to their own language. We retained the idiomatic homebrew of spellings such as "nocked out his brains" and "valueable artickles" in the journal of Elizabeth Dixon Smith (1847). When Robert Haswell (1788) writes, "I had given posative orders to our people not to fier . . ." we did not correct him. To be consistent, we have deleted most of the bracketed material and notes in published works by previous editors who may have felt the need to clean up the texts. We wanted to preserve what Henry Thoreau spoke of as "presentness" or "greenness," which gives character and interest to diaries and letters.

In spite of this commitment to authenticity, we still made a few changes in these texts: we added white space to clarify sentence boundaries; we standardized the dating and format in diaries and letters; we gave the first year of a diary entry, then left the year out until a new year; in letters, we used the basic form of the original, but rearranged or deleted parts of them, e.g., we simply couldn't publish an entire 26-page letter about the first known ascent of Mt. Jefferson by whites. Consistent with the rest of the *Oregon Literature Series*, we generally have not indicated our omissions with ellipsis points. In diaries, we excerpted enough to show the diarist's style and situation, but readers are always encouraged to consult the original as listed in our bibliography.

Our next step was finding a way to structure our voluminous materials. Again, we agreed to divide Oregon—this time into its most well-known geographical regions: Eastside and Westside. We then arranged the materials for each subregion chronologically, usually by date of composition. By using this design, we intend to highlight regional differences and similarities. For instance, Preston Gillette's 1860 journal from Astoria shows that he visited and traded with a friendly Chinook hunter, while Julia Gilliss's 1866 letters from Fort Dalles record the slaughter of Native Americans in southeast Oregon. To frame the selections, we gave each a title.

With these responsibilities divided, Terence O'Donnell and I made a last division: even though we both found, worked on, shared, and present both kinds of texts in this collection, I would write a brief introductory essay for diaries (Part II), and he would write the same for Oregon letters (Part III).—S.A.

II. Introducing Oregon Diaries: A Dialogue

Over the years, critics have not been kind when evaluating the efforts of Oregon diarists. In 1948, for instance, scholar H.B. Nelson wrote: "There is no more reason for regarding the diaries (and) journals of the early settlers as literature than there is to regard a windmill a steam engine" (Nelson 82). Thus, I may reasonably start by raising a frequently asked question:

"Are Oregon diaries literature with a capital "L"?

No, not in any narrow canonical sense. However, these thirty-three examples are rich in literature's most essential trace elements: careful observation, idiosyncratic voice, revelation of interior life, a quest for emotional insight and integrity, a mix of image and statement, original language, dramatic immediacy, a sense of place, character, voice, risk, adventure, and story. Diaries can have the dramatic suspense of mystery novels in which resolutions are only gradually revealed. In this collection, the poignant 1972-73 diary of thirteen-year-old cancer victim, Nora Longoria, a Mexican-American schoolgirl from Nyssa, Oregon, leads the reader to an implied tragic ending. Reading Judge Deady's 1871 diary immediately draws the reader into his amazing Portland social life. From Shaniko, consider Mary McKinley's description of her hard-luck life "in a five-cent house out of a nine o'clock town." Places, people, and events come alive in such writing—rural and urban, dry and wet, east or west of the Cascade Range.

"Do people who write diaries intend them as literature—is that their purpose?"

No, not intentionally—with some exceptions. The reasons and circumstances for keeping diaries are extremely complex and varied. Some are traditional: to prevent forgetting during daily routines, to develop writing skills, to do personal accounting, to gain self-knowledge anywhere, to relive the past, to find the release of solitary confession. In this volume, Emily Trevett (1894) identifies some of these better-known purposes:

> As a child I was trained to [keep a diary] & I dare say it did me both good and harm, good in teaching me to express myself easily in writing, harm in as much as it led me to pay too much attention to my own ideas and feelings. During the last eight years, since leaving school, there has been a great deal of nonsense written in my so called journals & much of it deserves a very hot fire, but in beginning again it is with the determination of doing an entirely different kind of writing. Reading George Eliot's life has given me the idea of it. She notes down the most interesting events of her life regularly, with simplicity & sincerity. Sometimes she expresses her feelings without sentimentality or exaggeration. It is evidently written neither for posterity nor for her friends but for herself. I rite so much to my friends never to return to me that it will be good to keep some record for my own future pleasure.

Others purposes include "self-improvement," a tradition made popular by the published works of Benjamin Franklin, and found here in the diary of Lane County inventor and gadfly, Henry Cummins (1858). Diarists such as Haswell (1788), Clark (1805), Douglas (1826), Glover (1875), and Sullivan (1985) participate in the Hakluyt Society tradition—recording their journeys of exploration and discovery for civilization. Writing as she crosses the plains to Oregon, Elizabeth Wood represents the nineteenth-century emigrant tradition in this collection, a diary type later gathered and studied in the monumental *Covered Wagon Women: Diaries and Letters from the Western Trails: 1840-1890* (1983) by Kenneth Holmes and in Lilliam Schlissel's *Women's Diaries of the Westward Journey* (1982). Haralambos Kambouris (1914), a Greek emigrant railroad worker and poet, represents the emigrant diary tradition continuing in the twentieth century. For Oregon poets and prose writers, the diary has served as a place to gather rough materials for later autobiographical books: Whiteley's *The Story of Opal* (1920), Pratt's *A Homesteader's Portfolio* (1922), and Sullivan's *Listening for Coyote* (1988) all began as diaries under isolated and remote circumstances. Diaries also serve their writers as places to order, understand, and survive major change: the challenge of adolescence, as in the diaries here of teenagers Grace McCrary (1899) and Robert Keyes (1922); the challenge of some new role, as in Linus Pauling's preparations for college (1917) or in the diary of fire lookout Cindy Donnelly Fairchild (1973). Diaries may also begin and end because of a particular life crisis or emotion—loneliness, marriage, war, death. Sr. Miriam Murphy (1981), a painter and Marylhurst nun frustrated by a feeling of waning creativity, began her Intensive Journal when she was in her seventies. When chaos needs the order which language can give to experience, diaries get written.

"What kinds of people keep diaries?"

There are no easy stereotypes here. Many diarists are amateur writers, many are not. As novelist and critic William Maxwell has pointed out, diaries "do not spring from prestidigitation or require a long apprenticeship" (viii). Gender and age are not barriers to such writing: girls, boys, women, men, young, and old—all appear here in this most democratic of genres. Judged by this collection, class, education, and economic status don't seem to stop anyone from keeping diaries. These selections are by authors ranging from the wealthy and well-educated federal judge, to the middle-class grade-school teacher with average education, to the poor and semi-literate ship's clerk. Ethnicity— when joined by literacy—seems to be no barrier: railroad worker and poet Haralambos Kambouris kept a lyric-laced diary in demotic Greek about his southern Oregon experiences.

"If diaries are so widely used by so many different kinds of people, why don't we study them more often for their factual information?"

A diarist's account may not be factually reliable—for a variety of reasons. The diarist may not be able to recognize the breadth or depth of his or her motives. Lord Byron, the English poet, wrote in his own diary, "I fear one lies more to one's self than to anyone else." If Byron is right about our tendency to self-deception, any private version of reality may be skewed, and any diarist may alter the facts to fit the diarist's view of events. Also, any diary—published or unpublished—may be factually inaccurate. For instance, the diaries here of youthful Florence Hofer (1910) and traveler/ writer Thomas Farnham (1839) were significantly added to after the experience was over. The language has been changed. Should they still qualify as "true" reports? How can we tell without the original? Elizabeth Dixon Smith reported in 1847 that Elizabeth Markham said she "brained" her son with a rock while they traveled on the Oregon Trail, but the Oregon census shows that Markham's son, Edwin Markham, arrived in the Willamette Valley in good health and became a poet there. Elizabeth Markham's hyperbole or irony in her diary may be impossible for a reader to detect.

"For what audience does the diarist write?"

This is more ambiguous and complex than it might first appear. As suggested earlier by Emily Trevett, her diary modeled on George Eliot was to be "neither for posterity nor for her friends but for herself." Should readers believe a diarist when she makes such a declaration about audience? One scholar says clearly that we should not. Since the late 1970s, American diary literature scholar Steven E. Kagle has read thousands of texts while collecting representative diaries for his comprehensive three-volume survey listed in the bibliography. By the time Kagle wrote his second volume (1986), he came to believe that "almost all, if not all, diarists envision an audience for their entries...even those who profess horror at the idea that anyone else might see their 'private confessions'." He qualifies this opinion by noting that the diarist's audience may be an idealized self, a future self, or a partial self, but it "is not the diarist, at least as he or she exists at the precise moment the entry is being written" (Kagle, *Early Nineteenth* 5). Who is that "listener within" for whom the diarist writes? Who is the audience being invented? Who shouldn't be listening? Such questions have no simple answers.

"Are there some other formal ways to read, study, and understand the diary as literature?"

Given an awareness of the basic rhetorical context, I would say "Yes, there are many, but consider at least one." Kagle's three-volume survey seems to describe four general types of American diaries: the earliest type is a *spiritual journal* in which "authors...sought to find evidence of their place in the divine scheme either directly through religious experience or indirectly through finding a pattern in the world God had created," and which served as confessional, confidant, and weapon against despair (Kagle, *Early Nineteenth* 104). Practiced intensely by the seventeenth-century Puritans, by later Protestant sects, and by missionaries, this type of American diary is represented here by Sister Miriam Murphy (1904-83) who noted in 1977 that she was attracted to keeping a journal because "the 'process' . . . reinforces the faith dimension of my life. I believe in the indwelling spirit . . . [and because keeping a journal would] "help my spiritual life of prayer and a sense of God's presence in my life." For further examples, readers might also review the diaries of early Oregon missionaries.

Kagle's most common type, a *diary of situation*, is "created to record a special activity or to perform a limited role. Once that situation is ended they usually stopped" (*Am. Diary Lit.* 142). Here, we present most of the rich sub-genres Kagle identifies: *diaries of travel* (Smith [1847], Wood [1851], Glover [1875], Sullivan [1985], and Thomas [1986]); *exploration* (Haswell [1788], Clark [1805], Douglas [1826], and Miller [1899]); *settlement* (Humphrey [1860], Pratt [1911], Steinhoff [1910], and McKinley [1922]); and *war* (Bensell [1864], C. E. S. Wood [1878]). While Kagle's study also includes diaries of *romance* and *courtship*, we do not include them here. However, I have added two important sub-categories to *diary of situation* omitted by Kagle: diaries of *work* (Watson [1900], Marshall [1907], Vincent [1922], and Fairchild [1974]); and diaries of *childhood/adolescence*—(McCrary [1883], Keyes [1921], Hofer [1910], Pauling [1917], and Longoria [1972]).

The longest, most complex type Kagle identifies is a *life diary* in which "the habit of diary-keeping itself is the motive; and therefore, extensive diary production continues even when a diarist's activities change" (Kagle, *Late Nineteenth* 99). The voluminous *life diary* is represented here by various writers—Cummins (1858), Deady (1871), Trevett (1894), Trimberger (1916), Casteel (1931), and Daniel Mote (1930). A self-educated eccentric, Mote describes his frustrations with quack cures, his love of Tolstoy, the collapse of the international stock market, and the bank closures in his own community. Despite the wide range of topics in diaries such as Mote's, the *real* subject matter is always the needs of the diarist's self at different stages. *Life diaries*, like all diaries, reveal the development and concerns of an individual who records personal experiences at regular intervals over a significant period.

Kagle's last type of diary, *literary notebooks*, is the most likely among all diaries to be published and considered as "literature." They are "used to improve [the author's] writing and as a sourcebook that might be mined for materials to be used in their public writing" (Kagle, *Early Nineteenth* 104). These are represented here by Pratt (1911), Whiteley (1920), and to some extent by Sullivan (1985), who probably used his field notebooks as the base material for *Listening for Coyote*. While Kambouris might also be included here, there is no evidence that he ever published his poems written while traveling in Oregon. This may also be the largest under-represented body of writing in our collection, since there are undoubtedly hundreds if not thousands of writers' journals in Oregon.

"Based on your travel, research, and reflection, do Oregon diaries create any dominant impressions?"

Over and over, I'm left with the profound impression of the exact moment, of the diarist, and of his or her need for company—for someone to talk to. Talking to the page seems to resolve loneliness into solitude. Also, while I found several previously unknown Oregon Trail diaries still in the hands of families, the overland diary is more a subset of Oregon's extensive diary literature than a quintessential or dominant diary type. Some Oregon diarists feel compelled to include objects tucked between the pages: locks of hair, pressed roses, plant samples, playing cards, religious medals, etc. Other diarists add drawings: Mary McKinley (1922) drew stick figures in the margins of her diaries; Charles Marshall (1907) drew detailed diagrams of ore chutes and pipelines at the R. and S. Mine in his diary; Dr. L. H. Vincent (1922), a physician serving the isolated mountain community of Sisters, made his lengthy typed diary a scrapbook of photographs, invitations, letters, and colored pencil drawings of his immediate surroundings. One such drawing, reproduced in this volume, shows his little stove, a rocking chair, a book, an ink well and a man's pipe resting on a small table near a partially curtained window. The caption reads, "I sit here and read and smoke and prospect through my fenestrium." In some Oregon diaries, the words seem to generate the need for an even more graphic image—as though the writer felt the language too limited or limiting to render the moment.

"Why are we as readers so attracted to diaries? Is it merely that we relish eavesdropping upon those who are talking on paper; who are only half-certain that someone, someday, maybe be listening?"

No one disputes that we delight in the diary's apparent authenticity, integrity, and content—both literary and historical. As Dr. L. H. Vincent says, "I intend to record . . . such matters as will give a natural touch to the scene and enable one to *vision these times. A picture is not true nor interesting that paints only the sublime."* Like Dr. Vincent, Maxwell also reminds us that the enduring virtue of diaries lies in the fact that "they tell what happened—what people said and did and wore and ate and hoped for and were afraid of . . . in detail after unimaginable detail."

These are rewards enough for any eavesdropper! But Maxwell adds something which goes more deeply to the heart of the matter: diaries "refresh our (own) idea of existence." For the diarist as well as the reader, they "hold oblivion at arm's length."

Shannon Applegate
Yoncalla, Oregon

III. Introducing Oregon Letters

Portland, Oregon
August 1994

Dear Reader,

Most letters are very boring," writes Felix Pryor in his introduction to *The Faber Book of Letters*. He's right and he isn't—to use an Irishism.

Having read hundreds and hundreds of these communications written in Oregon between 1830 and 1980, Shannon Applegate and I might indeed agree with Pryor's charge that letters in general can be a bore. On the other hand, those who received the *personal letters* in this collection prove that Pryor is wrong. "The only pleasure I find in this wooden country is your letters," writes the photographer George Hazeltine to his new bride. He was alone in Canyon City in 1863. "I could never get along without letter papers and magazines coming pretty frequently. I always consider them my best friends," writes Cynthia Horning in 1876 to her friend in Lake County. What is more pleasing to the ego, the heart, than those pages just for us? What better gift?

The repartee of conversation, good conversation, is delicious, but limited: "I wish I'd said . . ." or "I was too shy to tell . . . ." But in a personal letter, we have the distance shyness needs, the space that telling the whole truth may require. In this collection, for instance, Rufus Matthews, a professional gambler, may have never had the courage to tell his mother—face to face—that he was cheating everyone in town, but he tells her here in a letter. Polly McArthur may have left out something important from her childhood memory of Portland's Chinatown if she had just told her story after dinner one night. Hood River settler Shizue Iwatsuki wrote, "I wanted to tell my sadness to my mother, so I wrote letters . . . ." Later, she decided that even her letters were too truthful for her mother, so she burned them in her stove.

Time to discover our thoughts, to organize, to reflect and revise—these are added benefits of writing personal letters. In this collection, there are several types of personal letters that show why people need such time: when Oregonians are caught up with action—building summer camps (Nunn), walking on thousands of frogs (Sutton), fighting barbarian thieves (Kam Wah Chung), climbing Mt. Jefferson (Lewis), watching a bronc riding contest (McGuire), riding into a deer hunting camp (Tippett)—they may be too busy with living to write. However, the day or week after the demands, the excitement, the danger, the difficulty, the challenge of action are over, people frequently sit down and write a record to share with others and to keep for themselves. They want to reflect, remember, relive, reconsider—in letters.

Other types of personal letters included here that require time to pass and/or very careful language include love letters (Hazeltine), letters to old friends about childhood (Colvig and Higginson), thank you or bread-and-butter letters (McNary), letters by travelers to those at home (Gilliss, Robbins, Reber, Lewis), and most frequent of all in this collection, letters to family and friends about major life events—birth, growth, change, moves, loss, death. (They are too numerous to list.)

Letters also become engaging because of their traditional form and its variable conventions. "Honored Madam" was a favored nineteenth-century form as was "Reverend

Sir." In this collection, "Dear Beloved Anna," "My Dear," "Little One," "Dear Folks," "My Dear Brother and Sister"—these show the range of personal salutations here. And for farewells, General Joel Palmer is most traditional with "I am, Sir, your obedient servant"; Abigail Scott Duniway most political with "Affectionately yours for Progress"; Pinto Colvig most informal with "Howdy"; Kenneth Reber most direct with "Love." A cultural variation on these English complimentary closings can be found in the Chinese Kam Wah Chung letters which traditionally end with "I bow to you" and "I wish you wealth."

Of course, not all Oregon letters are personal intimate correspondence between two people who know each other. There is also another general type of communication included here we might reasonably call *public letters* with many subdivisions: letters to an editor (Burnett, O.C. Applegate, Sutton), letters to government authorities (Chinook, Hull, Waldo, Tittinger, Bush), letters to researchers (Iwatsuki, Duniway, Scharff), prolocutor letters written on behalf of a group (Winnemucca, Urizar, Stone), letters as legal documents (Judson), and business letters (H. Miller, Lees, and Kam Wah Chung). The broad scope of this collection includes a sample of such public discourse written— in many cases—to a larger and frequently unknown or impersonal audience. These public letters intend to solve problems, to make something happen, to document facts, to make transactions, to influence public life, politics, legislation. Unlike *personal letters*, such *public letters* may or may not be welcomed by the person who receives them, and they may or may not be intended for publication or some kind of permanent record, and they may demand a reply. Most often, they begin with the conventional "Sir" or "Madam," maintain apparently formal address throughout, and end as formally as they began with "Sincerely."

In early nineteenth-century Oregon, both personal and public letters—as well as the wide range of letters between them—had no easy, fast, frequent, or dependable means of transportation. Letters of credit, letters of introduction, and personal letters were all carried by hand, horse, or ship, and were frequently entrusted to a friend or acquaintance heading in the same general direction as the addressee. In one of his letters to the *New York Herald* in 1844, Peter Burnett states that his letter will be sent by Hudson's Bay Company ship, the *Columbia*, which was leaving Fort Vancouver in a few days. Sailing first to Hawaii, or the Sandwich Islands as they were called in those days, his letter could take months to arrive in New York. Tallmadge Word states that all the letters he sent overland in 1845 were lost. Eugene Skinner tells his sister he has received no letters for twelve years after he came to Oregon.

However, no colony can become an authentic place if people there cannot communicate—personally or publicly—with the rest of the world and among themselves. Thus, in 1846, the Provisional Government created a postal department with service of sorts to Oregon City, Fort Vancouver, and a few locales in the lower Willamette Valley. In the words of one commentator, the service soon "languished" and it was not until Oregon achieved territorial status that two federally appointed postmasters were installed at Astoria and Oregon City. Regular mail service by ship was established between California and the Columbia River in 1850, and in that same year, Eugene Skinner reports he became postmaster in Eugene City. Eventually, over forty post offices were established in the Oregon Territory. In The Dalles of 1866, Julia Gilliss told her parents that she heard every steamer that brought the mailbag up the Columbia about 8:00 p.m. She further reports that the arrival of the mail was a major evening social event in their home. However, through the 1860s and later, remote regions east of the Cascades and away from the Columbia River still may have had only weekly or monthly mail service. From Ochoco in 1873, Kate Robbins wrote that "Tomorrow is mail day and I hope to get letters . . . ." Rachel Colver noted in 1864 that family members did not know where to send letters to Idaho, so all she could do was send them—with hope—to the closest city.

Then, as now, no place becomes a town until it has a post office, for a post office is the imprimatur, as it were, of a community. The absence of a nearby post office was a decided hardship in early Oregon—as two personal letters included in this collection show. "I should consider *that* the worst feature of frontier life," wrote Cynthia Horning in an 1876 letter. In 1873, Jesse Applegate measured his remoteness in rural Klamath County by stating that a letter "was brought to me at my sheep ranch, more than fifty miles from any post office."

In addition to symbolizing a new community's identity, the post office also provided a social service, for it was there, day after day, year after year, that people going for their mail encountered one another. This continued until the turn of the nineteenth century and the introduction of rural free delivery. The rural mail box with its red flag was no doubt looked upon as a great convenience, but may have further isolated the Oregon farm families included in this collection—the Hawleys, the Stirewalts, the Donaldsons, the Steinhoffs, the Tippetts, the Robbins, the McGuires. With roadside mailboxes and star routes, there was no longer any need for all families in a rural community to call at the post office in town. In short, rural free delivery was a strike against what we now call "community."

But there was worse to come for letters—especially personal letters. Until the turn of the nineteenth century, there were only three common ways for people to communicate: face-to-face meetings, letters, and telegrams. Then came the telephone. It tended to decrease the isolation of rural life—and Oregon was predominantly rural well into the present century—while it also further increased rural isolation by decreasing the need for face-to-face communication. The telephone seemed to take over more and more from the personal letter as means of communication. The mailbox, meanwhile, became polluted with an endless stream of public junk sometimes called advertising.

In several important respects, however, the telephone never can and never will be able to replace either type of written communication—and all the variants between them. For one thing, a *personal* letter still signifies a special effort taken for just the addressee. Also, both *personal* and *public* letters—unlike telephone calls—can be kept. The permanency of letters: that is one of their great virtues. Without them, what would we know of the adventures of overlanders such as Peter Burnett?—whose *public letters* were published in newspapers in both New York and Iowa. What would we know of the intimate revelations of a cheating gambler named R.B. Matthews?—whose *private letters* to his mother appear here for the first time. What would we know of the community's conscience without prolocutor letters by Sarah Winnemucca Hopkins, Rev. Stone, and Felix Urizar, and an anonymous soldier?—who all spoke for an invisible group of people who had not received justice from their community. What would we know of a lonely bachelor's life in the Klamath wilderness, a distraught mother's life in Tillamook after her son died, the daily nightmare of the Vietnam War, a judge's plea to save the Oregon Cascades? Yes, letters both personal and public can be read again and again. They are tangible, concrete, lasting records of adventure, affection, sympathy, tragedy, and love.

Also, letters—from personal to public—afford us a special knowledge of the everyday past, for they are commonly filled with the concrete details of daily life—details which biography and history may generalize away or disregard in favor of safer, more abstract, more self-adulatory, less controversial themes. For example, the letters here of Julia Gilliss, a young army wife in the Oregon of the 1860s, give us lively descriptions of rooms and gardens, pots and pans, carts and clothes, and she also becomes an authentic witness to the widely unknown slaughter of Native Americans in southeastern Oregon. Both Pinto Colvig, famous as Bozo the Clown, and Ella Higginson, famous for her poems and stories, have given us here intimate insights into their childhoods in Jacksonville and La Grande, and so created intimate portraits of unknown Oregon small towns seventy years ago. Henry Miller, the richest man in the cattle industry, reveals the hidden policies he used to manage his ranches in Harney and Malheur counties when depression hit the country in the 1880s. The letters of Chinese gold miners—published here for the first time—show us the dangerous life of the Oregon gold frontier.

So, though the telephone is handy, it is ephemeral, its messages written on water. Garrison Keillor, in an essay on letter writing, has put it well: "You can't pick up the phone and call the future and tell them all about our times. You have to pick up a piece of paper."

One last virtue of the letter, and another reason it will never disappear may be worth noting here: the letter is the most adaptable and popular literary device in English. Columnists such as Ann Landers use letter format every day. St. Paul wrote his New Testament theological treatises as letters. Novels, essays (like this one), and poems can be written as a series of letters. In this collection, we see that same adaptablity of letters as they become many different things: a series of letters can be edited into a diary (French, Ad. Wilson); a letter can become family or local history (Skinner, Findley, Colver, Colvig, Higginson, Iwatsuki); a letter can become a promotional tract (West, Burnett); a letter can become an annual report (Hawley); an exchange of letters can become a debate (Applegate cousins); a letter can become an autobiography (Duniway and Iwatsuki); a letter can become an expose (Brenne, Kam Wah Chung); a letter can become a magazine article (Lorenz); a letter can become a court deposition (Judson, O.C. Applegate); a letter can become an advisory (Horning, Burnett, J. Applegate); and finally, a letter can become free self-analysis (Haycox); and, finally, every penitent's confessional (Matthews).

Because Shannon Applegate and I were limited by time, budgets, and pages, we did not entirely succeed in our endeavor to find all of Oregon's letters and diaries in every nook and cranny of the state. However, we have an impressive scope—from personal to public—in the following pages. We hope you enjoy this first anthology of Oregon letters and diaries.

Yours sincerely,
Terence O'Donnell

Westside

Robert Haswell
1768-1801

The shaping of the place now called Oregon began in primordial time. About ten thousand years ago, the great cataclysmic events may have been over. Exploding mountains, lava floods, draining seas, the massive, dragging glaciers—all this cosmic tumult finally seemed to cease and landforms seemed to come to rest in the contours we see today. About this same time, the first human beings appeared, Asiatics coming here by way of a land bridge from Siberia; those people we now call Native Oregonians. These people lived here for at least ten thousand years, and developed their own complex cultures, technologies, trade networks, societies, laws, languages, and literatures without any significant European contact.

Then, one day about four hundred years ago, Native Oregonians looking out to sea ("the river with one bank," they called it) may have seen floating toward them what looked like a huge, black-bodied bird with strange wings. What they saw riding the ocean swells was, in fact, a Spanish galleon under sail, for by the mid-eighteenth century Spanish mariners were exploring the Northwest coast—searching for the fabled Northwest Passage, searching for a great river believed to issue from this coast, searching for good harbors for the galleons crossing the Pacific from the Philippines. (See *Varieties of Hope* and *The Stories We Tell* of the Oregon Literature Series for examples of Native Oregonians' stories of sighting European ships.)

In the last quarter of the eighteenth century the Spanish were joined by the British, likewise searching for the great river and for the Northwest Passage. But all failed in their quest. Meanwhile a Boston sea captain, Robert Gray, engaged in the fur trade, sailed the Northwest coast. In May of 1792 he succeeded where the others had failed. He crossed the bar of the great river and named it for his ship, the *Columbia Rediviva*.

However, this was not Gray's first landing on the Oregon coast. In 1788 in his sloop, the *Lady Washington*, he anchored in what is now called Tillamook Bay and went ashore, the first known landing of Americans in Oregon. In his log, one of the ship's officers, Robert Haswell, described that landing, and the tragedy which ensued. His log was first published in the *Oregon Historical Society Quarterly* (*OHQ*) 29 (1928). See Don Berry's novel *Trask* (1960) for a fictional treatment of this tribe and place.—T. O'D.

The Death of Marcus Lopius at Tillamook Bay

Saturday, August 16, 1788

On the 16 we had pleasant weather with a moderate breze to the eastward   at this time an amazing number of the natives were alongside with boiled and roasted crabbs for sale which our people purchaced for buttons etca.   they had allso dryed salmon and buries in abundance.

Having nothing else to do but wate for the next days tide to depart, Earley in the Afternoon I accompaneyed Mr. Coolidge onshore in the long Boat to amuse ourselves in taking a walk while our boat was loaded with grass and shrubbs for our stock   we took all the people in the Boat who were affected by the Scurvey our number in all amounted to seven   the disposition of the people seemed so friendly we went worse armed than ordinery   we had two Muskets and three or four Cutlaces   we boath took our swoards and each of us a pistol on our first landing   we visated there Houses and such victles as they eate themselvs they offered us but they are so intolerable filthey there was nothing we could stumac except the frute.

They then amused us shewing there dexterity with there arrows and spears they then began a war dance   it was long and hedious accompaneyed with frightfull howlings   indeed there was somthing more horrid in there song and the jestures which accompanied it than I am capable of Discribing   it Chilled the bludd in my vains. The dance over we left the natives to themselves and walked along the beach to the boat where the people were cutting grass and only one or two of the Natives with them   we went past the boat a little way but within call to a small sand flatt in hopes to find some clams   while we were digging for these shell fish a young Black man Marcus Lopius a native of the Cape de Verd Islands and who had shiped Captain Grays servant at St. Jago's being employed carieng grass down to the boat, had carelessly stuck his Cutlas in the sand   one of the natives seeing this took a favourable oppertunity to snatch it at first unobserved and run off with it   one of the people observing him before he was quite out of sight called vehemonantly thretening to shoot him in hopes he would abandon the stoln goods and make his escape but I had given posative orders to our people not to fier but in cases of the most absolute emmergence when for self defence it might be nesecery.

'Twas the hollowing of our people that first roused our attention and we immediately flew to know the cause, we were informed of the sircumstance adding that the Black boy had followed him in spite of every thing they could say to the contorary.

I was struck by the daingerous situation the ladd was in and feared its concequences doubting of there being a posability of saving him from the impending danger, but resolving no project should go untried without hesitation ordering the boat to keep abrest of us we ran toward the village   we mett several Chiefs persons whose friendship we had taken every oppertunity to obtain by kind youseage and liberal preasants   Indeed it seemed before this period we had fully effected it   to these people Mr. Coolidge offered several articles to them of great value to bring back the man unhurt, this they refused intimating there wish for us to seek him ourselvs. I now remarked to Mr. Coolidge that all the natives we saw were unusualy well armed having with them there bows arrows and spears however we proceeded still further and on turning a clump of trees that obstructed our prospect the first thing which presented itself to our view was a very large groop of the natives among the midst of which was the poor black with the thief by the colour loudly calling for assistance saying he had cought the thief, when we were observed by the main boddy of the Natives to haistily aproach them they instantly drenched there knives and spears with savage feury in the boddy of the unfortunate youth. He quited his hold and stumbled but rose again and stagered towards us but having a flight of arrows thrown into his back and he fell within fifteen yards of me, and instantly expiered while they mangled his lifeless corse.

We were now by our passing a number whom as I remarked before we supposed to be our friends situated between two formidable parties. Those we had passed being reinforsed by a great number from the woods they gave us the first salutation by a shower of arrows   Our only method was to get to the boat as fast as posable for this purpos we turned leaving the dead body; for it would have been the highth of imprudence as our Number was so small to have attempted its rescue   we made the Best of our way for the Boat assaulted on all sides by showers of arrows and spears—and at length it became abso-lutely nesecery to shoot there most dairing ringleader which I did with my pistol   Mr. Coolidge and one man who was with us followed my example and Mr. Coolidge ordered those who were in the boat to fier and cover us as we waided off for the boat could not come within a considerable dist of the shore. But undaunted by the fate of there Companions they followed us up to the middle in water and slightly wounded both Mr. Coolidge and myself in the hand and totaley disabled the person who was with us onshore who fainting with loss of blud lay lifeless several hours and continued to bleed a torant till the barb of the arrow was extracted, we jumped into the Boat and pushed of and were soon out of arrow shot   when we found this they launched there Canoes intending to cutt us off indeed they were well situated for it but some were timid some were bold and not half paddled but keeping a constant fier from the boat they came bairley within arrow shot before we were nigh the sloop, and they returned towards the shore as soon as we got onboard we discharged two or three swivel shot at them and in a few Moments not one Canoe was to be seen all having fledd, duering the whole of the night it was dismal to hear the hoops and houlings of the natives   they had fiers on the beach near the spot where the ladd was killed and we could see great number of them passing too and froo before the blaze.

I must confess I should not have lett them enjoy there festervile so peasabley had I been Cap. Gray but his humanity was commendable.

William Clark
1770-1838

Several years after the Boston sea captain Robert Gray entered the Columbia River, President Thomas Jefferson determined to send an expedition overland to the Northwest. To head the expedition, he chose his secretary, Meriwether Lewis, and he in turn chose William Clark, an army comrade, to share the command.

The expedition had at least three purposes: to plot a route between the Missouri and Columbia rivers and thereby facilitate travel and trade; to report on flora, fauna, geography, ethnography, and linguistics of the region; and to establish friendly relations with the Indians. The expedition departed from St. Louis in spring 1804 and reached the lower Columbia River in November 1805. They first camped on the north bank of the Columbia, described below in an excerpt from Clark's journal entry of November 19, and first published as *History of the Expedition Under the Command of Captains Lewis & Clarke* (1814). In December, they crossed the river to a place they named for local Indians—Fort Clatsop.—T. O'D.

American Explorers Meet the Chinook Nation

Tuesday, November 19, 1805

I arose early this morning from under a Wet blanket caused by a Shower of rain which fell in the latter part of the last night, and Sent two men on a head with directions to proceed on near the Sea Coast and Kill Something for brackfast and that I should follow my self in about half an hour. after drying our blankets a little I set out with a view to proceed near the Coast the direction of which induced me to conclude that at the distance of 8 or 10 miles, the Bay was at no great distance across. I overtook the hunters at about 3 miles, they had killed a Small Deer on which we brackfast, . it Comened raining and continued moderately untill 11 oClock A.M.

after takeing a Sumptious brackfast of Venison which was rosted on Stiks exposed to the fire, I proceeded on through ruged Country of high hills and Steep hollers to the commencement of a Sandy coast which extended to a point of high land distant near 20 miles. this point I have taken the Liberty of Calling after my particular friend Lewis. at the commencement of this Sand beech the high lands leave the Sea Coast in a Direction to Chinnook river, and does not touch the Sea Coast again below point Lewis leaveing a low pondey Countrey, maney places open with small ponds in which there is great numbr. of fowl   I am informed that the *Chinnook* Nation inhabit this low countrey and live in large wood houses on a river which passes through this bottom Parrilal to the Sea coast and falls into the Bay

I proceeded on the sandy coast and marked my name on a Small pine, the Day of the month & year, &c. and returned to the foot of the hill,   I saw a Sturgeon which had been thrown on Shore and left by the tide 10 feet in length, and Several joints of the back bone of a Whale, which must have foundered on this part of the Coast. after Dineing on the remains of our Small Deer I proceeded to the bay distance about 2 miles, thence up to the mouth of Chinnook river 2 miles, crossed this little river in the Canoe we left at its mouth and Encamped, on the upper Side in an open sandy bottom.

Thursday, November 21

the Womin of the Chinnoook Nation have handsom faces low and badly made with large legs & thighs which are generally Swelled from a Stopage of the circulation in the feet (which are Small) by maney Strands of Beeds or curious

Strings which are drawn tight around the leg above the ankle, their legs are also picked with defferent figures, I saw on the left arm of a Squar the following letters *J. Bowman,* all those are considered by the natives of this quarter as handsom deckerations, and a woman without those deckorations is Considered as among the lower Class they ware their hair lose hanging over their back and Sholders maney have blue beeds threaded & hung from different parts of their *ears* and about ther neck and around their wrists, their dress otherwise is prosisely like that of the Nation of *War ci a cum* as already discribed.

Maney of the men have blankets of red blue or Spotted Cloth or the common three & 2½ point blankets, and Salors old Clothes which they appear to prise highly, they also have robes of *SeaOtter,* Beaver, Elk, Deer, fox and cat common to this Countrey, which I have never Seen in the U States. they also precure a roabe from the nativs above, which is made of the Skins of a Small animal about the Size of a cat, which is light and dureable and highly prized by those people. the greater numbers of the men of the Chinnooks have Guns and powder and Ball. The Men are low homely and badly made, Small crooked legs large feet, and all of both Sects have flattened heads. maney of the Chinnooks appear to have Venerious and pustelus disorders. one woman whome I saw at the Creek appeared all over in Scabs and ulsers &c. . . .

Christmas. Wednesday, December 25

at day light this morning we we awoke by the discharge of the fire arm of all our party & a Selute, Shouts and a Song which the whole party joined in under our windows, after which they retired to their rooms were chearfull all the morning. after brackfast we divided our Tobacco which amounted to 12 carrots one half of which we gave to the men of the party who used tobacco, and to those who doe not use it we make a present of a handkerchief, The Indians leave us in the evening all the party Snugly fixed in their huts. I recved a presnt of Capt. L. of a fleece hosrie Shirt Draws and Socks, a pr. Mockersons of Whitehouse a Small Indian basket of Gutherich, two Dozen white weazils tails of the Indian woman, & some black root of the Indians before their departure. Drewyer informs me that he saw a Snake pass across the parth to day. The day proved Showerey wet and disagreeable.

we would have Spent this day the nativity of Christ in feasting, had we any thing either to raise our Sperits or even gratify our appetites, our Diner concisted of pore Elk, so much Spoiled that we eate it thro' mear necessity, Some Spoiled pounded fish and a fiew roots.

David Douglas
1798-1834

David Douglas, a Scottish botanist, visited the Pacific Coast several times between 1825 and 1833 using the Hudson's Bay Company's Fort Vancouver as his headquarters. His Oregon travels in the Willamette Valley, the Blue Mountains, and the Umpqua and McKenzie river drainages resulted in the naming of more than fifty tree species including trees now known as Douglas-fir (*Pseudotsuga menziesii*) and the sugar pine (*Pinus lambertiana*). Called "Grass Man" by the Native Americans he met while in the Umpqua region, Douglas was at last guided to *nátele*—the tree noted in his diary as "my long-wished *Pinus.* . . ." In the rainy autumn of 1826, while lying on the wet grass with his gun beside him, Douglas wrote about his first sighting of "this most beautiful and immensely large tree. . . ."

Douglas's life of discovery and adventure ended tragically when he was only thirty-six years old: he was gored to death by a wild bull while exploring the Sandwich Islands—today's Hawaiian Islands. The following exerpt is taken from *Journal Kept by David Douglas During His Travels in North America 1823-1827* (1959).—S.A.

Seeking Magnificence
A BOTANIST FINDS A DOUGLAS COUNTY PINE

Wednesday, October 25, 1826. Upper Umpqua River

Last night was one of the most dreadful I ever witnessed. The rain, driven by the violence of the wind, rendered it impossible for me to keep any fire, and to add misery to my affliction my tent was blown down at midnight, when I lay among *Pteris aquilina* rolled in my wet blanket and tent till morning. Sleep of course was not to be had, every ten or fifteen minutes immense trees falling producing a crash as if the earth was cleaving asunder, which with the thunder peal on peal before the echo of the former died away, and the lightning in zigzag and forked flashes, had on my mind a sensation more than I can ever give vent to; and more so when I think of the place and my circumstances. My poor horses were unable to endure the violence of the storm without craving of me protection, which they did by hanging their heads over me and neighing. Towards day it moderated and before sunrise clear, but very cold. I could not stir before making a fire and drying part of my clothing, everything being completely drenched, and indulging myself with a fume of tobacco being the only thing I could afford. Started at ten o'clock, still shivering with cold, although I rubbed myself with my handkerchief before the fire until I was no longer able to endure the pain. Shortly after I was seized with a severe headache and pain in the stomach, with giddiness and dimness of sight; having no medicine except a few grains of calomel, all others being done, I could not think of taking that and therefore threw myself into a violent perspiration and in the evening felt a little relieved. Went through an open hilly country some thirteen miles, where I crossed the river to the south side near three lodges of Indians, who gave me some salmon such as is caught in the Columbia and at this season scarcely eatable, but I was thankful to obtain it. Made a short stay and took my course southerly towards a ridge of mountains, where I hope to find my pine. The night being dry I camped early in the afternoon, in order to dry the remaining part of my clothing. Travelled eighteen miles.

Thursday, October 26

Weather dull and cloudy. When my people in England are made acquainted with my travels, they may perhaps think I have told them nothing but my miseries. That may be very correct, but I now know that such objects as I am in quest of are not obtained without a share of labour, anxiety of mind, and sometimes risk of personal safety. I left my camp this morning at daylight on an excursion, leaving my guide to take care of the camp and horses until my return in the evening, when I found everything as I wished; in the interval he had dried my wet paper as I desired him. About an hour's walk from my camp I was met by an Indian, who on discovering me strung his bow and placed on his left arm a sleeve of racoon-skin and stood ready on the defence. As I was well convinced this was prompted through fear, he never before having seen such a being, I laid my gun at my feet on the ground and waved my hand for him to come to me, which he did with great caution. I made him place his bow and quiver beside my gun, and then struck a light and gave him to smoke and a few beads. With my pencil I made a rough sketch of the cone and pine I wanted and showed him it, when he instantly pointed to the hills about fifteen or twenty miles to the south. As I wanted to go in that direction, he seemingly with much good-will went with me. At midday I reached my long-wished *Pinus* (called by the Umpqua tribe *nátele),* and lost no time in examining and endeavouring to collect specimens and seeds. New or strange things seldom fail to make great impressions, and often at first we are liable to over-rate them; and lest I should never see my friends to tell them verbally of this most beautiful and immensely large tree, I now state the dimensions of the largest one I could find that was blown down by the wind: Three feet from the ground, 57 feet 9 inches in circumference; 134 feet from the ground, 17 feet 5 inches; extreme length, 215 feet. The trees are remarkably straight; bark uncommonly smooth for such large timber, of a whitish or light brown colour; and yields a great quantity of gum of a bright amber colour. The large trees are destitute of branches, generally for two-thirds the length of the tree; branches pendulous, and the cones hanging from their points like small sugar-loaves in a grocer's shop, it being only on the very largest trees that cones are seen, and the putting myself in possession of three cones (all I could) nearly brought my life to an end. Being unable to climb or hew down any, I took my gun and was busy clipping them from the branches with ball when eight Indians came at the report of my gun. They were all painted with red earth, armed with bows, arrows, spears of bone, and flint knives, and seemed to me anything but friendly. I endeavoured to explain to them what I wanted and they seemed satisfied and sat down to smoke, but had no sooner done so than I perceived one string his bow and another sharpen his flint knife with a pair of wooden pincers and hang it on the wrist of the right hand, which gave me ample testimony of their inclination. To save myself I could not do by flight, and without any hesitation

I went backwards six paces and cocked my gun, and then pulled from my belt one of my pistols, which I held in my left hand. I was determined to fight for life. As I as much as possible endeavoured to preserve my coolness and perhaps did so, I stood eight or ten minutes looking at them and they at me without a word passing, till one at last, who seemed to be the leader, made a sign for tobacco, which I said they should get on condition of going and fetching me some cones. They went, and as soon as out of sight I picked up my three cones and a few twigs, and made a quick retreat to my camp, which I gained at dusk. The Indian who undertook to be my last guide I sent off, lest he should betray me. Wood of the pine fine, and very heavy; leaves short, in five, with a very short sheath bright green; cones, one $14\frac{1}{2}$ inches long, one 14, and one $13\frac{1}{2}$, and all containing fine seed. A little before this the cones are gathered by the Indians, roasted on the embers, quartered, and the seeds shaken out, which are then dried before the fire and pounded into a sort of flour, and sometimes eaten round. How irksome a night is to such a one as me under my circumstances! Cannot speak a word to my guide, not a book to read, constantly in expectation of an attack, and the position I am now in is lying on the grass with my gun beside me, writing by the light of my Columbian candle—namely, a piece of wood containing rosin.

Peter Burnett
1807-1895

Encouraged by missionaries, fired by a belief in Manifest Destiny, desiring free and fertile land as well as a healthy climate, many border-state Americans such as Peter Burnett embarked on the Oregon Trail beginning in the 1840s. The wagon trains customarily departed from Missouri in the spring, reaching the Willamette Valley in the autumn after two thousand miles and six months of arduous travel.

The wagons—on average ten feet long with two-foot sides—were stocked with tools, clothes, seed, perhaps a harmonium, a clock, and the staples: bacon, beans, sugar, salt, coffee, and often a keg of whiskey. The travelers' books would frequently include the Bible and *Pilgrim's Progress.*

The trail held hardships: shortages of grass for the cattle, raging rivers to cross, harrowing mountain descents, death by disease, drowning, and the accidental discharge of firearms—far more deaths from these causes than from attacks by the Native Americans.

The trail also held pleasures: a good camp site, a dance to fiddle music, a spirited prayer meeting, a wedding. The young in particular appeared to enjoy themselves. "We had dancing every night, buffalo hunting every day," wrote Jacob Harlan. "There was plenty of frolic and where there are young people there is always lovemaking," wrote Susan Parish. (See *Varieties of Hope* and *From Here We Speak* of the Oregon Literature Series for other texts on this subject.)

One of the most perceptive and literate of the wagon train people was the Missouri lawyer, Peter Burnett. His letters written along the Oregon Trail first appeared in 1844 in the *New York Herald* and are taken here from *OHQ* 24 (1923). After settling near Portland, Burnett also wrote letters home describing aspects of the Trail. Later from "Falatin" or "Fallatine" Plains, his two versions of Tualatin Plains, Burnett wrote describing conditions in Oregon. (His reference to "Pakenham's mission" refers to negotiations to resolve the boundary dispute between Britain and the United States, a dispute settled in 1846 with the drawing of the present boundaries.) In 1850, Burnett became the first American governor of California and eventually became a wealthy banker there.—T. O'D.

Crossing the Plains
LETTERS FROM A TUALATIN PIONEER

Linnton, Oregon Territory
ca. February 1844

New York Herald
James G. Bennett, Esq.—

Dear Sir:

In my former communication I gave you some account of our trip as far as Elm Grove, fifteen miles from the rendezvous. On the twenty-fourth of May we crossed the Walkalusia, a tributary of the Kansas, about twenty yards wide, clear running water, over a pebbly bed. We let our wagons down the bank (which was very steep) with ropes. There was, however, a very practicable ford, unknown to us, about one hundred yards above. We here saw three Potawotomie Indians, who rode fine horses, with martingales, bridles, and saddles. We found very few fish in this stream. On the twenty-sixth of May we reached Kansas River, which was too high to ford; and we prepared a platform, by uniting two large canoes together—and commenced crossing on the 29th. On the 27th we held a meeting, and appointed a committee of three to make arrangements for crossing the river. The committee attempted to hire Pappa's platform (a Frenchman who lived at the crossing,) but no reasonable arrangement could be made with him. Before we had finished our platform, some of the company made a private arrangement with Pappa for themselves, and commenced crossing. This produced great dissatisfaction in camp. On the 28th Pappa's platform sank, and several men, women, and children came near being drowned, but all escaped with the loss of some property. As yet no organization, and no guard out. Wagons still coming in rapidly. On the thirtieth of May two Catholic missionaries to the Flathead Indians arrived and crossed the river. The Kansas is here a wide stream, with sandy banks and bottom. I suppose it to be about a quarter mile wide at this point. The water was muddy, like that of the Missouri River. We finished crossing on the thirty-first of May. Our encampment was on Black Warrior Creek; very uncomfortable, as our stock were constantly sticking fast in the mud upon its banks. On the first of June we organized the company, by electing Peter H. Burnett commander in chief and Mr. Nesmith orderly sergeant. On the 4th we crossed Big Sandy, a large creek with high banks. Last night we had a hard rain. Last evening we saw several of the Kanzas chiefs, who visited our encampment. Our usual mode of encampment was to form a hollow square with the wagons. When we organized we had about one hundred and ten wagons and two hundred and sixty-three men, all able to bear arms. On the 5th we crossed the East Fork of Blue, a large creek, and a tributary of the Kansas, and on the 6th, in the evening, we crossed the West Fork of Blue, a small river, about fifty yards wide. Contrary to our expectations, we found it fordable, by propping up our wagon beds with large blocks of wood. We encamped for the night on a level prairie, dry and beautiful. In the night we had an immense thunderstorm, and torrents of rain. Half the tents blew down, and nearly the whole encampment was flooded with water eight inches deep. We were in a most uncomfortable predicament next morning, and nearly all wet. We this day met a war party of Osages and Kanzas Indians, consisting of about ninety warriors. They all rode ponies, were painted, and their heads shaven, and had one Pawnee scalp, with the ears still to it, and full of wampum. This scalp had tolerably long hair upon it, and they had divided it into some five or six different pieces, some with an ear to them, and some with part of the cheek. The Kanzas and Osages are the most miserable, cowardly, and dirty Indians we saw east of the Rocky Mountains. They annoyed us greatly by their continual begging. We gave this war party bread and meat, and a calf; they said they had eaten nothing for three days. Two of this party were wounded severely, one in the shoulder and the other in another part. They had killed but one Pawnee, who had wounded these two before he fell. The Kanzas Indians, however, did not steal from us, except perhaps a horse or two which were missing, but which might have escaped back to the Kanzas River. On the 7th we removed our encampment one half mile to a place we supposed to be dry; but in the night another severe storm of rain succeeded, and again flooded half the encampment. On the 8th we traveled five miles to a grove of green elm trees, and it again rained in torrents, but our encampment was upon high ground this time. P. H. Burnett this day resigned the command of the company in consequence of ill health. On the 9th the clouds dispersed, and we traveled five miles to find wood, where we dried our clothes. The company now separated into two parties, one under the command of Capt. Jesse Applegate, and the other reorganized by electing William Martin commander. Martin's company had about seventy-two wagons and one hundred and seventy-five men. On the 10th we met a company of four wagons from Fort Larimer, with furs and peltries, going to Independence. They had with them several buffalo calves. As yet we saw no game of any kind, except a few straggling deer. This day Mr. Casan and others saw the corpse of an Indian in the prairie; his head had been cut off and was badly scalped, and left to be eaten up by the buzzards. This, no doubt, was the same Indian killed and scalped by the war party of the Osages and Kanzas. On the 11th we had a fall of rain in the evening, before dark, but none in the night. . . .

Your friend,
P.H.B.

Linnton, Oregon Territory
1844

New York Herald
James G. Bennett, Esq.—

Dear Sir:

In my letter of the 26th instant, I continued my account of our trip to our last encampment on the waters of the Blue. . . .

On the twenty-second day of June, we saw the first band of buffaloes, which contained about fifty, of all ages and sizes. Out of this band two were killed. They were found in the plain close to the river, and were pursued on horse-back. Perhaps no sport in the world is so exciting as a buffalo hunt. The fox chase sinks into insignificance when compared to it. The mode of hunting this noble animal is very simple. They are generally found upon the wide plain beyond the sand hills, as I before stated, and you will almost always find them grazing near the head of some hollow leading up near them. When you approach him you must get the wind to blow from him to you; because if you scent him, you will hardly run off, but if he scents you, he is certain to scamper. The sight of the buffalo is very dull, but their sense of smell is very acute. I one day saw a band of about one hundred buffaloes on the opposite side of the river from us, and about two miles off, running parallel with the line of wagons, up the river. When they came directly opposite us, so as to strike the stream of wind, which blew from us directly across the river, they turned suddenly off at right angles, and increased their speed greatly. They had evidently scented us. If you have the wind of them you can approach within a very short distance, near enough to kill them readily with the rifle. When you fire, if you remain still, and do not show yourself, the buffalo will perhaps bring a bound, and then stop, and remain until you have fired several times. If he is wounded he will lie down. If several guns are fired in quick succession it alarms the band, and they all move off in a brisk trot; but if you load and fire slowly you may often kill several before the balance leave. I have seen three or four lying within ten yards of each other. When you have fired as often as you can, and the buffalo have retired beyond the reach of the balls, you return down the hollow to your horses, and having mounted, you approach as near as possible before you show yourself to the animal; and when he sees you, your horse ought to be at the very top of his speed, so as to get near him before he gets under full speed. You may dash at a band of buffaloes not more than one hundred yards off, and they will stand and gaze at you before they start; but when one puts himself in motion, all the rest rise instantly, and those lying down will not be very far behind the others, as they rise running. Although they seem to run awkwardly, yet they step away rapidly, and if you lose much time you will have a hard run to overtake them. The better plan is to put your horse at the top of his speed at once. This enables you to press upon the buffalo at the first of the race, and when you approach within fifty or sixty yards of them, you will find that they can let out a few more links; but if a bull is wounded, even very slightly, the moment you press hard upon him he will turn short around, curl his tail over his back, bow his neck, and face you for a fight. At this time you had as well keep at a convenient distance. If you keep off about fifty yards he will stand, and you may load and fire several times; but you had better not fire at his head, for you will not hurt him much if you hit him, for the ball will never penetrate through the skull bone. Whenever you bring one to bay, if the country is not too broken, and your horse is good, there is no danger of his escape, as you may shoot as often as you please; and whenever you give the animal a deadly shot he will kick as if kicking at some object that attacks him. The buffalo, when excited, is very hard to kill, and you may put several balls through his heart, and he will then live, sometimes for hours. The best place to shoot him is behind the shoulder, at the bulge of the ribs, and just below the backbone, as to pass through the thick part of the lungs. This is the most deadly of all shots; and when you see the animal cough up blood it is unnecessary to shoot him any more. When you shoot them through the lungs the blood smothers them immediately. The lungs of the buffalo are very large and easily hit by any sort of marksman. If you pursue a buffalo not wounded, you may run up by his side, and shoot off your horse. The animal becomes tired after running at the top of his speed for two or three miles, and will then run at a slow gallop. The buffalo is a most noble animal—very formidable in appearance—and in the summer has a very short soft coat of fine wool over his body, from behind his shoulders to his tail. His neck and head are covered with a thick mass of long black wool, almost concealing his short thick horns (the points of which just peep out), and his small eye. This animal has a great deal of bold daring, and it is difficult to turn him from his course. . . .

Your friend,
P.H.B.

Falatin Plains, Oregon Territory
Nov. 4, 1844

Dear sir—

The emigrants are all arriving, and will be here in a few weeks at furtherest, and I expect to receive other letters and papers. I have now an opportunity of writing a hasty letter, as one of the H. B. Co's ships, the *Columbia*, leaves Vancouver in a few days for Sandwich Islands.

Our country is most beautiful, fertile and well watered, with the most equable and pleasant climate. Our population is rapidly increasing, and the country is making progress in wealth and refinement. I have never yet before seen a population so industrious, sober and honest as this. I know many young men who were the verist vagabonds in the states, who are here respectable and doing exceedingly well.

Our crops the past year (1844) have been most bountiful, and we have a full supply of wheat for our consumption, and a large quantity for exportation. Large numbers of cattle are raised here which are never fed or sheltered. Many men have from three to four hundred head of cattle. Sheep can be had in any desirable number, as the H. B. Co. have a large flock, and many private individuals have a large quantity.

Ere this reaches you, perhaps you will have learned that we have a regular government in most successful operation in Oregon. When I first reached this region about one year ago, I thought any attempt at organization might be premature. I had not, however, been here long before I conceived that a government of some kind was inevitable. It grew out of stern invincible necessity. Our commercial and business transactions were considerable. Difficulties were daily occurring between individuals in relation to their "claims"; the estates of deceased persons were daily devoured and helpless orphans plundered; crimes were committed and the base and unprincipled and reckless and turbulent were hourly tramping upon the rights of the honest and peacable. A civilized population, numerous as we were, could not exist without government. The thing was impossible. We therefore organized a government of our own.

We have no money, no means. I was a member of the Legislature. I had most of the business to do. We passed a tax bill, appointed an assessor and permitted every man not to pay a tax if he chose so to do; but if he did not pay, being able, we disbarred him from suing in the courts as plaintiff.

At the same time we passed acts to protect all bona fide settlers in their claims to the amount of 640 acres. The tax bill operated like a charm. Nearly all the population paid without hesitation.

We selected a tall Tennesseean, Joseph L. Meek, for our sheriff. He had been in the mountains with Wm. L. Subblett for eight or ten years, is exceedingly good humored, very popular, and as brave as Julius Caesar. The first warrant he had delivered to him was issued for the apprehension of a very quarrelsome and turbulent man who resisted Meek with a broad axe, but Meek, presenting a cocked pistol, took the fellow *nolens volens.*

We now have five counties and two terms of the circuit court in each county in every year. We have but one judge, who discharges the duties of probate judge, chancellor, and what not; in fact, we have only as yet circuit courts and justices of the peace.

Our government was intended only as provisional, to exist until some regular government could be established. We adopted the statute laws of Iowa which were applicable to our condition, and not modified by our legislature.

We are now waiting most anxiously for the result of Pakenham's mission; and if the two governments have not settled the question between them, the moment the fact is known, there will be one universal movement made. A regular convention will be held and a constitution adopted (republican no doubt), and an independent government put in operation at once. Necessity will compel us to the step. The population of this country are no doubt desirous to live under the government of the United States, but if she will never do anything for us, we must and will do it for ourselves. The people here are worn out by delay, and their condition becomes every day more intolerable. I speak to you with great candor, for you know me, and know that I withold nothing and disguise nothing. We are well satisfied that the United States Government, as well as Great Britain, could not object if we form an independent government for ourselves situated as we are.

Treaties must be made with the Indians, and many other things of importance must of necessity be done. The practice of law has commenced, and I have several important suits on hand. Our population about doubles every year and our business trebles. We will soon have a printing press and paper of our own. We can then publish our laws. I have a fine claim, perhaps among the best in Oregon, situated in one of those most beautiful prairies called Fallatine Plains. I am in excellent health. Mrs. B's health has improved, and my children are all well, fat and fine.

Your Friend
Peter H. Burnett

Tallmadge Word
1817-1848

The Northwest fur trade began in the last quarter of the eighteenth century. Trade goods were exchanged for pelts with the Native Oregonians, and the pelts were sold in the Far East, with the profits used to purchase tea, spices, and other commodities.

In 1811, John Jacob Astor established a fur-trading post at the mouth of the Columbia, naming it Astoria. In 1824, the Hudson's Bay Company established a major post at what is now Vancouver, Washington. The trade flourished until the early 1840s when the supply of beaver declined.

Tallmadge Word (also known as Wood) arrived in Oregon in the 1843 migration. He was murdered at the California mines in 1848. The letter which follows describes his earlier life as a trapper in the trade. It first appeared in *OHQ* 3 (1902). Also see Osborne Russell's *Journal of a Trapper* (1955), and *A Majority of Scoundrels* (1961) by Don Berry.—T. O'D.

A Hunter's Life Is a Dog's Life
A FUR TRAPPER'S LETTER

Clatsop, Clatsop Co., Oregon Territory
February 19, 1846

Dear brother:

It was with pleasure I received yours of March 8, 1845; also one from Cyrel at the same time (Nov. last, 1845), and was happy to hear of general health, and that I am blest with the same, and have been ever since I have been in this territory; and, in fact, I have not had an hour's sickness for five years past. You ask me to give a sketch of my travels since I first arrived in Missouri.

I was some of the time in employ of Fur & Trading Co., and some of my time a free trapper. A hunter's life is a dog's life, exposed to all kinds of danger and hardships, and but little gained at last, but men soon get so accustomed to it that in a short time they fear neither man, musket, or the D——, and there is so much nature, romance, and excitement in their way of living, that they soon become much attached to it, for it is much easier for a white man to become an Indian, than to reverse the thing. I have been compelled to hunger to eat mules, horses, dogs, wolves, badgers, ground hogs, skunks, frogs, crickets, ants, and have been without food of any kind for six days and nights. Cats, dogs, or anything else, is right good eating meat at such times.

At another time we were four days, and three out of the four compelled to fight our way as we traveled, but hungry men are fond of fight and fear nothing, and so we walked through. You may think crickets and ants rather small game to shoot at, and so it is, but we have another way of taking them, which is by going in search, early in the morning, when the crickets (which are in some parts very numerous and as large as the end of your thumb,) by the coolness of the air and dew are very stupid, and climb to the top of weeds in great numbers that the sun may get a fair chance at them; they are at such times easily captured by jarring them off into a basket and then roasting them with hot stones,—feathers, guts, and all,—and make very good eating—when one gets used to it. The ants are taken by sticking a stick in the center of their hill, and making a fire around it, which compels them to ascend the stick, and from that to the bucket or sack; in this way a meal is soon procured. But those times are all past with me.

Elizabeth Dixon Smith
ca. 1808-1855

Elizabeth Dixon Smith wrote one of the most quoted overland diary entries in Oregon history. While traveling in 1847, Smith witnessed a prime example of marital stress upon the trail. The boy named John survived his mother's hyperbole—according to the 1850 federal census. The woman Smith refers to in her diary entry was Elizabeth Markham, the mother of one of the West's best-known nineteenth-century poets, Edwin Markham. Elizabeth Markham was also a poet and suffragist—an "advocate of the ladies' cause." (See also *From Here We Speak* of the Oregon Literature Series.)

Like many overland diarists, Elizabeth Dixon Smith wrote in a terse ungrammatical style. Nonetheless, her message was vivid and moving. For example, when her husband Cornelius Smith died in February of 1848 in a lean-to shack in the tiny settlement known as Portland, Smith wrote simply: "rain all day this day my Dear husband my last remaining friend died." A year and a half later, Elizabeth Smith married a widower named Joseph Geer. She died in 1855, less than a decade after her arrival in Oregon.

In 1848 she included excerpts from her overland diary in a letter to Indiana friends from which the following version is taken. A copy of this diary and numerous annotations are found in Kenneth Holmes's *Covered Wagon Women* (1983).—S.A.

Protest, Fire, and Hyperbole on the Oregon Trail

Wednesday, September 15, 1847

layed by this morning   one company moved on except one family   the woman got mad and would not budge nor let the children   he had his cattle hitched on for 3 hours and coaxing her to go but she would not stur I told my husband the circumstance and him and Adam Polk and Mr. Kimble went and took each one a young one and cramed them in the wagon and her husband drove off and left her siting   she got up took the back track travled out of sight cut across overtook her husband   meantime he sent his boy back to camp after a horse that he had left and when she came up her husband says did you meet John   yes was the reply and I picked up a stone and nocked out his brains   her husband went back to ascertain the truth and while he was gone she set one of his waggons on fire which was loaded with store goods   the cover burnt off and some valueable artickles   he saw the flame and came runing out and put it out and then mustered spunk enough to give her a good floging   her name is Marcum she is cousin to Adam Polks wife

Elizabeth Wood
1828-1913

The Oregon Trail experience for women—many of whom had not been eager to start on the journey—was often more difficult than for the men. Keeping house in the heat and rain and dust, caring for children in a jolting ten-foot box, keeping apparel clean and in repair when it was torn, worn, caked with dust, stained, and rank with sweat: these were all heavy chores. At some camps the women had to carry water for long distances, and some found the gathering of buffalo chips for the evening fire a repellant task.

"The females are heartily tired of the toilsome journey," wrote an army officer who encountered the 1845 migration. Despite these difficulties, some women traversed the Trail with remarkably high spirits as, for example, Elizabeth Wood, who arrived in Oregon in 1851. Her journal entries below, first published in the Peoria (Illinois) *Weekly Republican* (1852) and reprinted here from *OHQ* 27 (1926), recount her experiences as a 23-year-old woman along a portion of the Trail.—
T. O'D.

A Young Woman's Trip to Oregon

Sunday, June 29, 1851

This morning we start with a company of 25 wagons, and commence the ascent of the Rocky Mountains: we go up some very high hills, called the Black Hills, which are very handsome to look at, as they have shelves of rock around them, between which are cedar bushes growing, which adding to the beauty of their appearance, and looking as if they were fashioned by the hand of art. The water is so bad here, and the milk from our cows so strongly impregnated with alkali, that I have substituted coffee as a beverage. The ground is white with alkali, and the cows get it by feeding in the grass. This substance made some of our company sick before they knew what was the matter.

Friday, July 4

We have been traveling among the hills and the monotony has been relieved by the ever varying beauty of the scenery and the pleasantness of the weather. Today we traveled till noon, and then stopped to get a Fourth of July dinner and to celebrate our nation's birthday. While making the preparations, and reflecting at the same time of what the people of Morton and Peoria were doing, and contrasting my situation with what it was this day last year, a storm arose, blew over all the tents but two, capsized our stove with its delicious viands, set one wagon on fire, and for a while produced not a little confusion in the camp. No serious injury, however, was done. After the storm was over, we put up the stove, straightened up the tent, and got as nice a dinner as we had upon the "Glorious Fourth" in Morton last year. We then took care of our game, consisting of 5 black-tailed deer, 1 antelope and 3 buffalo. Last of all we went to hear an oration delivered by Mr. S. Wardon. For your amusement I will give a description of my dress for the occasion: A red calico frock, made for the purpose in the wagons; a pair of mockasins, made of black buffalo hide, ornamented with silk instead of beads, as I had none of the latter and a hat braided, of bullrushes and trimmed with white, red and pink ribbon and white paper. I think I came pretty near looking like a squaw.

Saturday, July 5

We found a squaw, which we suppose had been hung up a tree, perhaps alive, as it was lying at the foot of one, and had been, probably, placed there several months previously. She had $5. worth of beads about her.

Sunday, July 6

Every week we find different soils, different weeds and different grass. We find wild pepper, camomile, and a great many things I didn't expect to see. We are now a hundred miles from the fort (Laramie), and we find three cabins with white folks living in them. It seems strange to meet any person living here, away from civilization, among the Indians, wild beasts, and the Sand Hills, where nothing can grow for man's sustenance.

Monday, July 7

We have got where the horny toads are, and they are very poisonous. They resemble the toad, except that they have a tail as long as one's finger and horns upon each side as thick as saw teeth.

Friday, July 25

Since last date we camped at the ford where emigrants cross from the south to the north side of the Platte. On the south side there are a great many graves, as if whole families had been swept off at once, and the wreck of every description of property taken out by the emigrants. We stopped near the Red Buttes, where the hills are of a red color, nearly square, and have the appearance of houses with flat roofs. We have left the Platte, which we followed for 500 miles; traveled over the Sand Hills, where the wind blew the pebbles against my face almost hard enough to fetch the blood; camped by a spring almost cold enough to freeze your face and hands if you washed in it; passed over the sage plains; came to the Sweet Water River, and it did look sweet, too, after traversing a country of nothing but sage, without a spire of grass or a drop of water. We also passed Independence Rock and the Devil's Gate, which is high enough to make one's head swim, and the posts reach an altitude of some 4 or 500 feet. We found dead oxen, of which our company lost several, and any amount of wagon wheels, strewed all along the road. One of the strangest sights to me, in the month of July, was the snowy mountains, covered with their everlasting snows. On Saturday, July 19, we reached the top of the mountains, and found the roads as level as the streets of Peoria. Passed the Pacific Springs, and commenced the descent, which was here so gradual as barely to be perceptible. Came to bad roads after a while and found worse hills going down the Rocky Mountains than when ascending. We had hills to climb so steep we could hardly get up, and so sidelong that we have to tie a rope to the underside of the wagon, let it extend over the top, and then walk on the hill above and hold on to the rope. When we gain the summit, we then have to go down one a great deal steeper; everything that is not tied in the wagon falls out, and it would be amusing for a disinterested person to stand at the top with a spy glass and witness the descent of a train down one of these terrible looking hills. You would see the women and children in advance seeking the best way, some of them slipping down, or holding on to the rocks, now taking an "otter slide," and then a run till some natural obstacle presented itself to stop their accelerated progress, and those who get down safely, without a hurt or a bruise, are fortunate indeed. Looking back to the train, you would see some of the men holding on to the wagons, others slipping under the oxen's feet, some throwing articles out of the way that had fallen out, and all have enough to do to keep them busily occupied. Often the teams get going so fast down hill it is difficult to stop them to double lock, and when, at a still steeper place, there is no stopping them at all, the driver jumps on the near wheel ox and the whole concern goes down with a perfect rush until a more level place is reached. So you see we have some "hair breadth" escapes, and a jolly time of it if we could only think so.

Tuesday, July 29
The road goes between high hills and rocks, and we have to drive over rocks so large it seems as if the wagons would break, and they would if they were not good ones. If we were the first that ever went along here, I should think we had come to the end of the road for we can see but a short distance before us, and it seems as if the high mountains ahead had to be climbed but could not.

Saturday, August 2
Cold weather; the leaves on the trees are killed with the frost.

Sunday, August 3. Oregon
Snakes and grasshoppers rule here; but of the former I mean the Snake Indians instead of the genuine serpent. This morning, by way of variety, we were treated with an Oregon blow, the wind coming in such furious blasts that we had to hold the plates fast to the tables, and make our repast the best way we could. Though it is now August, "dog days" with you, yet here it is quite cold and "winter is coming." The weeds are as dry and brown as they are in Illinois quite late in the fall. One of our company is doubling his money on his goods. Cloth that can be bought for 16 cts. in Peoria he sells for 75 cts. per yard; coffee 50 cts per lb., and tea that cost him five bits a pound he readily sold for

$2. As money-making is the "order of the day," I engaged in some profitable speculations in a small way and realized quite a handsome profit comparatively to the cost of the articles sold. For instance, I disposed of a worn and faded dress to the Indians for $3.50, which was purchased when new, in Peoria, at 10 cts per yard—other things in the same proportions.—Here the roads were so bad, as we went over the steep hills and clambered over the rocks, I could hardly hold myself in the wagon. Sometimes the dust is so great that the drivers cannot see their teams at all though the sun is shining brightly, and it is a great relief to the way-worn traveler to meet with some mountain stream, meandering through a valley, after traveling for miles over these rough and dusty roads, through a country where every blade of grass has been dried up, with the drouth that generally prevails here at this time of year, except in the bottoms along the river banks, where we can yet get feed for our cattle. One day we only made seven miles through a very deep sand.

Wednesday, August 6

We passed Fort Hall; met a company of Indians, moving; they had their ponys packed with their goods until one would suppose nothing else could be got on them; but on the top of their "plunder" the little papooses were tied, to keep them from falling off. Some of the ponys were rode by the squaws, with a papoose lashed to their backs, and in some cases one or two at their sides, or if one, something else to keep up the equilibrium. There were about 20 families of these Indians, seeking for winter quarters. One morning at the break of day I was awakened by a disturbance among the cattle, which had got frightened at the barking of a dog. They run against the wagons, broke the wheels and tongue of ours, and bawled and pitched around till they finally got loose and run off in an estampede. For a while all was confusion in the camp, and we expected to lose some of the cattle. They kept on running until something in the distance frightened them back again, and they returned as furious as they went, when the men with great difficulty managed to stop them. The captain ordered all the dogs to be killed, and in obedience to his commands, our faithful "Tray" was shot. Some of the company were not disposed to comply with this sanguinary, though I believe necessary, decision of the captain's, and threatened retaliation in case their dogs should be killed. So, after repairing, we started on our journey with the expectation of having another run-a-way scrape; an expectation which was shortly realized. We had not gone far when the train commenced running. I was on the pony, and he did not seem disposed to lag behind, but made every exertion to come out "first best" in the race; as I had nothing but a man's saddle I jumped off, after getting in advance of the train, and you may imagine my position, with the whole train coming towards me, and the clouds of dust so thick that I could not see them. The last I did see of them they were running three or four teams abreast and making as much confusion as only such "critters" can when they get frightened. Cattle here are as different from what they are in the states as day is from night; and I think a little as Mrs. W— says, that they are paying up for the abuse they received at the start. They have been maltreated, cursed and hallooed at all the way, but now the men durst not speak loud to them they are so easily frightened. We are waiting for our cattle to be found; hunted till the afternoon, and have lost our best yoke. The two Wilson families lost so many they had to join teams and go on with one wagon. While hunting for the cattle one of the company was shot at by an Indian, who missed his mark. This afternoon we traveled four miles to another camp ground, and had another frightful runaway before stopping. The dogs, now, are all killed; but the cattle get frightened at any thing, and sometimes at nothing. We dare not ride in the wagons, for the cattle are perfectly wild—and I believe the people are too, for they don't know what they are doing.

Saturday, August 9

Started and drove all the loose cattle ahead; the men, women and children also go ahead of the teams, or far enough behind, so as not to frighten the cattle. In this wild region we cannot milk our cows any more than so many untamed antelopes. Perhaps they smell the wild animals, or scent the Indians; though the dogs frightened them in the first place. After experiencing so many hardships, you doubtless will think I regret taking this long and tiresome trip, and would rather go back than proceed to the end of my journey. But, no, I have a great desire to see Oregon, and, besides, there are many things we meet with—the beautiful scenery of plain and mountain, and their inhabitants, the wild animals and the Indians, and natural curiosities in abundance—to compensate us for the hardships and mishaps we encounter. People who do come must not be worried or frightened at trifles; they must put up with storm and cloud as well as calm and sunshine; wade through rivers, climb steep hills, often go hungry, keep cool and good natured always, and possess courage and ingenuity equal to any emergency, and they will be able to endure unto the end. A lazy person should never think of going to Oregon.—Our cattle, by treating them kindly and speaking to them gently, are beginning to get a little tame, and we can now venture to ride in the wagons. Here we have very little grass, and have great difficulty in finding enough for our stock; what there is, is dried up, but the cattle eat it.

Friday, August 15
We have found some good grass, and the cattle are into it up to their eyes; it looks like timothy, off at a distance, just ready to mow.—At one place here we have had to drive our cattle down 2000 feet to water; in doing this we were obliged to leave a cow, which had not strength to walk after the fatigue of going down and up this mountain of a hill.—Again, there is no grass, but the soil is of an ashy nature, very mellow and consequently dusty, and produces nothing but the sage brush. On further we come across warm springs (not the boiling springs) oozing out of the top of the ground; a cold spring is near by. On the opposite side of the river from us is a spring flowing out of the wall of a rock, large enough to turn a mill; it is a very beautiful stream, clear as crystal, and runs so rapidly that it looks white as ice as it flows over the rock, and roars like a mill race. We got some salmon of the Indians here.

Monday, August 18
We passed the Salmon Falls, at which place Capt. Taylor's company caught up with us; one of his women had got her arm broken going down a steep hill, where the road was only wide enough for a wagon, at the side of which was this woman. I wonder she was not smashed to pieces.—

Tuesday, August 19
This morning we expected a fuss with the Indians; one shot from across the river and killed a cow, and then snapped his gun many times at the men, some one of whom had killed the Indian's dog. This, in my opinion ought not to have been done. It is not always that the Indians are the aggressors; when they are it is well enough to chastise them, even with severity, but it is certainly a wrong policy, and results in much mischief, very often to unoffending people, to molest these ignorant and revengful savages even by killing a dog.

Thursday, August 21
We forded the Snake River, which runs so swift that the drivers (four to a team) had to hold on to the ox yokes to keep from being swept down by the current. The water came into the wagon boxes, and after making the island we raised the boxes on blocks, engaged an Indian pilot, doubled teams, and reached the opposite bank in safety. It is best in fording this river to engage a pilot.— The "Telegraph Company," as we call them, who passed us in such a hurry on the Platte, have left their goods and wagons scattered over the mountains. We find them every day. Their cattle have given out, and I have seen several head of them at a time which had been left dead at the different camping places on

the road. We drove too slow on the Platte, and the "Telegraph" hurried too fast, and while our cattle are comparatively strong and in good condition, and will enable us, if we have time before the setting in of winter, to reach our destination, theirs are so worn out from hard usage that it is doubtful if they get through at all this season. We have met some "packers," and they inform us that we are too late to cross the Cascade mountains this season.

Monday, August 25

Palmer's company found a dead man, shot through the heart, supposed to be one of the returning packers.

Tuesday, August 26

A poney was stolen by the Indians last night. We are now camped with three companies, and an encampment of Indians is near us; but we are not afraid of them when they come in sight. It is only when they keep out of sight, and hid in some secret place, near enough to see us, that they are to be feared or will commit mischief, if they can. The Indians we have met with here are more savage, cunning and treacherous than any we have yet seen. At one place they had cut a road through the willows, so that they could come up to camp after night undiscovered. The willows were not cleared quite up to the road, but a short space was left to hide in ambush, so that the enemy could attack us by surprise. They know where we have to camp, and often see us when we are not aware of it. If a company is large enough they are too great cowards to attack it, but watch an opportunity to steal.—Our captain has at last resigned, and had sufficient cause for so doing. It is our desire to travel with a captain, and not with a tribe whose insubordination will not allow of one.—Here we find balm of gilead trees, which when dry, make very good fuel. Some of them are large enough for saw logs, and it is very pleasant to see trees again after traveling hundreds of miles over the sage plains.—We have forded Boisee River, passed the Fort of that name, and the second time forded Snake River, which we have left never to return, and on Thursday the 4th of September pitched our tents upon the top of a high mountain; but away up above us are mountains still higher. These are the Wind River Mountains. Here we left Dr. Perkins, of Indiana. His team gave out, and he waits for another company.—This is a dismal morning, as it has been raining; the hills are very slippery, and before us is a mountain that looks as if it could not be climbed. We are at one of those places where the way cannot be seen twenty steps ahead, but as we proceed openings are found to let us through, and where others have been we can go. It is snowing in the mountains while it is raining in the valleys.

Anonymous Soldier

The Rogue River Wars of 1853-56 had their beginnings in conflicts between miners and the Native Oregonians in southern Oregon. Volunteer military units were formed in the Willamette Valley and southern Oregon to fight in the conflict. The following letter by an "anonymous" volunteer appeared in the Salem *Oregon Statesman* on October 18, 1853—and "anonymous" since the volunteer's sympathetic understanding of the Native Oregonians of the region might well have earned him severe reproach from many of his less understanding comrades. The letter was also published in *An Arrow in the Earth* (1991) by Terence O'Donnell.

The Rogue River Wars ended with the removal of the Native Oregonians of southern Oregon to reservations. The volunteers billed the federal government $107,287.20 for their "services." For further information on their mercenary motives, see House Executive Document No. 99, 33rd Congress, 1st Session, pp. 2-5. Chief John of the Rogues said: "It is not your war which had killed my people but your peace."—T. O'D.

A Rebuke for Racists, Settlers, Bureaucrats, Mercenaries, and Thieves

October 18, 1853

Editor, *Oregon Statesman*
Salem, Oregon Territory

A few years since the whole valley was theirs alone. No white man's foot had ever trod it. They believed it theirs forever. But the gold digger come, with his pan and his pick and shovel, and hundreds followed. And they saw in astonishment their streams muddied, towns built, their valley fenced and taken. And where their squaws dug camus, their winter food, and their children were wont to gambol, they saw dug and plowed, and their own food sown by the hand of nature, rooted out forever, and the ground it occupied appropriated to the rearing of vegetables for the white man. Perhaps no malice yet entered the Indian breast. But when he was weary of hunting in the mountains without success, and was hungry, and approached the white man's tent for bread; where instead of bread he received curses and kicks, ye treaty kicking men—ye Indian exterminators think of these things.

A Soldier

Calvin B. West
1814-1854

Calvin West had high hopes when he settled in the beautiful Umpqua River country in 1853 and began finding supporters for the Baptist academy he intended to establish, though he missed his wife and five children, who were still in Ohio. Nothing he had done in his adult life to that point had proved either lucrative or stable. But he was determined to change all that with a new start in the wonderful rural settlement of Garden Valley.

In 1854 West returned to his family and packed them up for a long sea journey to Oregon via Panama. He had never been happier in his life, he claimed. His plans for a Baptist school were maturing. Teachers would arrive soon. He described the perfect site for a family home to his wife.

At the Panamanian village of Virgin Bay, however, many of West's shipmates contracted cholera. In all, thirty passengers died en route, including West, who apparently caught the disease while assisting the ship's surgeon. What would have been southern Oregon's first Baptist school was not to be. The following letter was first published in *Calvin B. West: An Obscure Chapter in the History of Southern Oregon* (1961). The original is housed in the Special Collections, Knight Library, University of Oregon.—S.A.

Oregon Is a Wicked Paradise, Washington a Children's Heaven

A MISSIONARY'S LETTER

Garden Valley, Oregon Territory
January 23, 1854

My Dear Beloved Anna—

Last evening I wrote a letter in answer to Ma's and yours of Nov. 8th, which I received night before last. (Saturday eve.) And now I am set down to converse a little with my Dear children. And what shall be our subject my Love? Do you say Oregon—or Heaven. Take your choice—did you say Oregon before you thought? Well then listen. Oregon, you know, is a large , though not so very large, country, embracing extensive ranges of lofty mountains, covered with tall straight evergreen timber trees; with here and

there a mighty towering mountainous Peak, reaching miles into the sky, covered with perpetual snow, and seen from many hundred miles distant.

. . . within the borders thus environing the intervening country, lie spread out the most beautiful Valleys, meandering Rivers, Creeks, rivulets and Rills; and these fringed with a low growth of trees, schrubs and vines gay in blossoms or more inviting still in bounteous lucious fruit, ever emitting an arrowmatic fragrance equalled only by the tropical Isles of the Sea. . . .

May be you have not heard of the grand division of this Country. You know we have a great River here; this separates the two countries. On one side it is called Oregon; the other side is named in honor of a man sometimes called the Father, and sometimes the Savior of his Country. I live in Oregon, but the other country is reported to be far—far better than this; very many are moving there, both from here and all parts of the world.

It is so healthy here in Oregon, yet it is much more so there, just the opposite side of the River. Here we have some colds, and occasional pains. There, they say, the people never take cold nor ever suffer the least pain. In Oregon, children must become men and women very quick; but then of course they must grow old, too; but on the other side of the River, I understand they never become old. Do you ask me if I believe this? You know, my Dear, that I am quite credulous, easy to believe. But I think there is this advantage, to credulity: the credulous are easy of faith. You see I am inclined to believe *all*. So we will go on. In Oregon people sell and drink liquor, gamble, fight and even murder sometimes; but nothing of this kind exists on the other side of the River. All are very pious there, yes, all, for they have a law that none shall live on that side unless they are true Christians. I think by this time you are wishing to live there. I too have thought much of it. But they have no preaching nor teaching there. I suppose they are good and wise enough without. So what could I do there? You may ask what they do who live there? I suppose they just enjoy themselves as children would in a large, fine, grand house; filled with everything good, sweet and beautiful. Some folks do not appear to think of anything but enjoyment, you know, caring but little to aid others in the way to happiness. I do not say this is the case with the people on the other side of the River. But I think I am content to remain in Oregon and try to reform the wicked and inform the ignorant.

Your Devoted Husband
C.B. West

Nancy Judson
1830-?

In nineteenth-century Oregon, affairs of the heart were as subject to success or failure as they are today. The letter which follows was addressed to the Territorial Legislature, at that time the only body authorized to grant a divorce and which in Mrs. Judson's case it did.

However, such cases commonly have two sides. Mrs. Judson's husband, Lewis Hubbel Judson, a missionary who came to Oregon in 1840, wrote to his sister several months following the divorce to describe his former wife as "that apology for a woman." It is difficult to know where the truth lies.—T. O'D.

I Cannot Live with Mr. Judson

A WILLAMETTE VALLEY WIFE PETITIONS THE LEGISLATURE FOR DIVORCE

Polk county Oregon Territory
November 15, Ad 1858

I humbly Beg of the Legislator of oregon to grant me a bill of divorcement for I cannot live with Mr Judson he misuses me in everry shape he is capable of doing he has knocked me down and scolded me and beemeaned me in everry shape and lyed on me as bad as one could lly on another and does not Provide for me Nor the family as he aught to do But has squandered all that father has givin mee and has squandered every thing wee have in the world and has mortgaged my land and his and it is all gone and he is not able to support me nor the Children neither is he capable of taking care of us the children are ragged and go not fit to bee seen and have to depend on the Neighbors for their bread and do not get mutch of that I have not lived with Mr Judson since the first of last December Ad 1857 from that time to this I have had to support my self as best I could and the children has been Poorly taken care of for they have had to take care of them selves in a maner that is too of them for I have one of them with me sending him to scool the yongest a little boy the other too is down at Clatsap where he keeps them have stalved and half naked My Children has never bee to school of any consiquenc and he never will sende them I have three children one little girl 10 years olde the 10 day of next december one boy 12 years old 22 of February next the yongest is alittle boy 7 years olde the 26 day of may next and he knows more than all the rest for I have been sending him to school ever since wee parted Now if it will please your honerable boddy to give me a bill and give me the Children I will every Pray ec

I ever remain your humble friend
Mrs Nancy Judson

Henry Cummins
1840-1901

Henry Cummins believed that a diary ought to be a tool for self-improvement and self-evaluation. He greatly admired Benjamin Franklin, who recommended keeping diary-like inventories for similar reasons. Cummins spent his youth in rural Lane County. While living in Eugene City he helped initiate lyceums, lectures, and debates to stimulate himself and his circle of intellectual friends. He planned a "Great Pantheon of Science" which he intended to stock with his own and other geologic and scientific collections. Restless and ambitious, Cummins began a series of moves in 1864 to the eastern United States.

After clerking for the legislature in Salem, he left Oregon. Moving to Idaho for a time, he became involved with state politics. Later, he resided in Washington D.C. and bragged about hobnobbing with such powerful national figures as Salmon Chase, Chief Justice of the United States. He told Oregon family members and friends about various schemes and dreams including the establishment of a ship canal from New Orleans to the Gulf of Mexico, and the founding and organization of the Postal Telegraph Company.

Eventually, Cummins moved to New York City, where he died at age 62. Many admired Cummins's "meteoric genius" but believed, as did the Eugene man who wrote his Oregon obituary in 1901, that Henry "died poorer than he ought to have been (and) was a good deal in advance of the average citizen in intelligence though not in practical methods of plodding through the world . . . like the draft horse." The following selection is taken from a microfilm of Cummins's diary located in Special Collections, Knight Library, University of Oregon.—S.A.

Perfecting the Self in Eugene, Then Going East Forever

January 6, 1858

btained a Phrenological chart of my cranium, of C. Lafollet. $1.00

January 17

Took a pleasure walk upon Skinner's Butte. & made some genealogical discoveries. The rock of which the greater part of the eminince is composed is pillars of rock from three to five feet long and a bout two feet in diameter and having from four to seven sides; being entirely separated from each other by a thin layer of dirt.

March 10

Read an Essay on Tobacco—16 pages—a Lecture on Tobacco—11 pages and other articles on the same weed amounted to twenty-six pages.

March 29

Had the company of Mr. E.L. Applegate as a visitor. Conversed on Philosophical, Scientific and humorous and religious, historical subjects. read newspapers & c. played violin & c. & c.

May 8

Went to Eugene City to see about getting to teach a school. Spent a couple of hours conversing with Prof. J. H. Rogers and looking at valuable books that he had lately received from Gen. Lane.

June 14

I will here state that I wash my teeth every day, neither chew nor smoke tobacco, nor use anything that tends to keep the mouth otherwise than clean. Drink no tea nor coffee, nor anything stronger than milk. And I am very strict about my diet, and the result is so beneficial that I would advise every person both young and old to adopt the same rules

June 24

Studied Natural Philosophy—Hydraulics. Studied Phonography. Split, pealed and ricked one hundred rails. While working, I engaged my mind on the Subject of "Free Moral Agency," and collected some important ideas. Attended to the daily ordinance of ba(thing) ptism, which is an excellent ceremony. Played the violin. Practicing rigidity of Diet, which is strictly vegetable. And my drink nothing stronger than water. So help me tater.

June 25

Laid out a plan of study for the future. Which is: To devote the next five or six years to reading, and acquiring general information, & then commence studying particular subjects. Amen.

June 26

Perused the *Pacific Journal,* the first paper every printed in Eugene City. And am happy to say that of all the Papers published in Oregon, I consider it by far the best. It is "Devoted to Physical, Intellectual and Moral Improvement." And the articles that graced this first sheet are certainly calculated to accomplish the desired end. I am personally well acquainted with the Editor, Mr. Rogers, having received Moral and Intellectual instructions from him for nearly a year; and I am also personally well acquainted with Mr. Wilson; and know both to be men of excellent character.

July 15

Read two hundred pages in Mrs. Sigourney's *Letters to Young Ladies,* in the subject of Knowledge, Industry, Domestic employment, Health and Dress, Manners and Accomplishment, Sisterly virtue, Books, Friendship, Cheerfulness, Conversation, Evening Thoughts, Superficial Attainments, Benevolence. The beautiful and exalted thoughts set forth herein, clothed in such elegant, yet plain language, certainly ought to find place in the mind of every Young Lady. They can, there find Advice of the purest character; and if they are discouraged, there they can find sweet consolation and encouragement. If they have done anything amiss, there they will find reproof, which will not only point their misdeeds, but will also point the better path to pursue.

August 24

Walked about two miles for exercise. Entered the holy sanctuary of contemplation. . . . Bathed.

March 14, 1859

Was a little insulted by a large man striking me in the face. I took a stool and attempted to hurt him, for which I repent &c. &c. &c. &c. &c. &c. &c. &c. &c. &c.

September 30

Read 80 pages in the *Life of Fanny Hill*, a book which has a good aim in view that of giving us peep behind the curtain of the life of woman of pleasure. Yet it enters rather much into detail and the scenes represented are not much fitted to cultivate virtuous thoughts in the minds of its readers; and I also read 50 pages in the Private Life of Byron . . . a book not of a very moral nature. It shows us how the so-called great men conduct themselves in Private life, which is, in a way, not at all disirable, expecially to a person of moral disposition.

January 27, 1860

Attended the debate of the young men's debating club in company with a young lady. Opened and closed the debate, also made one speech during the main discussion. Negative gained the decision. The question was, Resolved that woman ought to have equal privileges with men, religiously and politically. Had several hours conversation with a young lady after the debate.

August 7

Finished reading Sumner's speech on the admission of Kansas, showing the barbarism of Slavery and the unconstitutionality of its extension—the greatest speech that i ever read on the subject.

September 24

Practiced healing a little—relieved a little brother from a fit or spasm, caused by a morbid state of the stomach and bowels, having a slight touch of the diarrhea,—did it by bathing in slightly hot water. In the evening bathed him in tepied water and kept wet compresses on him till about ten o'clock at night when he became almost entirely relieved.

October 30, 1861

Arranged my lecture on temperance, wrote the outline, It consisted of an answer to the question, "Why do men who have joined the pledge return to drinking again?" The ground that I took was that man is not altogether the subject of his own acts—that is he is governed by his organization and circumstances both of which are beyond his control.

Eugene Skinner
1809-1881

Eugene Skinner may rightly be considered the founder of one of Oregon's best-known cities—Eugene. Skinner and his wife and children traveled overland to California in 1845. They journeyed to Oregon by horseback in the spring of 1846, following the old Hudson's Bay Company trappers' trail. The children were carried in baskets attached by rawhide strands around the pack saddle arms. In the summer of 1846, Skinner marked his claim by building a windowless and doorless cabin on the place that would one day be called Skinner Butte. At that time, it was the only settler's structure between Sacramento and the upper Willamette Valley.

Skinner briefly returned to California during the 1849 gold rush. The townsite of Eugene was platted in 1852. The following letter was written in 1860 to Skinner's sister Phoebe and was first published in the *Lane County Historian* in 1976. Skinner's papers are located in the Lane County Historical Museum.—S.A.

Oregon Is Not Wealth, but Contentment and a Conscience Clear of Offense

Eugene City, Oregon
March 18, 1860

My Dear Sister

Yesterday evenings mail brot a long and welcome letter from you of date of Jany 20th 1860. . . .

It is now some 12 years since I have had the pleasure of getting a letter from you direct, before the one last evening . . . you are a Stranger to this far off west and those that inhabit it, and the beautiful scenes which surround us in Oregon but could you but see our land of enchantment—& we could be once more together in this Country, we would try to live our childhood days over again and I still hope to see you and our brother in this country yet: the trip is not a long one nor very expensive, and then I think that you and your kind companion in this Country could make a good living.

Though the Country is new, we have no aristocracy and no high style of living   Still we enjoy life as well as those who roll in luxuries. My Dear wifes health for a few years past has not been of the best, but she has now passed that critical period in woman and she is now. . .well and becoming Stout & hearty. She is 46 years old as for our children they no nothing of Sickness They are all verry larger of their ages. Mary is as tall as I am & will outweigh me The next Leanora is more slender. Phebe is robust and is as much like the original in our younger days. St. John is said by all to be as Smart as the Smartest. Amilia soon will be five years old & I think the Smartest of them all. The four older are going to School, as this place there is a Cumberland Presbyterian College, a primmarie School, and a high school. The high school building is on my claim a little over ¼ mile from our house, the professor is an excellent man a Graduate from Dublin College. I made the arrangement for him to teach for 5 years from first of December last, and am in hopes that my children will by that time have acquired a good education   Mary, beside the usual English, is studying French. I intend to have her as well the ballance to thuraly understand Mathematics   She as well as St. John are quite good in figures. Leanora is more dull, Phebe wont work Spends her time in reading   Our school has about 50 students many of them young women from 18 to 25 years. The District school ¼ mile from our house has some 60 to 80 children mostly small. The College 1½ miles from our house has some 80 to 100 students Our little town has from 900 to 1000 inhabitants, One Episcopal Church, One Old School Presbyterian . . . and one Methodist Meeting House, 8 stores, 2 drug stores, two Hotel two Saloons, two Printing Offices, three Black, one tin & sheet Iron factory, one Goldsmith, 3 Waggon Shops, two Livery Stables One market, one Shoe Shop, two Saddle & Hemp makers one saddle tree maker, One Grist & One Saw mill. . . . One door and Sash factory two Cabint Shops, and one Post Office and your humble Servant has been for the last ten years Post Master.

In the month of november last we had a full of some 2 inches of snow one night— the next morning it looked Irregular to see Tomato Pumpkin Cucumbers & Bean blossoms Peering through the Snow it was all gone by ten o clock and the vine Continued to blossom until about the middle of Dec. . . . Ice formed on the Ponds . . . none in the stream, to the thickness of 3 inches which the boys used for skating . . . my Peach & Almond trees are in full bloom Strawbury Bloom have been seen every month this winter. . . . Stock require little or no feed in Oregon in winter unless near a town. I have some 100 h of cows & stock cattle and they have no feed this winter except what nature provides, upon the whole will candidly say that was I offered all—and be Compelled to live there or live oregon on a bare subsistance I would take Oregon as it is nothing more than a bare subsistance that we have in any country, tis not wealth, but Contentment and a Conscience clear of offence that makes the sum total of this life I am tolerable well off in property.

Your brother
Eugene

Preston W. Gillette
1825-1905

Founded as an American fur post in 1811, Astoria passed to British control during the War of 1812 and was renamed Fort George. With the transfer of the Hudson's Bay Company headquarters from Fort George to Fort Vancouver in 1824, the settlement went into decline.

In 1846, American immigrants began to settle in the locale and soon thereafter Astoria's salmon industry began. Among the immigrants was Preston Gillette, a young bachelor, law student, and nurseryman who arrived with the 1852 migration. Gillette started his nursery near Astoria in 1853 and stocked the new business with plant material sent by sea from his father's nursery in Ohio. After leaving for a gold rush, Gillette returned to Astoria and became a representative in the legislature for his region. The following are excerpts from Gillette's unpublished 1860-62 diary written at his Astoria nursery. The complete document is located in the Clatsop County Historical Society, Astoria.—T. O'D.

At Home and Almost Alone for Ten Years
AN ASTORIA BACHELOR'S DIARY

Saturday, January 12, 1860

The rainy and stormy character of the day kept us confined to the house. So we made a sort of wash day, or job of it: mending old pants sewing up rents, and on buttons. A vary unpleasant occupation, yet sometimes necessary to a bachelor. I generally go to town on Saturday, and did intend to go today,—more, I suppose from force of habit, than from press of business. But the rain prevents it. On account thereof, I feel a little disappointed. But why should I? I have pleanty to eat, drink and to ware, and a comfortable house, and Johnny's a tolerable companion. I attribute it, to a craving of the natural wants of man. The want of society—Society of the opposite sex *too*.

Monday, January 14

This has been a stormy, unpleasant day, more than half of which we were compeled to remain in the house.

As we sat eating some delicious Baldwins, that grew on the two large trees, just back of the house, the thought occured to me that it would be well enough for future refference; to note down a short sketch of my operations, from my first settlement on this place. I first visited Clatsop County in Nov 1852, shortly after my arrival in Oregon. I remained about two weeks in the County, when I left, satisfied that I could not find a place to sute me.

After traveling over the greater part of the Willamette Valley in quest of a "claim," not being able to buy such as I wished, and finding none vacant that I would have; I again returned to Clatsop in Feb 1853, and bought the South part of what is my present farm. For which I paid $187.50. There was about the 6th part of an acre cleared on it, just at the river landing. Where stood a log cabin, in which myself and Thom Scott and I held our "claims" jointly. The line running through the middle of the house enabled us to fulfil the requirements of the Donation Law, "that each claimant should reside upon his own land." The small cleared spot at the landing, was done principaly by the indians. It seems to have been a village, or camping place, occupied by them from time immemmorial. The indian name for my place is "Kolotska," Old "Twilch" the elk hunter informs me that this was in old times, his "illahee" home, that he was born there. Twilch was an old man. And remembered Lewis and Clark when they were here. The filthe and offal of the camp had made the ground exceedingly rich. They buried their dead in the back part of what's now the "mills" (my) orchard, where we burned up many bones (I burned up a wagon load of human skulls and bones when I cleared the land, where the north part of the orchard stands) in clearing the land. I found the skeleton of an arm and hand from the elbow down complete, on which was 5 brate rings.

The first spring after my arrival, I cleared and planted (with potatoes and vegitables) about ½ acre.

Sunday, March 17, 1861

The Steamship *Panama* arrived this morning from San Francisco. She stoped 3 hours at the dock, & took in wood. The news from the Atlantic States indicate that *disunion*, or *civil war is inevitable*. The Southern Congress is now in Session at Montgomery Al. Hon Jeff Davis of Miss. is President of the Southern Confedracy. During the night my boat draged her anchor and went ashore damageing her so much that I had to leave her to be repared, & we were compleled to borrow a boat to come home in.

Monday, March 18

Fair weather yet. We planted Peas, latuce Parsnips & carrots today. According to the Dutch signs. However we planted the root crops in the wrong stage of the moon. But we resurved one half of the Parsnip bed to be planted in the "dark of the Moon."

Saturday, March 30

Showers and Sunshine alternately all day   John started to the Plains this morning and left me all alone. I have been grafting pear trees all today. After I finished my supper I made myself a good fire & seated myself; I was museing upon passing events & had nearly fallen asleep in my chair, when a rap at the door aroused me. I found old McEwan, almost exhausted from fatigue & exposure. He had been lost in the wood & traveled a great distance through the wet brush;—he had waded shoughs & creeks until he was thoroughly saturated with water & mud, or, at least his clothes were. The Jaunt was enough to out do a young man much less a man of 80 years.

Sunday, March 31

The Storm still continues, and the rain still pours down almost unceasingly. I found Old Luck, with a young calf this morning.

Monday, April 8

In obedience to a summons to appear at Astoria on 9th, I started after dinner, calling on my way for Mr. Jeffers & wife, who accompanied me. We encountered a savere squal in our passage across the bay; but received no damage. On reaching town, I found President Lincolns inaugural address. Everybody seems to be pleased with this document. It seems perfectly adapted to the Spirit of the times.

Tuesday, April 9

Court convened this morning, pursuant to Notice. Judge Wait on the bench. I was drawn uypon the Grand Jury. which body sat near two days, when it adjourned without any bills. There were but 3 or 4 cases Before the Court & yet it was in session 3 days. My old friend D. Ingalls was devorced from his wife.

A novel excitement exists in town on the question of prayer or no prayer in Schools. A question arose, whether School Should be opened by prayer. A Few favored it, but a large majority opposed it. No little fanaticism & angry spirit was manifested. One of the cases that occupied the attention of this originated upon a difference of $12, but a Small Sum for either party to loose. By the time it was decided it cost the Plaintiff $500. So much for "lawing."

Tuesday, May 7

The news from the Atlantic States this morning was of a painful and startling character. It indicates that the older States are Soon to be in a blaze of Civil War! Federal troops were attacked in the city of Baltamore on their way to Washington. Southern ports are to be blockaded etc. O, My Country! Where now is your boasted permancy and durability? Where is the cherished boon of our fathers, that has been our proudest boast for near a century?—The Federal constitution—Broken, and trampled upon—where now is that once brillint constelation of Stars, and the waveing Stripes? Are they disserved and scattered? May it not be So—

Monday, July 1

I took another hunt for the old mare but was unsuccessful. In the afternoon Elijah and I went to town. The news from the States is unimportant.

Thursday, July 4

At 4 o'clock I was awakened by the boom of the independence gun at Astoria. The Morning was beautiful and after a vary early breakfast started for the celebration on Clatsop Plains. We reached the appointed place in due time, where we found the American flag proudly waveing over the assembling multitude.

The Citazens in the nighborhood brought in an abundance of provisions which was spread upon a table already prepared in a beautiful grove upon Col. Taylor's farm. After the reading of the Declaration, by Mr. Deardoff, Rev. Mr. Thompon & Mr. Callender made Some vary appropriate remarks. I was then called upon, and am proud to say that my little Speech created conciderable Sensation. The Sesessionists that were there looked black as thunder clouds. Mr. Deardoff then made an excellent speech; and then came the feast.

I must not omit mentioning the name of "Twilch," the old indian elk hunter. He is a very old indian and knew, and saw Lewis & Clark when they wintered here in 1805 & 1806. He sayes that my home was at one time his home, or "illahee," and that of his people for ages back. That it was an old indian village, and had been for ages. Twilch, visits this river about once in every 8 or 10 days, to hunt. He always stops at my place, and asks me for powder, shot, or something to eat. I never refuse him, often buy elk meat or duck, from him. He was so old when the white people came here, that he did not learn to speak English, or even Jargon well.

Saturday, July 6

Each day, for some days past we have had a little mist in the morning one evening. Strawberries are abundant yet. They are later than I ever knew them. The bees acted much as if they were going to Swarm, but they did not. The price of bees, is growing up very fast. Three years ago, a good hive of bees was worth $125.00 in ready cash. Now they can be had at $20 to $25. Honey, until last summer was worth $1.00 per lb. It is probably now worth 50 cts. I hoed potatoes all day.

A Journey to the Mines! Monday, April 14, 1862

I have ocupied the last two week in arrangeing my busines & makeing preparations for a trip to the Salmon river gold mines. I am inclined to apologize to myself for takeing such a step at this period, haveing so far successfully resisted the many temptations that have been afforded, in the scores of previous gold excitements. But I have remained at home, almost alone for the last 10 years; and have now resolved to take a cruse—not confidently, indeed, scarecely expecting to make anything.

Having put my place in charge of Elijah & made the necessary arrangements; I started this evening on the Multnomah, in company with about 15 of my neighbors. The boat left the wharf amid the shouts and cheers of our Astoria friends. Their many well wishes, & big guns fired, were flattering tokens of their regards. I took with me, a horse, blankets, a change of clotheing & money enough to defray my expenses there & back.

Harriette Applegate
1845-1862

Gertrude Applegate
1841-1867

Gertrude Applegate

Harriette and Gertrude Applegate were first cousins living less than a mile apart in Yoncalla, Oregon. When the Civil War began, each held her own opinion about the conflict that also divided several hundred thousand American families. Harriette, like most of the large family clan named Applegate, fiercely believed in the Union cause. Gertrude was to elope with a Southern sympathizer from nearby Jacksonville—an act which caused her father Jesse Applegate such anger and anguish that he scratched her name out of the family Bible with a pen knife. Harriette, an aspiring artist and writer, died at sixteen before the war ended. Gertrude died of tuberculosis at age twenty-six, just five years after Harriette. Both Harriette and Gertrude were writing to another cousin, Theresa Applegate, who had moved to Ashland. These letters are from the voluminous Applegate family correspondence in the Special Collections of the Knight Library, University of Oregon. See also *Skookum: An Oregon Pioneer Family's History and Lore* (1988) by Shannon Applegate.—S.A.

Yankee and Pacifist

TWO COUSINS ARGUE THE CIVIL WAR FROM YONCALLA

Yoncalla, Oregon
May 13, 1861

Dear Theresa,

I think now is the time for women to assert their rights, for they should all have the right to fight. If the southern women are embroidering flags and rattlesnakes why can't the northern ones have spunk enough to tear them down!! We heard that when Jo. Lane landed he raised the secession flag and began to make a speech. The women broke loose, tore down the flag and burnt it in the street, and beat him out with rotten eggs. There has been talk of Jo. Lane trying to raise his flag at Roseburg, but if old Jo does, there will be a fight in Umpqua, for our Republican men there say that they will not bear it!!! If they do stick it up, I hope their women will tear it down. . . . How I would glory in burning their treacherous rattlesnake. Their emblem is well chosen! The South is sinking and the sooner it is down, the better. Our President has come under many difficulties and he is showing himself worthy of his office. I am not afraid for our Union for I know the just God will not give the power into hands of these oppressors of the human race.

Your Cousin,
Harriette Applegate

Yoncalla, Oregon
February 12, 1862

Dear Theresa,

What an awful state this continent is in now. His Satanic Majesty is certainly loosed upon it, and has, for the time, undisputed sway. How do you stand on the War? . . . I am the only "peace man" in the family. I think I would vote for a compromise, anything to stop, anything I say, to stop the shedding of blood. I am eager in the cause of liberty, I would like to see every slave free, yet to gain this effect the country will have to be steeped in debt that we shall never see ended in this life, yea, in many more lives to come. I would rather be at quits. Don't blame me for such sentiments, I am but a woman with a woman's weak brain and soft heart. I am a deep "sympathizer" but not a sympathizer of rebels but with the widows and the orphans, the desolate home circle, the famine and the misery, that is why I would compromise. I can but see the utter folly of it. For when the "storm dieth not, and the fire be not quenched" as long as slavery exists this war will go on and on and this generation will expiate the sin of it as will other generations to come.

Your cousin,
Gertrude Applegate

Royal Augustus Bensell
1838-1921

Royal Augustus Bensell came to California with his father from Wisconsin during the Gold Rush. In a fever of patriotism, Bensell and a number of other Californians volunteered for Civil War duty. Forming a group called Company D, they were assigned to Fort Yamhill in Oregon's Coast Range. "This rowing after the Siwash is no part of a soldiers duty," observed Corporal Bensell in the diary he kept for three long years as he fought rain, hunger, and monotony. Instead of fighting the blood-drenched battles endured by other Union protectors far to the east, Bensell rounded up Indian families and came to believe that "A Soldier is a Slave." He grew to despise Indian Agents and privately condemned the callousness of officials who "expect the Blind to see, the lame to walk, and all Siwash to subsist on nothing." The Chinook Jargon word *Siwash*, a corruption of the French word *sauvage,* was commonly used until the 1930s.

Bensell's pithy and often insightful diary (the original is housed in the Special Collections, Knight Library, University of Oregon) provides a fascinating lens through which to view the desultory life of a Civil War soldier obliged to serve his time in Oregon. Bensell later became one of Newport's earliest and most prominent settlers. The following selections are from *All Quiet on the Yamhill : The Civil War in Oregon, The Journal of Corporal Royal A. Bensell* (1959).—S.A.

Rowing after Indians Is Not a Real Soldier's Duty

A UNION CORPORAL'S DIARY FROM FORT YAMHILL

April 27, 1864

Clear. Break Camp by 8 o'clock and cross a sand-point five miles wide. Came to the Umpqua River. Stopt at Umpqua City consisting of a small grocery and a large untenanted Hotel. Here originally stood Fort Umpqua and among these bleak sand hills Jo' Drew established an Ind Agency. The remains of the garrison can be seen ready for shipment to Scotsberg, Government having left no one to take charge of the property at the time of its vacation. The Officers Quarters were expensive buildings. Some neat conservatories still stand, monuments of useless extravagance.

We walk down the River, two miles, and by dint of hard shouting aroused the ferry man over in Winchester Bay. He said tide was to strong to cross yet, so all hands found a shade and took a snoose. At 4 o'clock we commenced swimming the mules, 4 at once, two at each side of the small boat. The River at this point a good mile wide. We were two hours getting our mules over. Found a nice camping place. Had milk, eggs & Butter for Supper and potatoes. Turpin injured himself "ateing" this vegetable. When I come back I will speak more of this Boy. All Hands to Bed.

April 28

Clear. Broke camp by 10. Passed Umpqua Light house, now in ruins. This costly structure was built in '60 on a foundation of Sand and this when a fine, solid resting place was near at hand. The Keeper, (Ed Brin) a San Francisco Bummer, retains his "posish" and salary of $800 per annum. The oil and lamps lay exposed to wind and weather. One of the large iron Barge broken lose and drifted ashore, bids fair to remain a loss to U.S. Near all this waste of property is a large wrecked Schooner loaded with timber, the rigging gone, a large hole in her bottom into which the never ceasing surf dashes up and down the hatchway. Barnacles and musels hold silent carnival.

April 29

Clear. Run all night. The first camp surprised us, for there was not an Indian to be seen and everything indicated a premeditated departure. Tyee Jim felt certeain some body had "wa-wawed". I concurred   Going down the river, three miles below town, we captured 8 Indians and were suprised to find some of our anticipated game flown. (Ed Brin), engaged as secret agent by Harvey, was here, drunk. I accuse him of "blowing." This he denied. We tied our prisoners, and leaving three men to watch their camp until morning I started for the Camp over the Bay.

April 30
Clear. The Det left over the river came in early this morning with one Indian. "Tyee" Jim and two men go up to Capt Hamiltons. Find some lumbermen on a spree. Jim narrowly escapes being shot. The boys tho't they were to short handed and come back. I went of to town. Empire City is the county seat of Coos County. There is not over a dozen families in the place, one large Mill which turns out lumber, broom-handles, & and lathe, doing a good business. The employees are decidedly "Roughs." Caught some Siwash to-day.

May 1
Clear. Pike, Plunkett, Clark, Mr. Harvey, & Luce (Mill-man) go up Coos River 25 miles to-day after some Indians. Find at the head of tide water a small ranch owned by one De-Cuys. He had a pretty little girl, some 8 years old. We got two Squaws and a Buck. After getting in the boat I was surprised to hear one of the Squaws (old and blind) aske me, "nika tika nanage nika tenas Julia." I complyed with this parental demand and was shocked to see this little girl throw her arms about old Amanda De-Cuys neck and cry, "clihime Ma Ma." DeCuys promised the Agent to school Julia. We started back with the tide. Got home at midnight. Good night.

May 2
Clear. Yesterday, thro' the influence of Ed Brin, Tyee Jackson's band came in and expressed a "close tumm tumm." One Charly Metcalf who run off the Agent of last year tried the same game on Lt Herzer who after taking a reasonable amount of abuse took a musket and give Mr. Metcalf one minute to leave in. The lumbermen up these bayous and Sloughs are the roughest of men. Nearly all are married to Squaws or else have a written obligation that will marry rather than allow the Ind Agt to deprive them of their concubines. They conceal the Indians, warn them, and otherwise enhance the difficulties of catching the red devils. There are yet some 60 Indians on North Bend Slough, Kitchen Slough, and Coquile River. We arrive after rough voyage across the Bay at camp by midnight. The fact of the business is, this rowing after Siwash is no part of a soldiers duty.

Rachel Colver
1789-?

Rachel Colver was the grandmother of Martha Ann
Colver Sisley, to whom the following letter was
addressed in 1864. Martha Ann and her husband, miner
and farmer Lewis Sisley, lived near other members of
the Colver family in the small southern Oregon
community of Phoenix, where they operated a stage
stop until 1862. After hearing about Idaho gold strikes,
Lewis Sisley gave in to the same restlessness that
originally led him to the Oregon country. He headed
for the eastern mines, later sending for his wife Martha
Ann and children Frank, Donna, and Letty.

This letter concerns Sisley and Colver children who did
not survive the frontier experience. Evidently, both
Martha Ann and her mother—not named here—lost
offspring in the early 1860s. Martha Ann's grandmother
writes not only to give comfort but also to vent her own
loneliness and grief. The loss of a child, whether in
childbirth or as a result of disease or accident, is a
common theme in letters and diaries of pioneer-era
women. The practice of photographing a dead child was
popular all over the United States, particularly in the
1860s, a period some historians call the "Sentimental
Era." Members of the Sisley family eventually settled in
the Baker City area, where a copy of this letter was
found among other family papers.—S.A.

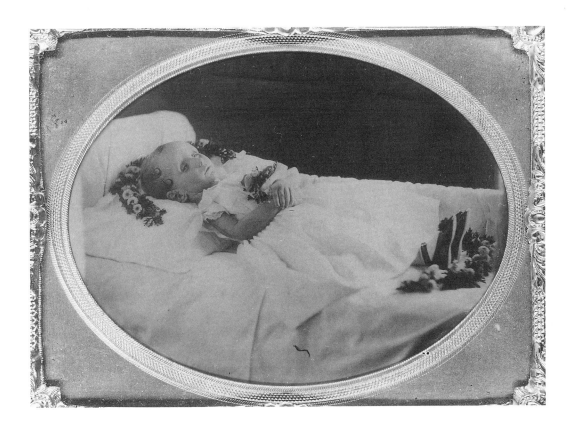

My Brightest Flowers Have Faded
A GRANDMOTHER'S LETTER TO HER GRANDDAUGHTER SO FAR FROM HOME

third day of august, 1864

Phoenix, Ore.

Dear Martha sisley

O h! I was so glad to hear from you. I hope you will take comfort with your pretty family. dont work too hard, martha. Dont troble your self about mony to pale (fence) in little Dudey's grave   I got mr Sprague to pale it in shortly after you left   he done it nice and then I got it painted white   I wish you could see it. Little frances and little quincy are paled in together   poor quincy died very hard   he was several days a dying   mr. foudray sat by him night and day till he died   mr. sprague drest him for his grave. We got his likeness taken after he was dead   I look at it often every day   it was so hard for your poor mother with him to part. It has made them feel lonely. Martha Abi and Donna have written to you About the time they thought you had got settled but they did not know where to direct there letters and they sent them to bannock citty   Martha my grandchild write often and tell me about litttle frank, and little donna and little letty   I never expect to see you again only in Memory. Let us remember each other   I am in my seventy-fifth year since the first of last August   i have not long to stay   "My brightest flowers have faded away." farewell tis but a little word   I am saddened by farewell, martha sisley

Your grandmother,

Rachel Colver

Ellen Hemenway Humphrey
1839-1930

Ellen Hemenway Humphrey worked hard as did most pioneer women in Oregon. After coming via wagon train to Oregon in 1853, she lived on her parents' Donation Land Claim five miles west of what was then known as Eugene City. She kept her diary in pencil. Many farmers and farm families in rural Oregon kept similar diaries during the nineteenth and early twentieth centuries. Such accounts served a number of practical purposes, including information on weather and planting cycles. Ellen Hemenway Humphrey seemed to think it important to keep track of the kind of work she did. Perhaps it increased her sense of accomplishment.

In 1978 a descendant, Edwin A. Simpson, became interested in her hard life as a Willamette Valley farmer's daughter in the 1860s. Using a magnifying glass and great patience, Simpson deciphered her handwriting and published a limited edition, *Diary of Ellen Hemenway Humphrey* (1978). While the language of this slim diary is terse and gives little insight into her feelings about her existence, her brief daily entries reveal the many ways in which women's work has changed. The following excerpt is taken from a transcription of the entire diary located in the Lane County Historical Museum.—S.A.

Work, for the Night Is Coming

A LANE COUNTY FARM WIFE'S DIARY

Tuesday, June 23, 1868

Trimmed a dress and sack for Walter. Cut out a waste for myself. Yesterday Pa brought our rolls home will have some spinning to do.

Wednesday, June 24

Made a white waste.

Thursday, June 25

Cut and made a dress skirt. Mrs. Evans called.

Friday, June 26

Made an apron for Ann. We quit making cheese for a while having made 42 or about 600 lbs. Urban hauled a load of wood.

Saturday, June 27

Cut over a sack. Spun some yarn. Volney came home from the shooting mach with a quarter of beef.

Sunday, June 28

We went to church at Driscal's schoolhouse. Preaching by Miller and Finkins and Charles Richeson.

Monday, June 29

Washed four quilts. Urban hauled wood. Making three loads Pa sent a letter to Mores concerning some land.

Tuesday, June 30

Sewed. Urban hauled wood.

Wednesday, July 1

I did an ironing. Ma and Pa went to Eugene. Urban hauled.

Thursday, July 9

Quilted. Frank got thrown from a horse and hurt very badly.

Friday, July 10

Finished the quilt this morning. I made a riding skirt. Volney invented a revolving rake. Urban hauled wood, Georgy here today.

Saturday, July 11

Spun today.

Sunday, July 12

Read.

Monday, July 13

Went to my farm with Frank. Went through the orchard and prospected for fruit. Spun the afternoon.

Tuesday, July 14

Spun. Also cleaned out my old stove.

Wednesday, July 15

Washed. Pa turned the sheep out.

Thursday, July 16

Thur. Ironed.

Friday, July 17

Knit a footmat.

Sunday, July 19

Read Life of Christ and got to the 425th page.

Monday, July 20

Made a rug.

Tuesday, July 21

Helped Ma tie a wool bed.

Wednesday, July 22

Made a chair cushion-made and mended stockings.

Thursday, July 23

Made Walter a pair of stockings.

Matthew P. Deady
1824-1893

By the 1870s, there were several established towns in the Willamettte Valley, six with their own colleges, some with opera houses, libraries, and the other accouterments of a cultivated urban life. Most impressive of all, a railroad now ran from Roseburg to the Northwest's largest city, Portland.

One of the most distinguished citizens of Portland in this period was Judge Matthew Deady: U.S. District Judge for Oregon, a founder of the Multnomah County Library, President of the Board of Regents of the University of Oregon, and a jurist of national repute. The diary Judge Deady began in 1871 and continued until his death in 1892, and from which the following excerpts are taken, is considered by some scholars as one of the most important diaries produced in nineteenth-century Oregon. The diary was published as *Pharisee among the Philistines: The Diary of Judge Matthew P. Deady 1871-1892* (1975). The "Edward" referred to in the diary is the Judge's son, while "the Hall" refers to a private school for girls.—T. O'D.

The Place Was Crammed with the Elite

THE DIARY OF A FEDERAL JUDGE IN PORTLAND

March 1871

Stout died on Saturday, March 4, at 7 minutes to 10 oclock. Wife and I were both there. He had not spoken since early morning to any one. Funeral procession left Stouts residence at 10oclock, Judge Upton, Trimble, Dolph and myself acting as Pallbearers. There was a large procession of the members of the bar, firemen and carriages notwithstanding the inclemency of the day. We marched down Jefferson St. to Third and thence to the Roman C. Church. There Mass was celebrated and The Requiem sung. Archbishop Blanchet made a few remarks. He thinks in French and attempts to speak in English and the result is not very intelligible. But he is an excellent old man and a very good illustration of a combination of the wisdom of the Serpent and the harmlessness of the Dove. The services were conducted by Belgian Priests whose Latinity smacks strongly of Low Dutch. From the church the procession proceeded down Stark St. to the ferry, where the Pall-bearers dropped out and poor Stout was taken across the river. What will become of his poor widow and children?

Monday, July 24

Mailed letter to E. Applegate in reply to one from him, advising him to keep his boots and shirt collar clean if he went east to lecture, and that a toothbrush regularly used would be a favorable introduction to a Boston audience.

Monday, December 18

Commenced going to my chambers in a hack. Snow fell Sunday night. B., sheriff of the county, died Sunday evening and was buried with a great demonstration on Tuesday, by Methodists, Odd Fellows, Masons, and Common Councilmen. He was naturally a good fellow, but the office of sheriff brought him in contact with vicious influences that he had not the stamina to resist. The newspapers and societies say that he died of inflammatory rheumatism, but I know that he died of a putrid fever which was brought on by the virus of clap getting into his blood and poisoning it, and his wife came pretty near dying from the same cause. . . .

Monday, June 24, 1872

Today is the twentieth anniversary of my marriage. We celebrated it in a modest dinner and bottle of claret. The wedding took place on Thursday at 4 oclock P M in the first cabin built on the Henderson place on south Yamhill. The time which has rolled by has not chilled our youthful affection, but on the contrary, I think I have grown more uxorious with the changing years.

Wednesday, October 9

Attended the grand circus in the evening. Met the Pages there. A gloomy raw cold place. Every time I go to a circus I am disgusted with myself, and vow I will never go again. But when a year rolls around and the circus comes with it, the vagabond rises up in me, and I want to go again, and do.

Thursday, October 10

Attended Annie Holbrooks wedding at the Pres. Meeting House. The place crammed with the elite of the place. By the kindness of the pastor, Dr. Lindsley, I obtained a good seat in front of the bridal party. I shall remember him for this. This marriage ceremony was extempore and uninteresting, a very large part of it being a rambling prayer delivered with outstretched arms—stretched toward the congregation—and in white kid gloves. I took Miss Lydia home, and went into the Hall awhile where I met the family and Mr. Canfield of the North Pacific.

Thursday, December 26

Heavy rain, the first of the season. Attended a dancing party given by the British Benevolent Society at the Masonic Hall. Took Mrs. Deady and Alice. Very pleasant affair, and an excellent supper. Got home by 4 oclock. The Campbell women there but not much attention. The Count and Countess Portales there, but did not dance. She had a horrid eye. Said it was the effect of neuralgia. Heard since that she was drunk. One thing I know, she was as stupid as an oyster.

Friday, July 25, 1873

Attended church in the evening, and an informal party on the English ship *Middlesex* at Holladays wharf. Went on board at 10 oclock and came off at 4 A M. Small party. Tolerable Supper. Plenty of good sherry and champagne. Dancing on the Quarter deck. Danced with Mrs. H. and Misses Cardinel, Sherlock, Bacon and Dickinson. Took the latter to supper. Some good singing after supper. Slept 4 hours after I got home.

Saturday, August 2

The anniversary of Ollie Failings marriage. About 4 oclock awakened by cry of fire. Looked out & saw smoke in SE part of the city. Thought it a small fire and returned to bed. Got up at ½ past 7 and found 2 or 3 blocks burned. Went down town and remained until after 12 when fire subsided. The largest fire ever known in the city. It was the work of an incendiary and most likely of some wicked anti-Chinese fanatics. The fire department lacked a head or it might have been suppressed in the morning.

Saturday, March 17, 1877

This is St. Patricks day and the Kelts are out in full fig celebrating the misfortunes of Ireland. Best thing that ever happened to Ireland was when so many of them came to America and made room for the more practical and patient English and Scott. There is too much poetry and passion in the pure Irish to form or maintain a civil society. . . .

Sunday, March 18

Walked out with Henders in the afternoon. Down to see the *Ajax.*

Saturday, October 13

This week the news came of the surrender of Joseph. Howard has shown great energy and pertinacity in the pursuit. Because he didn't play poker, drink whiskey and fornicate, it was supposed or said rather by persons of that ilk or their flatterers that he couldn't fight Indians and therefore there was a move to supersede him at the start. If the government had purchased the few squatters whose groundless claim to Wallowa valley was the direct cause of this war, it would have been a very cheap preventative of this bloody and costly war. Joseph and his people have made a good fight of it, and from as noble and patriotic considerations as Bruce or Tell. . . .

Saturday, January 26, 1878

Gave Mrs. D. tickets for the "Mazeppa" matinee (Buckingham). My toe has been sore all week and I am still lame from it. On Wednesday evening attended Library meeting. Presented my set of the Statesman to the Library and a chip cut from a tree at Fort Clatsop by Mr. Smith in 1874 containing 2 bullets fired into it by some of the Lewis and Clarkes men in the winter of 1805-6, when they camped there. The weather has been warm all week but somewhat damp particularly today. Surrendered my paid-up policy. . . in the Life Association for $600 for a Tontine to expire in 1888 for $800 to a Mr. Corlyn, an agent of the Association. Corlyn is a native of St Louis and an agreeable fellow. I gave him a copy of the proceedings of the Pioneer Association containing my address.

Saturday, February 2
Wednesday evening I attended Mr. Eliots 3 lecture on his "broad" that he took last year. This one was upon Florence with a large digression upon Dante and Angleo. It was pleasant and entertaining. The little man was quite ambitious in some passages. His strong, resolute, nervous wife sat near me and I had a good opportunity to observe her. She never took her eyes off him during the hour of the lecture, and looked as if she was in labor with every line of it. Edward left for Yamhill yesterday. He is drifting about imagining that he is going to do something, but is not. I hope he will get through this period all right, but I am afraid.

Saturday, April 19, 1884
Edward came home last night very sick and out of his head with drink. We sat up with him all night or rather his mother did. This evening she and Dr. Strong took him in a carriage to the G. S. Hospital where he will stay until he is well. In the meantime I hope to get him on board a ship bound for Europe and if that don't save him from the demon of drink nothing will but the grace of God which I cannot command and may not deserve. . . .

Saturday, February 12, 1887
This day has been bright and clear, but the snow still hangs on in patches in the shady places. The legislature adjourned last night in a merry mood, and everybody breathes freer.

Harry De Witt Moore
1851-1878

Harry De Witt Moore was a native of Pennsylvania who graduated from West Point military academy in 1872. By the following year, 2d Lieutenant Moore found himself across the continent on the Oregon-California border fighting one of the last major Indian wars in America. Federal attempts failed to place members of the Modoc tribe on a reservation.

Lt. Moore and other soldiers found themselves trapped in a labyrinth of ancient lava beds near Tule Lake, California, by the Modoc under the leadership of Kientepoos (Captain Jack). For several months, fifty Modocs successfully evaded capture in a nerve-wracking and lethal game of hide and seek amid the lava caverns and tubes. The extended standoff was highly demoralizing to young soldiers like Moore.

The Modoc War ended in 1873, and Kientepoos and some of his followers were hanged. Lt. Moore died at Ft. Klamath in 1878. One unofficial version states Moore was also hanged; supposedly he slipped on a foot bridge and his wool scarf acted as a noose when it caught on a rail. The official report stated that he died by drowning, but on the remote outposts of the West where soldiers led lonely, monotonous lives, suicides were not uncommon. Moore's unpublished letter, part of which appears here in a slightly reordered form, was sent to a woman friend he never saw again. The complete letter and the papers of Harry D. Moore are located in the U.S. Army Military History Research Archives, Washington D. C. —S.A.

It Is Impossible to Catch Them

A LIEUTENANT'S LETTER FROM THE LAVA BEDS

Camp in the Lava Bed.
—50 yards from Capt. Jackson's camp
South shore Tule Lake, Cal.
April 29, 1873

My Dear,

We have been in this delectable place (the promised land I call it—the name induced by the closeness of resemblance of its features to the descriptions I have read of that country,—with one slight difference, scarcely worth chronicling, (I give it up I can't spell it, you know what I mean) that, instead of flowing with milk and honey, as that land is represented to be,—this flows with rattlesnakes and scorpions—) just exactly two weeks, as shown by the Farmers' and Mechanics' Almanac, and a year and a half as indicated by the appearance of my raiment. I inadvertently looked into a ten-cent mirror hanging against a rock, where an officer had been indulging in a shave, the other day, and was just on the point of saying, "Go away, poor fellow, I haven't anything for you and besides it's against my principles to encourage beggars," when it suddenly occurred to me that I was looking at my own image. I believe if I were to walk through the streets of Pottsville, or any other town, I would be arrested in ten minutes for vagrancy, and fined ten dollars and the costs.

I live in a den of rocks,—which I have had constructed on the most scientific principles as regards ventilation. —It is covered with a tent-fly as a protection against the rain,—a function which it does not perform entirely to my satisfaction or comfort, on account of sundry holes, the results of long service. I am very comfortable considering (?). I have plenty of blankets and a nice bed of tules,—a species of white bull-rush which grows luxuriantly on the shores of the lake. I frequently awake however, with an unpleasant sensation of having a rattlesnake or a scorpion for a bed-fellow. There are so many around that it is more than probable, that some adventurous fellow will, one of these nights, make his way into one of our beds. . . .

You have, undoubtedly ere this reaches you, read accounts in the daily papers of our last fight with the Modocs and of the massacre of the last detachment sent out against them on the 26th. All the accounts of our doings here that I have seen have been very much exagerated, and, in many instances, statements have been made which have no foundation on fact. It may interest you to read a true narrative, by an eye witness and participant. . . .

You have probably heard ere this of the terrible massacre of Major Thomas' command, which went out on the 26th to see if a trail could be found, over which mortars and howitzers could be packed. There was no reason in the world for sending troops out for this purpose. We have, as I have already stated, a company of Indian Scouts, enlisted for just this kind of duty. However, Maj. Thomas, 4th Artillery, was sent. Of course, he had no alternative but to go. He had about sixty-five men. He got very close to the Indian camp without receiving a shot. He had completed his reconnaissance; had ascertained as far as he could the nature of the country and the approaches to Jack's place, and was about returning, when the Indians opened fire upon him. . . . Four of the five officers accompanying the expedition were killed and the other dangerously wounded and now lies in a very critical state,—Lt. Harris of Philadelphia. Not an officer escaped; even the Surgeon, Dr. Samig, was wounded twice, while dressing the wounds of an enlisted man. Twenty-four men were killed on the spot and twenty-one wounded and missing, and four officers killed and two severely wounded.

It was a horrible thing. The tragedy began at half-past ten and the troops did not get out until after dark.

It was so intensely dark that night, that they were unable to find the killed and wounded, although they were within eighty yards of them all night. Conceive if you can the suffering, the terrible anxiety of the wounded that night, when they heard our troops throwing up breastworks and thought they were Indians preparing to slaughter them in their entirely defenceless position in the morning. Those who went out—I was not among the number—say it was a most horrible sight. Dead and wounded, officers and men, in one confused heap. All the wounded are in the hospital on the other side and oh what a horrible sight it is to see them in all their agony. I never fully realized what a horrible thing war is, until I came out on this trip. I want no more Indian fighting of this kind in mine. It is bad enough in Arizona where a troop of Cavalry can surprise an Indian camp kill fifty or sixty and not lose a man. In fighting there the danger is not much greater than in deer hunting. But among these rocks every one must look out for himself, officers and men, and the officers stand the worst chance of all. The Indians have been allowed to visit our camp until they have become thoroughly acquainted with all the officers, and of course where they can make a selection in an engagement, they will pick off the officers first.

We have all adopted the precaution of discarding all insignia of rank and it would be a difficult matter to tell us from enlisted men. I wear a private's uniforms, no straps or stripes, and a white broad-brimmed hat. I have discarded boots and taken to government gun boats. I doubt if you would consent to dance the German with me in my present garb or even to admit me into your house.

I must confess that I see no way of bringing this war to a successful termination, either without, or with, a great sacrifice of human life. We can drive them from any position they may take, but from the nature of the country, rough and broken-up in the extreme, we cannot well surround them; for as soon as they see our tactics—and they are not lacking in intelligence I can assure you—they scatter out, each Indian for himself and will not allow themselves to be surrounded. They can glide among these rocks like snakes, and it is impossible to catch them, and by drawing them from any position they may hold,—we gain nothing,—for the Lava Bed includes a hundred and fifty square miles of the roughest ground to be found anywhere on the face of the globe I think, and they can retreat from one place to another equally as strong, and keep it up ad finitum. We can't starve them, for the country surrounding the Lava Bed abounds with cattle and however perfect our system of vigilance, they can get all they want. They have abundance of ammunition, and are by this time all armed with our improved breech-loading Springfield rifle, which they have taken from our dead. They can always keep up their supply of cartridges by going over the lines we have occupied in an engagement —so many being lost by our men. If we move against them at all, it must be with our whole force.

Your sincere friend,
H. D. W. Moore

Oliver Cromwell Applegate
1845-1937

Oliver Cromwell Applegate was the sixth son of Lindsay Applegate, a pioneer and Applegate Trail blazer. O.C., as he was known, spent a lifetime working with Oregon's Native Americans, especially the Klamath Tribe, which gave him the honorary name of *Blywas' lo kay*—Golden Eagle Chief. During the Modoc War, O.C. served as a scout and interpreter. In 1876 he was appointed as an Indian Agent. His sympathetic if paternalistic view of Oregon's Native peoples and his abiding interest in the lore and legends of Crater Lake (where a mountain peak was eventually named in his honor) have made him an enduring historic figure.

He fought for the inclusion of Crater Lake in the National Parks system and strongly supported the creation of the Lava Beds National Monument. Before moving to the Klamath country, he lived briefly in the Yoncalla region with other branches of the Applegate family. While there he witnessed the troubles of a Klickitat Indian man, Dick Johnson, which he recalls in the following letter to former Superintendent of Indian Affairs, editor, and author, Alfred Meacham. Meacham published this and other letters in his book *Wigwam and Warpath* (1875). (See *Varieties of Hope* of the Oregon Literature Series for more of Meacham.)—S.A.

Eight Greedy Men Lived around Dick Johnson's Farm
A LETTER TO EXPOSE RACIST CRIMINALS

Swan Lake, Oregon
September 10, 1873

Hon. A. B. Meacham: —

Dear Friend,

A Klik-a-tat Indian, named Dick Johnson, came to my father's house in the Willamette valley, and worked for him on his farm, prior to the year 1850. In that year my father removed to the Umpqua valley, and soon after Dick Johnson, with his wife (an Umpqua), and mother and stepfather, called the "Old Mummy," followed up and asked permission to cultivate a small portion of my father's farm. This they were allowed to do. They cultivated these few acres in good style, and found time to labor for father and other farmers, for which they received good remuneration.

In 1852, Dick Johnson, under the encouragement of my father, Uncle Jesse, and other friends, took up a claim in a beautiful little valley about ten miles from Yoncalla, where my people resided. This place was so environed by hills that it was thought the whites would not molest Dick there. Aided by the old man and his brother-in-law, Klik-a-tat Jim, who came from the upper country to join him, Dick improved his farm in good style, built good houses and outbuildings, and fenced hundreds of acres. He was frugal, enterprising and industrious, and emulated the better white people every way possible, and was so successful in his farming enterprises that he outstripped many of his white neighbors. His character was above reproach, and, beside sending his little brother to school, he was always seen with his family at church on the Sabbath day. Unfortunately, there were greedy, avaricious white men living in the vicinity of Dick Johnson, who coveted his well-improved little farm. Eight of them—disguised—went to his place late one afternoon, and found Dick chopping wood in the front yard. They shot him in cold blood, and, as his lifeless body fell across the log on which he was chopping, his step-father ran from the house unarmed, and was shot also. The women, after being beat over the heads with guns and revolvers, finally made their escape to the woods, and took refuge under the roof of a friendly neighbor.

Klik-a-tat Jim—who came from mill about the time the old man was shot—was fired on several times, some bullets cutting his clothing, but, jumping into his house at a window, he got his gun, and the cowardly assassins fled. Although there was immense excitement throughout the country when this outrage was committed, and a hundred men assembled to bury Dick Johnson and the old man like white men, as they deserved, an ineffectual attempt was made to bring the offenders to justice, and *they actually lived for years upon the farm, enjoying the benefits of poor Dick Johnson's labor.* Our laws then scarcely recognized the fact that the Indians had any rights that were worthy of respect, and this most atrocious crime had to go unpunished, thus encouraging the Columbia Indians to greater desperation under Old Kam-i-a-kin, in the war of 1866-1867. Well it would be, for the good name of the American people, if we could point to but one isolated case of this kind; but truth and candor compel us to admit, that too many Indian wars have been occasioned by the greed and ruffianism of our own race.

Ever truly yours,
O.C. Applegate

Cynthia Horning
1853-?

Eighteen-year-old Cynthia Horning's prospects seemed dismal in 1870. The Benton County census listed her as a "housekeeper" on the Corvallis farm belonging to her German father. After her mother's death in 1868, Cynthia's responsibilities included raising nine siblings. As the decade dragged by, Cynthia commented and occasionally complained about her life in advice-filled letters to a younger friend, Anna Foster, of Lake County. "I never could get along without letters, papers and magazines coming pretty frequently," Horning confessed to Foster. "I consider them my best friends."

In 1883, at what she considered "a ripe old age," thirty-year-old Horning married Samuel Crape and may have moved to Portland with him. Anna Foster, living in the remote community of Summer Lake, surely missed her friend's lively letters. Difficult to decipher, Horning's letters used every inch of paper including margins upon which she frequently wrote sideways in a scrawl that was both microscopic and ornate. These letters were saved by Foster descendants, and are kept in a shoe-box in the Schmink House Museum, Lakeview. They have recently been carefully transcribed by Charlotte Pendleton.—S.A.

Advice to a Lake County Girl
from Her Best Friend in Corvallis

Corvallis, Or.
January 6, 1876

Miss Anna Foster

My Dear Friend,

I am going to answer your letter at once this time, in order that there may be no delay. "Delays are dangerous" says the old proverb and "procrastination the theif of time." I believe it, and in order to be on the safe side I will not delay, at least not for this once. I noticed some time ago in a paper that a mail route had been established in Lake county with Post offices in Summer Lake, Silver Lake and Chewacan valley's. I should think you would be glad to have a P.O. so near you after being so long without mail facilities. I should consider *that* the worst feature of frontier life. I never could get along without letters papers and magazines coming pretty frequently. I always consider them my best friends. I hope that you will all write more frequently in the future.

A great many deaths have taken place in Benton county this fall. One man whose wife died last summer lost four children in one week with scarlet fever.

Last Friday evening a difficulty arose at a dance in Kings Valley between Emmet Wrenn and Amos Halleck in which Halleck tried to cut Emmet's heart out—so he said (to eat) and succeeded in stabbing him several times in the breast and cutting his face up badly and almost cutting his throat. The officers are after Halleck who has left for parts unknown. Emmet will live so I heard, but he is badly wounded. Will Justice and Horace Crees got into a fight last week and Will put Horace's eye out. He may be sent to Penitentiary for it. I hear that there is such talk. I suppose that you are enjoying yourself going to dances as there is likely to be a good many of them at this time in the year. I wish that I could go with you to one or two. I used to like to dance, so well, maybe that I would again if I would only go. I suspect that you saw Bob—at the Christmas dance. You are cheif cook now are you! a good one I'll wager. Bob says so and he's a competent judge. I wonder what sort of houses you all live in anyway, I thought you already *had* a nice comfortable house.I have been thinking some about making the boy's quite a number of household elegancies, but am not sure that they would care for them enough to take them out. I visited a bachelor cabin with the Adams girls last summer and ugh! it makes me shudder even now to think of the filth I saw. If I thought our boys lived in such squalor I should feel very badly.

I am sorry to say that my health is improving so that I will not need to take a trip away from home. I suspect that I have written a splendid letter this time. I have been washing today and as I am writing George and Eddie are shooting from the front door at targets set up on the yard gate. I have been learning to handle a gun a little this winter. The boys think it prime fun to get me to shoot at blue jays. The birds never suffer much from my shooting. How did that trouble between Adams and Brown end we were all anxious to hear the last of it, as the Browns are such a revengeful race. Do you enjoy getting letters? then you must enjoy writing them too. Please remember that.

Your affectionate friend
Cynthia Horning

Corvallis, Oregon
February 14, 1876

Miss Anna Foster

My Dear Friend:—

Your good letter reached me two days ago and I hasten to reply to it. I am glad to know that you are going to school again, and I know that you will improve your opportunities. Your natural abilities are of the highest order and you must cultivate them and improve every moment. It is every man's (and woman's as well) duty to make as much of themselves as is possible. Too many young ladies are careless about their education and consider that because they are girls there is no need to know much. That marriage is the cheif end and aim of woman's existence, and towards that goal they bend all their energies. This is altogether wrong and if they could some of them hear the opinion the young gentlemen have of them I think they surely would go to work in earnest and try to stand before the world as responsible beings with thoughts and opinions of their own. I feel provoked enough with Tom and the young man that is staying here sometimes to wish I was a man long enough to thrash them both, they make so much sport of the school girls because they don't keep up with the boys. Girls *can* learn as fast as boys if they will and they ought to be ashamed not to. Woman's place in society and the world is not exactly the same as mans, but it is quite as high and she has just as great need of brains as man has.

Poor Frank! I wonder if Miss Elzora Pulora Victoria Josephine Hill has *dared* give my brother the mitten? If she has just tell her brother (if she has one) to look to himself when I make a visit to Summer Lake. Please write as punctually as you did last time. Good night,

From Your friend
Cynthia Horning

Corvallis
July 4, 1880

My Dear Anna:

While the others are getting ready for church I will begin a letter to you. I have been ready and waiting for half an hour and am getting rather impatient. I never did like to sit around half an hour or longer with my hat on waiting for a lot of boys to shave and primp, I suspect that you know how it is yourself, though, for you have two grown brothers. Talk of girls vanity indeed! They can not halfway compare with boys. I am thankful I wasn't a boy. I should be ashamed to believe that every time I saw a girl glance at me she was badly smitten and I had but to hint that I wanted a wife to have her throw herself in my arms. I am not meaning any harm to boys, they are very good creatures and I for one would not wish them to be different, or to be sent out of the world or anything else, we could not get along without the boys no matter how strong minded we felt, but ones own brothers you know my dear Anna they are much less apt to appreciate than other girls brothers.

Poor Anna what a hard time you must have!

Take warning by my example and dont live to be an old maid and always have to keep house for your brothers, I suspect that I will be of some use in the world but not a use that is very profitable to myself.

Write soon as you can.

Your sincere friend
Cynthia Horning

Polly Hewitt McArthur
1889-1943

Polly McArthur wanted to give her childhood doll, Eva, to her daughter. To capture both personal and local history, Polly wrote a series of letters addressed to the doll, which had been Polly's companion during her Portland childhood years, and gave these letters to her daughter Mary Law along with the doll. They were published as *Letters to a Doll* (1928). Because McArthur used the letter as a literary device, some of the conventions of the letter have been suspended.

The following letter describes Portland's Chinatown in the last years of the nineteenth century when the Portland Chinese community, though reduced by the anti-Chinese riots of that period, was one of the largest in the nation.—T. O'D.

Polly Hewitt McArthur is in the center

Letter to a Doll

Dear Eva,

For days I have been wanting to write you about the time I took you to my father's office. Do you remember the old Sherlock Building on Third and Oak Streets, with the elevator with panelled sides that was run so fast by the curly-haired Henry? And how we got off at the second floor without calling because Henry knew us?

You loved looking out the window when the police patrol, a black shut-in wagon drawn by two black horses, went, klanging its bell, to pick up some poor drunkard from the gutter. Sometimes it came back filled with Chinamen from a gambling raid instead. Then Father used to tell how nicely he would have the Chinese Sherlock Building done over after one of its frequent fires, all sanitary, and how in a week when he would go back he couldn't find his way around for the crooked passages and secret rooms. There was always a gambling den for fan tan, a Chinese card game. The Chinamen used to gamble behind a series of closed doors with police alarms to them. They never got caught unless they let in white people too often.

Then there were Chinese funerals in those days. Long processions headed by the hearse with black horses, followed by mourners wailing and beating devil drums to frighten off the devils. Next came the paper dragon, stretching almost a block, that was kept for funerals, and then dozens of closed carriages, every one in town when the Chinaman was an important merchant, filled with men from the dead man's "tong" or company. Every Chinaman belonged to a tong. That was their government, to which they owed obedience. The tongs were always fighting, sometimes it wasn't safe to walk down the street in Chinatown when there was a war on. If one Chinaman killed another the murder was always revenged. Once a great big Tartar cook was found stuffed-up a chimney with his throat cut.

Chinamen didn't often touch white people. They were very affectionate and fond of children, and took honest care of the houses where they worked. There were lots of Chinese cooks, gardeners, vegetable men and laundrymen in Portland when you were small. Father used to have a yard boy called Jack who gave us wonderful presents at Christmas and birthdays of colored silk handkerchiefs, dolls in Chinese costume, lichi nuts and tea. One year he gave Aunt Margie and me each a sword made of cash or Chinese bronze money with a hole in it, strung together on red cord. When I was five he bought "Bibi", as he called me, a picture of Fujiyama with little houses made of real mother of pearl on the hillside. You know, the one in the breakfast room now.

All the western railways were built by Chinese coolie labor. That was before the days of steam shovels, when cuts and fills were accomplished by shovel and pick and wheelbarrow. Now when you go to The Dalles or San Francisco and see the old curved right of way you will understand why the roads were not straighter.

Do you remember that all Chinamen wore queues, or long braids of their black hair with silk plaited into the ends, wrapped round their heads? And blue jackets with brass or real gold buttons, and full blue trousers? Cooks wore white jackets when at work and black satin slippers with thick felt soles on their feet. They all wore little round black silk caps like the crown of a hat on the street. The mandarins, or better class Chinamen, had a little red button on the top of the cap. The coolies at work outdoors used to wear wide sloping straw hats without crowns to keep off sun or rain.

When Aunt Bella drove us through Chinatown once we smelled the chickens fried in peanut oil and queer fish that the Chinese like and saw the medicine shops and the silk shops. Sometimes the medicine consisted of the scent pouches of skunks or a wild cat preserved in alcohol. All the bookkeeping in these shops was done on the abacus, or Chinese adding machine, which is nothing more than a set of wooden beads strung on a wire and worked by fingers. The Chinese can add like a flash in this way. The joss houses, or temples, were on the second storey, gilt inside and out, with much wood carving and vermilion paint and lacquer. The gods and devils sat in state on a dais at one end of the chief room. In front of them burned pots of incense. Chinese prayers were written on bits of paper which were then hung about the shrines. The signs alongside the doors of the shops, like the fronts of the joss houses, were elaborately carved and gilded, with many splashes of red. On the sidewalks, on teak wood stools or chairs, sat Chinamen smoking pipes and talking. Some of the shops held small congregations like the crowd in a popular club. Over the shop fronts hung balconies decorated with plants in beautiful pots. At Chinese New Years the streets were full of sweet-scented lilies, blooming in bowls. Every Chinaman, no matter where he lived, always had a lily growing in a bowl of water and stones, which he tended with anxious care. If it bloomed too soon before or too long after his New Years he had bad luck for the year, you see. I could run on all night about the dear Chinamen, we loved them so, with their funny lingo. Now the government won't let them in because they do not live like westerners. We have lost many a faithful friend who might have been. Goodnight my dear, no more this time,

Your loving
Mother

Emily B. Trevett
1869-1958

Emily Trevett with her husband, Dr. Richard K. Nunn, and brother-in-law

Emily Trevett, member of a pioneer Portland family, was educated at the exclusive Framingham School in Massachusetts. On her return to Portland at the end of the nineteenth century, she gave private music lessons and was active in the social life of the city. Also a political activist, she helped in the founding of local chapters of the American Civil Liberties Union and the Women's League for Peace and Freedom. The excerpts below from her journals of 1894-1901 contain the reflections of a serious and highly intelligent young woman. The complete unpublished journals may be found in the Oregon Historical Society, Portland.—T. O'D.

George Eliot's Life Has Made Me Ashamed
A PORTLAND SOCIALITE'S QUEST FOR KNOWLEDGE, REVERENCE, CONTROL

March 1, 1894

It is years since I have kept a journal with any regularity. As a child I was trained to & I dare say it did me both good and harm, good in teaching me to express myself easily in writing, harm in as much as it led me to pay too much attention to my own ideas & feelings. During the last eight years, since leaving school, there has been a great deal of nonsense written in my so called journals & much of it deserves a very hot fire, but in beginning again it is with the determination of doing an entirely different kind of writing. Reading George Eliot's life has given me the idea of it. She notes down the most interesting events of her life regularly, with simplicity & sincerity. Sometimes she expresses her feelings without sentimentality or exagggeration. It is evidently written neither for posterity nor for her friends but for herself. I write so much to my friends never to return to me that it will be good to keep some record for my own future pleasure.

Our Chinaman, Tom, has just gone downtown for registration. It seems to me a most unjust law which treats the Chinese differently from the other immigrants. But we have been unjust to them from the first to last.

March 2

Played the Andante & Scherzo of opus 14.2 and part of the chopin Etude in A flat. We are planning to have five afternoons of chamber music at our house beginning Sunday April 1st. They will only be possible in case we can get fifty subscribers at $2.50 a piece.

March 4

Every little while I have a fit of wondering where our time goes to, whether we should sleep less or know fewer people, or waste fewer hours on clothes & other prosaic matters. Other people read & write & do all sorts of other things & don't seem rushed. I keep a list of the books I read & it is pitifully small. Sometimes I reproach myself for not being more particular about my personal appearance & again for giving so little time to my friends & begrudging that time.

March 5

Read *Revue des Deux Mondes* for March. Interesting article on education in England. Comparative amount of bathing in the two countries. Article on Pardon, not from an ideally high moral standpoint. Long article on Character & Intelligence. Wanted to read it, but knew I wouldn't have time. Sketch of Darwins life in it, his love of music & of novels if they had good endings. He says a law should be passed against bad endings to novels. I am always interested to read of great men who love music. I feel it is a personal tribute, anything beautiful about music.

I earn part of the family's daily bread, of which I consume a greater proportion than I earn, I'm afraid, I have a certain reputation for being bright, & nothing more is asked of me. Last year when I had the Saturday mornings & they were a success of course the family expressed no great surprise though much appreciation. It was in a way no more than they had expected, but only in a general way. They have no particular idea of my ever doing or being much more than I am now. And I can't give up the old notion that everything is to come to me. When I read the life of any geat woman I compare every circumstance of it with the conditions of my own life & every trait of her character with those of my own. I suppose above everything else I have the idea of writing, and it is hard to realize that thousands of other young women in the world have the same idea, & that it comes to nothing. Perhaps all this is only exaggerated self conceit & self interest. Or perhaps the feeling is common to all humanity to be stirred in proportion as they think "I might have done this" or "I will do it someday." It is a feeling almost like jealousy of everything that has been done in or that is being done, in music, in art, in literature, as though I were defrauded of my share in the world's work. Oh, I know that this is all nonsense. People who are going to amount to anything in the first place choose one subject & keep to it. They have not a moments misgiving as to whether the have chosen the right one, that is their talent, their faculty. Then they are not drawn away from their work by love of pleasure or laziness or interest in outside things as I am. They have perseverance & determination.

March 12

One thing is certain. I shall never go back quite where I was before I read George Eliots life. It has made me too ashamed of my own ignorance & frivolity & low aims. The reaction is so strong now that I feel like making no more calls, seeing no more people as long as I am in Portland. The amusing part of it is that these are all people who had a more active intellectual life than I do, who all read the books I feel that I discovered years ago & can criticize them &

say that other books are better. But one naturally shews one's lowest side to people in formal social intercourse & they of course think me as frivolous & foolish as I think them.

August 6

Life continues interesting though I find it hard to realize that this—breakfast, dinner, lessons, mending, writing letters, arranging flowers, with a little visiting & reading is actually my life with a capital L. One waits for it to begin & will be waiting perhaps when it is past & gone. What part of it I wonder is my truest Life. The work surely, the daily tasks, are as great & pure & perfect a part of it as any. The American Man may not be as wrong after all to make his work the sum & substance of his existence rather than a trial to be endured till enough has been earned for a life of idleness. I am learning lately that almost all my opinions are as apt to be wrong as not. I feel it constantly in my arguments. I feel too that I am boundlessly conceited without cause to even be tolerably well satisfied with myself.

Am I more masculine than feminine, I wonder. Girls like me so readily, men care comparatively little for me. When I see every & any female with her love affair ending in a hubby & baby, I begin to wish myself the most sallow, ignorant, sour-tempered of them all with those blessings added. Strange that every woman should have a confidence waiting to be poured in your ear.

August 7

I finished up the evening with reading old journals. Dipping back into one's past is a rather dangerous occupation. There is so much one has forgotten or that one did not realize at the time. I know now the reason for my life's being a disappointment to me & to others if they would only acknowledge it—it is lack of seriousness, of ballast, I am too fond of pleasure to do my duty. Lately I am shockingly lazy. Housework & all distinctly feminine occupations are such a bore.

Rufus B. Matthews
1864-1940

Rufus B. Matthews travelled widely in Oregon from 1891 to 1897 with his third wife, the much younger Grace Smith Matthews, about whom little is known, but who is clearly the coauthor of the first of the following letters. A gambling man whose luck ran hot and cold, Matthews felt compelled to tell his mama everything in the letters he sent home to Roseburg. Spelling and punctuation were not Matthews's gifts, but he had a way of expressing himself that conveyed the highlights of his journeys in Oregon's wild, turn-of-the-century West. Matthews eventually owned a saloon in Roseburg and has the distinction of being the first Douglas County driver to run over a pedestrian—an accident that was apparently not his fault.

Matthews's brief description of a visit to the Beaver Hill Coal Mine in Coos County is the only known written contemporary record of life there. In 1894 a group of miners who had been working in Dowd County, West Virginia, came to the Coos Bay region with their families. They had been promised a living wage. But the presence of African Americans in the mines was fairly short-lived. Wages proved to be about ninety cents a day; no housing was available to them except leaking boxcars; layers of mud and constant rain made work in the mines especially dangerous. When complaints were filed, the manager accused miners of starting a strike, and they were ordered to pack up their families after paying for their board and lodging. Matthews's racist language was consistent with that of other Oregonians. African Americans living in Oregon were rarely treated respectfully; nevertheless, Matthews was clearly impressed with the kindness shown to him by Beaver Hill's black miners and their families.

Many other unpublished Matthews family letters are housed in the Douglas County Museum, Roseburg.— S.A.

The Roseburg Gambler Who Wrote His Mama Everything—Almost—and Invented His Own Spelling

Lakeview, Oregon
June 19, 1895

Mrs. B. T. Matthews

Dear Mother

We got back from Paisley last night a little after ten oclock and I thought I would write and tell you about our trip today. It is forty miles from here to Paisley four of us went over in a covered rig. We took our dinner with us. It is the greatest place I ever saw for fights. They had five fights in one afternoon. One of the men that went over with us got in a fight and got his eye blacked and his finger bit. I guess Paisley is alright but I don't like it. We went to a dance there and some of the men danced in there shirt sleeves and some with their hats on and others were drunk.

Grace & Bany

Marshfield, Oregon
July 19, 1895

Dear Mother

Your letter was received yesterday   was glad to here from you all   I dont know much to write this time but will tell you all I know   every thing is very dull know but I think it will git all wright—

there is a ball game at Coquille sunday   I am going to be there but the funniest thing of them all was a coon dance at beaver hill   I went up there   that was something I never seen bee fore   it was worth going to see   it is a coal mine   there must bee clost on 200 nigers there wimen and children if they dont have a time   they have a little town of there own   I just wish you could see it—one of the coons made me go and eat super with him   I was treeted fine. the ladies of the house was pretty black you bet but they were refind. they belong to the church. The dance comenced about 9 and you talk about your time   I had it   dident havt to have any introduction   they said git your own lady, have a time   I had it—you bet—they had everything to eat—was in the market and from the first set they comenced to eat. they cleaned everything out. I eat my self till I was all most sick. the coons think I am all wright, I will tell you moor about it when I come home.

If I can stick it out here till fall I will make some money. I am giting a new craps table made to day   well mother take good care of my Boy and your self.

Wright soon

> from
> *Bany*

> Angles Camp, Cal
> December 29, 1897

Dear Mother

I take the pleasure in answering your letter   I am glad to no you are all well and we ar the same   at present the town was full of life   Christmas they had another prise fight in the afternoon   the house was filled with people   it lasted 7 rounds and after the fight the majority of them got drunk and then it was an uproar from that till daylight—next morning   we have moore life here in one minute than you will see their in a month   I did not get anything Christmas.

I would like to come and see you all but I wont come now not for awhile yet I am makeing a little money all the time. I am $800 strong now   I am sure to reach $1000 if nothing hapens. Grace has made a litle sack to keep it in   we count it every day   nobody knows Ive got it here and the beauty of it is no body knows I am cheating them. everybody likes me here   they say I dont ack like a gambler. Good bye

> *Bany*

Charles Marshall
1882-1957

Charles Marshall, a mining engineer and surveyor, was born in Portland and educated at the University of Oregon. In January of 1907, he began to keep a diary of his experiences at the R & S gold mine on the Illinois River in Curry County. The mining "rushes" that characterized the newly opened country of southern Oregon in 1851 continued into the twentieth century.

Marshall and a partner were quartz or "rock" miners. Their method of ore extraction required capital and some expertise, as the meticulous diagrams in Marshall's diary indicate. Marshall also recorded mining folklore learned from occasional camp visitors. A prolific photographer, Marshall captured the images of many of his mining endeavors in various Oregon locations from 1903 to 1911. There is no record that he ever struck it rich. Marshall's unpublished diary, the source of this selection, is in Special Collections, Knight Library, University of Oregon.—S.A.

Gold Miners in a Siskiyou Mountain Winter

Thursday, January 3, 1907

We started the mill, but quit at noon. Trash clogged the screen in mill forebay and battery pipes repeatedly. At noon Higgins turned water out of upper ditch. Rain and heavy wind all day—snow practically gone at dark. Creek was very high all day. It cut a new channel around bridge at old camp. At dark weather turned colder, and some snow fell.

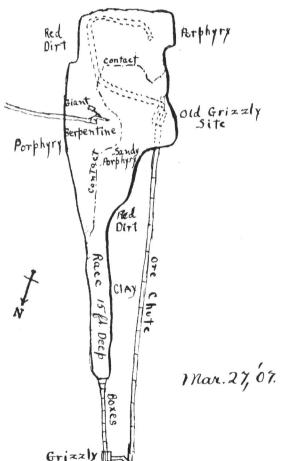

Sunday, January 6

We finished the cleanup, cleaning the plates, panning contents of mortar, etc. In afternoon we retorted the amalgam. The weather continued freezing all day again.

Monday, January 7

I went over to Bour's on my way to Grants Pass, reaching there at 9:30 A.M. The boat was out of water, and Pete Bour away hunting cattle. He returned at night. Reported Illinois river had been higher than for years. Within 2 ft of cable. His dog "Rats" drowned in Fall creek. Fishermen Aubrey & Jewell, with 2 trappers came in at 4:30 P.M. with 4 pack horses. Freezing, rain and snow in P.M.

Tuesday, January 8

Pete Bour and I launched the boat, and I went out to Selma. We met Jack Shade and White at Six-mile creek. The trail was slippery with ice, and cut up by storm of Jan. 3. Six mile ditch badly cut up. Two logs across trail. Weather clear and cold.

Amanda Smith Donaldson
1848-1916

Tillamook was the site of the first European landing on the Oregon coast by Captain Robert Gray in 1788. Gray called the anchorage "Murderer's Bay" because Marcus Lopius, one of his crew, was killed there by local natives (see Haswell entry, page 2 of this volume). In 1863, Amanda Smith of Nevada County, California, married Joseph Donaldson, and the new couple moved to Tillamook Bay. There, they established a homestead, started a dairy in 1867, raised a family of 16 children, and contributed to the cheese industry in the area. Among the family tragedies Amanda endured was the death of her 12-year-old son, Grover Cleveland Donaldson. His death is described in the following previously unpublished letter. The original may be found in the Tillamook County Pioneer Museum, Tillamook.—T. O'D.

A Mother Creates a Memorial Fund
after Her Boy Dies in a Hunting Accident

Tillamook, Oregon
ca. May 11, 1909

Dear Brother Willson,

Allthough I know your time is all claimed in your great variety of good works I cannot help asking a favor of you.

last wednesday May 4 Our Darling boy Grover Cleveland Donaldson the 5th of 7 sons aged 12 years June 17 1897 accidentally shot and killed himself while out shooting quails. I happened to notice him as he wrode of leasurely on his horse and watched him untill he passed out of sight little dreaming it was the last time I would be permited to see my Darling alive. he was on his usual trip after the Cows. he went and brought all but one and as he started after her he took a gun along to kill a few quails. he crossed to the oppisite side of Willson river a stream bordering our farm on the north tied his horse and went a short distance and shot a quail and it seems he was in a hurry to shoot an other and by accident the gun was discharged the contents entering his left side rungeing upwards shatering his side and left arm and in this condition I am told he drug his poor mangled bleeding body some distance towards his horse appearently in the hope of geting home to friends and relief. But the poor darling gave out and when found his forehead was resting on his right arm and he sleeping his last sleep. it was about ½ after 6 o'clock in the evening when the neighbors heard what they afterwards knew to be the fatal shot. About dark his papa got uneasy and started out to finde him but not Crossing the river, he faile to finde him so came home and with 2 of his brothes and a hired man started out again but as their absence was prolonged our eldest daughter at home Olive aroused the neighbors who turned out in full force and about midnight they found first his horse next his hat and next his precious body. poor Darling he was caried home tenderly cared for by kinde and sympathatic neighbors who prepared his precious body for its last resting place and on Thursday May 6 Six of his young friends and schoolmates acted as pallbearers and bore him from his late home to the herse where quite a procession followed to the school house where he had spent many happy hours with his schoolmates and in the attempt to gain knowledge their. the funeral sermon was preached by a Rev. Dieleson of the M.E. Church of this place to a large conggration of young and Old. most of his school mates were present and his many other friends besides 20 family relitives. I can not give the text or tell of the sermon as I am particully deaf and did not hear one word of the sermon.

Dear Brother this has been a sievere blow to me   I am the mother of 16 children 7 boys sons & 9 girls daughters and this is the first one called away since our first Born which went at birth   all the rest have been kindly spared up to the 4th of May when our darling Gleany was very sudenly called away. Our kinde heavenly father took the most exceptable one of member and now heaven seems nearer and dearer than ever befor for we have a very precious treasure there. What I wished to ask of you is this. Our dear boy always managed to have a little spending money of his own earnings the greater part of which he spent for the pleasure of others. But at the time of his departure he had $4.00 oweing to him. Now I want to start a little fund to be known as the Cleveland Memorial Charity or Missionary fund which ever it is used for. Starting with the $4.00 I will add to it in various ways a kinde of family fund for each member to contribute as they may and his friends will allso have an opportunity to contribute as they see fit bringing it to its highest rate on the 17 of June of each year that being our darlings birthday and I wish to make it a memmorial day for good. I expect to have a Childrens sermon preached to the children on the comeing June 17th and ever afterwards on that day. I hope to have it so arranged that a sermon be preached to the children and allso that our fund attain its fully growth on that day. Now I wish you to instruct me in what way to use our little fund to the best advantage   it will perhaps be small but I want to make it useful. He our darling has some posessions including a gun (not the one that killed him   that was borrowed gun) I expect to sell to swell the amount.

Now Brother Willson you may print this if you like. Makeing any changes you wish and if you do not print it please return it for which you will finde stamp inclosed. Perhaps you can not read this. Please excuse pencil and poor writeing.

Signed
Mrs. Amanda Donaldson

Florence
Hofer
1895-1984

The region of Newport, the locale of the following journal, originally was included in the Siletz Indian Reservation, which was established in 1856. The reservation extended 125 miles along the coast from present-day Tillamook south to the Umpqua River. When a large market for oysters at Newport's Yaquina Bay developed, the Siletz Indians were forced to abandon the Newport region in 1865. Shortly thereafter, a stage began to run between Newport and Corvallis, and at about the same time, Samuel Case built a tourist hotel called the Ocean House.

Gradually Newport became a summer resort for people such as the author of the following unpublished journal. Florence Amalie Hofer was 12 years old when she dictated this journal to her father, recounting her summer days in the Newport of 1907. The longer original document (excerpted here) may be found in the Lincoln County Historical Society, Newport.—T. O'D.

Pebbles Picked Up on the Beach at Newport

We have had a lovely summer at Yaquina Bay, and met many old friends. Our cottage is the same we have had for seventeen years, on Captain Olssen's block. Besides the cottage with two rooms, the big striped tent was up as usual, where the boys and papa sleep. We had a small tent for Miss Sabine Dent of Portland, who is one of the finest singers in that city. Aunt Florence was with us all summer, but papa and Mac did not arrive until August 21st. We all left Salem July 15th. Mr. Olssen was a Swedish sailor from the time he was a boy and sailed nearly all over the world. He had some great experiences with pirates in the Chinese rivers.

We had a visit from My grandma from Chicago. She enjoyed the beach very much, picked up a great many pebbles, and took long walks on the hills by herself. Papa gave her a shellbox full of candy for the children in Chicago at our annual picnic, where papa planked a salmon. She thought it was a funny way to cook a big fish on a slab of alderwood in front of a big fire in the open air. We had a game to blindfold the older people and lead up the path in the little canyon, turn them around a few times and then take the bandage off, and they were in the deepest woods only a block from home but did not know where they were. Grandma wouldn't play the game. She said she had never gone blindfold.

Papa had a surprise for the rest of us children. In the clear place where the picnic was he left a little evergreen tree just like a Christmas tree and when our backs were turned he hung a sack of nuts and candy on the tree for each of us. My brother Lawrence has built a boat this year and on Friday Sept. 7 he caught the first silverside salmon. We had it baked and then next day had some broiled. It tasted as good as trout. His boat did not leak a drop and we have had many rides in it. My dog Togo went with us over to the sandpit once. I did not clean off his feet and he got a lot of sand in the boat and papa scolded and cleaned it all out with a rag. Togo is a land dog but could swim if necessary.

This morning Sept. 10, we went across the Bay to the draw to get crabs, and little neck and Quohog clams. There was a little fog on the water, but we got all we wanted. The crabs creep and bury themselves in the sand, and boys spear them with a one-tine spear. When they are in the boat they turn them over on their backs and kill them instantly by spearing them through the heart. The Bay was smooth and when we came back the fog lifted. Sunday the wind was in the east and it was so warm for a time the candles in the tent melted. At noon a black squall came across the water and the hot spell was over, the wind blowing from the southwest and cooling off things like a refrigerator.

Mrs. Olssen dug a big pan of potatoes this morning and brought them to mama. Then Mr. Mitchell came along and papa asked her if she did not need a good man to dig for her. Mr. Mitchell is called the millionaire. He came from New York many years ago and lives all alone on the interest of his money.

We gathered a lot of huckleberries and blackberries for pies and jelly just above Mr. Berry's house. He is the only Irishman here and is a carpenter by trade. He is very jolly and let my brother Lawrence have nearly all the tools to make his boat with. Mr. Berry has a mystery about his life. He came, so the rumors say, from a large city where he was once an alderman, and owns enough property to keep him. We sent him a crab, and the other day two slices of salmon. He has a little garden, and would give anyone almost anything he has got. He had his ankle sprained and has to go on crutches. Nobody knows whether he was ever married or not but he is just as nice for all that.

Mr. Ford is another old bachelor who lives on our street. He is the finest carpenter in Newport, and yet Mr. Berry and none of them claim they could build a better boat than my brother has built. Mr. Ford can remodel an old house and make it into a modern cottage. Mr. Ford has a long beard and clerks in the postoffice store while the postmaster is away. My mama says the people of the neighborhood all rely on Mr. Ford. He is the stand-by of all of them, she says. She made him a pie several times and he brought us some string beans. Papa bought some down town and mama was scolding him because he did not get enough, and Mr. Ford's came in just right, and he might have heard her across the street.

Mama never scolds papa except when he lets flies in the house or does not buy enough of anything but candy. My dog has been sick but he ate grass and got well. He has the cheapest doctor bills so long as the grass holds out. We drove down town this morning with My Brother Mac to have the horse shod for his long drive over the mountains next week, when we are all going home to Salem.

Billy Neal is the oldest man who lives all by himself. He and mama are very friendly. He lets her have all his fresh eggs in preference to all the other women in the neighborhood. Mr. Berry says you might as well try to change a rock as get a woman to change her mind, once she has it made up in a certain way. He says he would never try to argue one out of anything. It's no use.

Uncle Billy Neal has rheumatism and trouble with the health officer. He does not expect to live long and says they have got too many sanitary rules to suit him. He says he has lived here so long he knows how, and don't need any old health board to tell him how to keep his premises in order, and I guess he is right. He keeps a cat and that is one reason why mama thinks he is about right, especially when she found out that he lets the cat come into the house. He has a long table in his parlor, and on that he has all the pots and keetles and jars. The walls of his room are pasted over with all the pictures of the pretty actresses he could find. Uncle Billy was handsome when he was young.

This morning Miss Dent, the boys and I went across the Bay to visit some of the old abandoned houses on the South Beach. Some of them were finished from the wreckage of the two big ships that went ashore about thirty years ago, and have the finest lockers, brass hinges and silver plated locks. The boys screwed some of them off but did not get anything worth very much, as most of them have been stripped. We came back in the skiff with a fresh wind from the south. Sounds as if we were going to have a big storm.

Papa drove to the lighthouse this morning and on the beach saw the dead body of a lynx or mountain lion, that some one had shot and skinned. A young man by the name of Charlton from Portland killed a bear yesterday near Otter Rock, not far from Wild Bill's place. Our horse was frightened by a bear the other day just across the canyon from our house.

The wind has been blowing from the south for several days, and Oscar says there will be a big rain tonight and we will have to stake down the tents. This morning we took a drive on the north beach, and I saw the dead lynx that some hunters killed and skinned. We stopped on the road out past the lighthouse and I picked some of the blue fringed gentians and Indian pink. Other flowers plentifull now are the everlasting flowers and the Indian pink, the pale blue asters, and the golden rod. We stopped in to see Mrs. Wilson's baby. He is a bright little fellow, nearly as white as the whitest white children, if his mother is half Indian. His grandma, Mrs. Meggeson was there, and Mrs. Kelly. Mrs. Meggeson is a Siletz Indian woman and has about a thousand acres of land and three tattoo marks up and down her upper lip. She has coal black hair that is beautiful. Mrs. Kelly, the mother of Mrs. Fitzpatrick, has a fine head of hair and when mama took her picture, she asked if she might take it down so that no one could say she had false hair. Hers is nearly white but long and heavy. She is whiter than Mrs. Fitz and has had three husbands. She is 83, and walks to the Lighthouse and back, about four miles. Mrs. Fitz has some fine daughters. They dress and sing and dance well and are as lively as their grandmother. They own the Monterey hotel, and my uncle Patrick gave us a dinner party there. Their hotel is in front of the big trees.

We are all going home on the 16th as the State Fair begins that week. Mrs. Croasman of Portland is coming up to the Fair one day and we hope she will come and see us.

Abigail Scott Duniway
1835-1915

Abigail Scott Duniway, Oregon's best-known and most indefatigable suffragist, came to Oregon by covered wagon at the age of seventeen. Despite her limited early education, she was employed as a Polk County school teacher at the age of eighteen. In the autumn that followed, "I met my Fate in Eola . . . in the person of my husband. . . ."

The challenges faced by the young but indomitable wife and mother form the subject matter of the letter that follows. These experiences were to profoundly shape Duniway's philosophy and fire her activism for decades to come. Other writings by Abigail Scott Duniway are included in *Varieties of Hope* and *Many Faces* of the Oregon Literature Series. Written a year before her death, this original unpublished letter was discovered in a collection of "women's miscellany" in the Special Collections, Knight Library, University of Oregon.— S.A.

Doing Double Duty
A SUFFRAGIST'S SELF-PORTRAIT

Portland, Oregon
April 11, 1914

My Dear Mrs. Booth:

Replying to your request of recent date will say, first, that my schoolday education was limited to a very few months in early childhood in Illinois, where I was born and lived to the age of 17 years. The school house, about a mile from our home on a farm, was built of logs, with one log omitted over the wall, for writing desks and a row of window frames. Benches, without backs, were used as seats, upon which we faced the center of the room, or turned toward the desks on the wall, as with our convenience, when studying or writing.

I have no recollection of learning to spell, or read simple words. Our busy mother must have taught us at her knee from Webster's Elementary Spelling Book. I smuggled this little, battered time worn volume—this first book I ever owned—across the plains, in an ox wagon, in 1852. I would give a handsome sum if I could find it now.

I attended school intermittently, for a short term, but was unable, from some physical ailment, to be classed as a "regular," so received little benefit. I was sent in the winter of 1850, for a few months. The school met in a primitive Cumberland Presbyterian Church, and the studies ranged from primary grades to Higher Arithmetic, Grammer, Geography, Philosophy, etc., with recitations called before a grizzly-headed teacher, who demanded elucidations of every person from self-taught statements made by students on a blackboard. My stay at this school was brief, as I was never a strong or healthy child, my numerous ailments resulting, as I afterwards learned, from self-imposed stints of heavy overwork, in my first decade of existence from which I am still a sufferer.

The loss of my dear mother in our six months journey across the Plains in 1852 brought to her large family an irreparable loss. We reached the village of Lafayette in Yamhill County, Oregon in the autumn of that memorable year, and I was called to the village of Eola, in Polk County, as a district school teacher in the following Spring. I remember taking a creditable examination and receiving a first days certificate, though I believe I was not questioned severely, except in the proverbial "three R's", in which I had been briefly thoroughly grounded by much less than a year's tuition all told.

I met my fate in Eola during that term of teaching, in the person of my husband, Mr. Ben C. Duniway, a young rancher and stock-man of Clackamas County, to whom I was married August 2, 1853 and taken by him to his donation claim, where I took up the burdens of a pioneer farmer's wife, mother and general drudge for everybody who came our way, chief of whom were bachelor ranchmen who found my husband's home a convenient rendezvous at meal-time, because his young wife could cook and wash for them, in addition to her regular duties for home and rapidly growing family. I was never contented on that Clackamas County farm, and my good husband, largely for my gratification, sold the place and bought another, a beautiful and commanding site in Yamhill County, where we lived for five years, or until a overdue debt confiscated the ranch and sent us to the village of Lafayette. A serious accident befell my husband, while negotiating for another isolated stock ranch, which changed all our plans and threw me back, or up, to my old gift as a teacher. But the tuition of my pupils was not enough to meet the needs of an invalid husband and growing family, so I fitted up a dormitory in the unplastered half-story extension over our cottage by lining and ceiling it with unbleached muslin and adding crude furnishings. I then advertised for young lady boarders and soon filled my quarters with a bevy of ambitious girls, who readily adapted. . . .

As it was impossible to secure domestic help, I would arise at three o'clock in summer and four o'clock in winter, to do a day's work in the kitchen before beginning my day's work in the schoolroom. We owned a lot overlooking much of the village, on which stood a square frame building, which I fitted up for school purposes. I taught school in this way, doing double work continually, in home and school room, keeping up and often ahead of my classes by opening the textbooks for the first time as they sat, expectant on the recitation seats before two blackboards. I cannot tell you how I caught this inspiration that led me through the baby instincts of all my many vicissitudes. But we sold the school in Lafayette, at a profit after nearly four years of strenuous effort, and removed to Albany, the county seat of Linn County, where I built a school house and resumed my teaching till I thought I could engage in merchandise. As this new departure ended my schoolteaching days, and left me equipped with a tolerably good English education and much practical experience, more varied than falls to the lot of almost any other woman I have ever known, I shall close this o'er-long letter rejoicing in the fact my humble efforts have borne in small degree in reshaping the affairs of my young friends in institutions of higher learning that none of them will be compelled to break new paths as I have broken them in my primary though erstwhile untrodden (?) fields.

Affectionately yours for Progress,
Abigail Scott Duniway

Haralambos Kambouris
1890-1965

Haralambos Kambouris was a highly romantic twenty-two-year-old Greek when he left his native Thebes for America in 1912. Hoping to make his fortune in America's West as well as avoid conscription into the Greek army, Kambouris tried to assuage his engulfing sense of loneliness by keeping a diary.

Written in his native Demotic Greek, Kambouris's slim black notebook is the only known diary of a Greek immigrant's experience between 1912 and 1915. (See *From Here We Speak* of the Oregon Literature Series for one of his poems.) His tribulations as a railroad worker in Oregon provide a glimpse into the perilously uncertain world of a transient ethnic laborer in the early twentieth century when Italians, Mexicans, Chinese, Greeks, Japanese, and other minorities helped build an increasingly industrialized West. Kambouris's translated diary, *Pages of My Life and Various Poems: My Leaving Greece for America and My Sojourn in America*, is located in the Manuscripts Division of the Marriott Library, University of Utah, Salt Lake City. The Oregon portion appeared in *OHQ* 80 (1981). Note: Dates in the following appear in both Julian and Gregorian calendars.—S.A.

Railroading in Oregon
A GREEK POET'S DIARY

Monday, October 8, 1913

It was the 8th of October, Monday, and we were at work. Since morning the day was cloudy and by 10 A.M. rain started to fall in fine drops and we are working in it. In this work there are three groups working, one Greek, one Mexican, and one Arab. Our group and the Mexican changed the rails of the track and the Arabs loaded the old ones on a freight train. Because of the rain the Arabs who were loading the rails stopped work. After lunch the foreman put us to load the rails. The train came at 1 in the afternoon and took us four miles away where we started to load the old rails.

The day was rainy and very cold, we could not feel our hands because of the cold. We had been loading rails for one hour. By bad fate a rail caught the left hand of my friend and partner Nicholas Boutsikos and fractured his two large fingers without anyone being aware of it. He only said, Haralambos, I hurt my hand. Immediately I ran to see. He was holding it with his right hand and his two hands were full of blood. The moment I saw them, I almost fainted because the two fingers were hanging by the skin. I took out my handkerchief and bandaged the hand. Then all the other workers came, and the interpreter took him to the hospital where they put medicines on it.

The following day at 8 o'clock, we left on freight no. 225 and at 2 o'clock in the afternoon we arrived at the town of Glendale, Oregon. There we were to work. As soon as the cars were ready, we went to the job and unloaded the equipment. As soon as we were finished, we put the handcars on the rails and went to our work. The work was two miles away, and we were going to work in a tunnel. The next day snow fell and we did not work all day, only 3 hours. In the afternoon we were transferred near our work.

In this operation there had been three gangs brought and none had stayed to work. They quit before they had even begun because inside the tunnel there was water and they wanted to replace the supports with new ones. It was dangerous for many reasons, and, also, very dirty and hard. For this reason they did not want to work there. This happened to us too in the first days; out of the 30 in our gang only 15 would come to work. I and A. Douros were not absent from work at all.

I fell one day because there was no light and injured my hand, but so as not to lose my day's wages, I bandaged my hand and went back to work. The work was not at all good.

Our feet were in water all day, and because of need, we remained and worked.

April 22, 1914

On the 22nd day of April the foreman again received orders to fire two laborers and Vasileos Liakopoulos and Lukas Douros were fired. After two days they left and went to Natron, Oregon, where my uncle Isidore Nakos had been transferred and there they obtained employment. After two days, Good Friday, Christos Santos left and went to Oregon City, Oregon, where he found work in a factory that manufactured paper . So there were of us who remained Andonios Douros, Gheoryios Tournavitis, Konstandinos Voulgaris, Konstandinos Tiganitis, Demetrios Haremis, and I. The next day was Holy Saturday and we went to work. In the afternoon George Tournavitis and Demetrios Haremis went and bought a lamb because the next day was Easter. And as Greeks we had to carry on our tradition. One thing was missing, there was no Greek church.

In the evening after we got off work, Gheoryios Tournavitis slaughtered the lamb and barbecued it so it would be ready the next day. Others had got the wood for the fire. I went to town and bought dye for the eggs. We had bought two barrels of beer, one 6 gallons and the other 8. As soon as God illuminated 27/14 April, Resurrection Day we got up and lighted the fire. As soon as the fire was ready we put on the lamb and began turning it. Seated near the fire we had the red eggs and said the "Christ is arisen," and drinking beer, we chanted the "Christ is arisen from the dead, etc."

Many Americans had come and admired the way we roasted the lamb on a spit, something they saw for the first time. Later I left the boys to barbecue the lamb and went to the railroad station to get a newspaper, and we saw that day that the protocol of peace had been signed by Greece and Turkey, and our joy increased even more. Resurrection is the day of greatest joy for Greek Orthodox. When the lamb was done, we ate it around noon, chanting the "Christ is Arisen" many times and whatever Resurrection psalms we knew. We sang other songs as well, drank beer, and became dizzy, and finished the celebration because we could remain no longer.

January 18, 1915

I had returned to Roseburg just in case I got work again with the New Year, as they had said that they would again start operations. Unfortunately, the New Year came and they did not put on workers. We waited day by day for them to begin. Came the 7th of January, 25th of December and still nothing. My uncle with his wife went to another town where some compatriots were to celebrate Christmas together I, alone and deserted, remained in Roseburg. The day of Christmas dawned I got up and after having coffee at 10 A.M. in the morning, I went to the postoffice to see if perchance I had a letter. Unfortunately, I did not find a letter. Thinking I was abandoned by friends and ignored by relatives, I broke into tears and quickly returned to the house. I shut the doors and windows, then I lay down on the bed and wept my misfortunes until sleep came and shut my tear-filled eyes. slept until 4 P.M. in the afternoon.

> The mother who raised me with golden dreams
> > And now she has lost me to a foreign land far off
> Those of us in strange land away from our parents
> > We are like lonely birds in a winter dawn
> Fate did not help her exiled children
> > And for this we are all forced
> From country, friends, relatives to be separated
> > Countrymen! if you want to be joyful
> Don't leave our sweet homeland

Elizabeth Trimberger
1892-1973

Elizabeth Trimberger began keeping diaries when she was ten years old—a practice that continued almost until her death at age eighty-one. Her first little notebook was a gift from a family friend in Mount Angel, where Trimberger lived with her devout Catholic and extremely strict German-speaking mother. Elizabeth Trimberger could not resist the luxury of expressing her own thoughts on the blank pages of her diary. There, she could not be contradicted and could disagree with her mother. Beginning a new notebook on April 18, 1912, she confessed, "I hardly know if I should or not write on this space, but it looks tempting."

As a long-time elementary school teacher, Trimberger encouraged her pupils to "Write! write! write! everyday!" She first taught at Crooked Finger School near Mount Angel. While she was there, her writing developed the humor and insight that characterized the majority of her diary entries. Her diaries also explored her literary interests, examined the motives of herself and others, and recorded her progress in "character improvement." Later, she married a Montana cowboy and lived with him and their five children in rural Douglas County.

Her grown children treasure their mother's unpublished diaries, from one of which the following selections have been taken. However, sometimes they express puzzlement over the contrast between the witty, life-loving private persona of the diaries and the serious, somewhat demanding public persona they knew as mother and teacher. The self depicted on the diarist's pages frequently differs from the self outsiders know. In her January 1917 entry, "Kitty" refers to Trimberger's saddle horse, and the acronym B.V.M. is short for "Blessed Virgin Mary."—S.A.

A Teacher's Life at Crooked Finger School

Undated 1916: Tuesday

Shall I adopt the measures in a teacher's code of ethics? Do they mean by Temperance "never" to smoke a cigarette? Do they mean by "unimpeachable morality" never to wade in the river, nor to climb a tree, nor to run, jump, swing, wrestle, jug, dance nor swim? Do they mean by discretion never to buy anything from peddlers? By economy not to invest in dancing slippers? If so I shall vote *no* on each one. I wonder if going to moving pictures is an avocation which "will bring the teaching profession into the highest respect." Or if wearing a red silk dress is in accordance with economy when dyes are scarce.

February 13
Two accidents to record, namely: (1) F.S. ran against H.W. and injured his face. particularly his left eye which was very picturesque in green and blue this afternoon. The teacher tied it up in a napkin. (2) The stovepipe fell down, and school had to adjourn at three. Not everyone can have such an accommodating stove-pipe! Miracles do happen occasionally. Even the best-wired stovepipes do sometimes "gang agley."

February 14
The Valentines fell thick and fast this day. "Love me, love my dog."

February 20
This evening there was no Holy hour for me. I had to keep house for two Italian orphan boys of my school. Their father is ill and unable to come home. We, i.e. M. and I, retired between 10 & 11 P.M. While at the supper table we talked of ghostly things when all at once there appeared a face at the window. I was frightened but recovered almost instantly. Looking the apparition straight in the eye, I found that it was only the "Schuderginkel" of the neighbor's house. He shrank slowly back and probably imagines that I did not see him. How little and mean it is to spy on another person! These people think it is wicked of me to associate with unbelievers. However I do not see the unbelievers in them but only needy orphans.

Tuesday, January ?, 1917

Marg. Sh. was the only scholar today. We rushed our work through and about noon Mr. Wourms (pronounced like ordinary angle-worms) put in an appearance and decreed on the strength of his directorship that school was to be closed until next Monday. I was glad because I had such a horrible time getting to school, the snow-laden wind nearly drifted me and Kitty into the fence-corner. (I must not forget to thank the B.M.V. for our safe arrival.) I decided to spend the afternoon sleigh-riding with M.S. but the snow was so deep and made my stockings wet. So I racked my brain for something to use for leggings. And I "hit" upon the old school flag in which the mice had raised a family, and who, upon the event of the young mice's "debut" into the exterior world had vacated & basely deserted the U.S.A. flag. Its red & blue was in tatters but the white was very strong. So round my legs it was wrapped as "First Aide to Injury" and after that I called them my "first aiders", for I wore them nearly every day of my unwelcome vacation. They did good service and I shall henceforth be very voluble in my praises of the "Stars & Stripes" especially the stripes.

October 8, 1918

School is rather empty these days. Some of the children must pick up prunes and others potatoes and so it is one long weary dawdle. It is difficult to be enthusiastic under these conditions.

October 17

The Crooked Finger school was suddenly called out today to fight fire. Mr. E. Schlacheter's house had caught fire on the roof near the stove pipe. He had called frantically for a half hour before any one heard him. Then he ran wildly about giving random orders to my little flock. The oldest, T.S., boosted himself up on the wall to the attic while J.B., a neighbor, climbed up the ladder which the teacher of Crooked Finger had hurridly placed. Then they began dousing each other with water one from the inside through the roof, the other from the outside along the same path. In three minutes the excitement was over.

October 22

After school I donned "clod-hoppers" and went to work in the dryer. I worked until 9:15 P.M. earning in all .85. My heel had the bad grace to come off while at work, and Mr. A. Bellinger was so kind as to nail it on before I had come home which happened about 10 P.M. The moon was large and bright and the mists rose from the land as I walked through the fields alone.

Linus Carl Pauling
1901-1994

Linus Carl Pauling was born in Portland, lived for five years in Condon, eastern Oregon, and returned to Portland where he attended Washington High School before dropping out prior to the last semester, to protest pointless classes. He graduated from Oregon Agricultural College (now Oregon State University) with a degree in chemical engineering in 1922. From 1922 to 1963 Pauling taught at the California Institute of Technology, the institution where he earned his doctorate in chemistry (minors in physics and mathematics) *summa cum laude*, and followed that with teaching an additional twelve years at other California institutions of higher education, including four years at Stanford University. From 1973 until his death he was affiliated with the Linus Pauling Institute of Science and Medicine in Menlo Park.

Linus Pauling has been described as a Renaissance man whose interests spanned theoretical chemistry, quantum mechanics, the common cold, and world peace. Much of his energy during the last twenty years of his life was devoted to research on the beneficial effects of vitamin C and other nutrients on the body.

In 1958, Pauling presented a petition to the United Nations opposing nuclear weapons tests, a document signed by more than 11,000 scientists worldwide, including Albert Einstein, Bertrand Russell, and Albert Schweitzer.

At Pauling's death on August 19, 1994, he remained the only person to have received two unshared Nobel Prizes, the first for chemistry in 1954, and the Peace Prize in 1962. He published several books and more than a thousand scientific papers, continuing to put out about a dozen papers a year well into his nineties.

The following excerpts are taken from his "Diary (so-called)," written in the autumn of 1917 before he enrolled in college.—T. O'D.

Oregon's Two-Time Nobel Prize Winner Prepares for College

August 29, 1917

Today I am beginning to write the history of my life. The idea which resulted in this originated a year or more ago, when I thought of the enjoyment that I would have could I read of the events of my former and younger life. My children and grandchildren will without doubt hear of the events in my life with the same relish with which I read the scattered fragments written by my granddad, Linus Wilson Darling. This "history" is not intended to be written in diary form or as a continued narrative—rather it is to be a series of essays on subjects most important in my mind. It will serve to remind me of resolutions made, of promises, and also of good times had, and of important occurrences in my passage through this "vale of tears." It is to be my Father Confessor—at times—and my companion at other times. Often, I hope, I shall glance over what I have written before, and ponder and meditate on the mistakes that I have made—on the good luck that I have had—on the carefree joyety of my younger days; and, pondering, I shall resolve to remedy these mistakes, to bring back my good luck, and to regain my happiness.

August 30

Tentative Resolutions.

I will make better than 95 (Mervyn's record) in Analysis (Math). (I made 99%/11% in Analytic Geom.)
I will take all the math possible.
I will make use of my slide rule.
I will make the acquaintance of Troy Bogart.
I must go out for track ~~as a high jumper~~, and *succeed*.

September 5

I have been reading a library book which I got yesterday. Its name is "Modern Chemistry and its Wonders", by Dr. Geoffrey Martin, an Englishman. It was written in 1915, and so contains references to the war and to "Kaiser William the Bad." The author makes the mistake, which I must avoid, of often saying such "as I pointed out in my former book 'Triumphs and Wonders of Modern Chemistry' 2nd Ed., p. 60." etc. etc. This mistake is very obnoxious; that is, the mistake of so often referring to your own "former volumes." Otherwise the book is rather interesting; containing, as it does, numerous anecdotes relating to chemistry.

Friday, September 7

This evening Lloyd and I, carrying about a dozen small photos and the same number of enlargements, went into Mason's Drug Store, 37th and Hawthorne, to see about getting their photo business. Mr. Mason said that if our prices were no higher than other places he would be glad to let us do his work, as he is not bound to anyone. He said Pope, the photographer at 26th and Hawthorne, who had done work for him, charged 75% of the amount paid by the customer for the work that he did. I suppose that is the general custom. Mr. Mason said that he would give us the next batch of films as a trial.

We also visited Doc Neubauer, at 39th and Belmont. He procrastinated, and prevaricated, exclaiming about the high quality of the pictures we showed him, but saying that he promised Henderson all his work. He said we could get his photo business next spring. Lloyd says that Henderson does not do Neubauer's work.

An ordinary week's business at Mason's store brings the photographer 6 to 10 dollars in the summer time, and about two in the winter.

Friday, September 21

Today I wrote to Mrs. Carton, 1461 Monroe Street, Corvallis, where Mervyn has boarded for two years, for rooms. I hope I will room with Mervyn there or at Mrs. Rust's. I will unless Mervyn lives at the fraternity. Aunt Goldie said that he was elected to the frat because of his excellence in math. I will accordingly get to join a frat. I must remember to take Spherical Trig. extra, as well as as much more math and other things as I can carry. If I can do as good as I did in high school without studying, I should be able to make over 95% at least in everything in college. I will do my best.

Sunday, October 7

Last night at the train I met Mr. Johnson, and his small son. He asked me if I was new, and said he was the head of the math department. According to the catalogue he is: Charles Leslie Johnson, B.S., Professor of Mathematics. I intend to take every one of the courses offered in Mathematics.

Charles Linza McNary
1874-1944

Charles McNary served his first term in the United States Senate soon after America entered World War I. Serving as the Senate's Republican leader for twenty-six years, McNary was described by his Democratic counterparts as a legislative genius. Harry Truman once said that McNary was the senate's hardest-working and most effective member. Richard L. Neuberger claimed McNary was Oregon's Thomas Jefferson, and Franklin D. Roosevelt viewed him as a potential president of the United States. McNary never ran for president, however, and his 1940 bid as vice-president on the Wendell K. Willkie ticket was a failure.

McNary claimed that the small-town values of the Pacific Northwest greatly influenced him throughout his career and had much to do with shaping his stances on conservation. Orphaned at an early age, and growing up on a pioneer homestead, McNary was always sensitive to people who suffered during hard economic times. He was especially sympathetic to those out of work during the Depression of the 1930s.

McNary described himself as neither liberal nor conservative. He advocated public ownership of waterpower and was called the "father of the Bonneville Dam." The McNary Dam was named after him in 1953. "I've always cast my lot with the voting groups of my state," he said. This point of view separated him from colleagues who took their cues from favor-seekers representing special interest groups.

The following previously unpublished letter demonstrating McNary's faith in the Oregon voter was written after McNary won the primaries during his second successful bid for the U.S. Senate. It was written to his friend Henry Hanzen, the editor of the Portland *Evening Telegram*. Hanzen's correspondence is located in the Knight Library, Special Collections, University of Oregon.—S.A.

After the Campaign, a Senator Thanks His Lion

May 30, 1918

My dear Henry:

This is Memorial Day and I will write you briefly. I have received a down-pour of congratulatory telegrams and letters and kept five girls busy.

I cannot adequately express to you my appreciation for the great work you performed for me during the last campaign. I attributed my tremendous majority in a large way to the efforts of you and John. I never felt at any time that there was serious danger, because I was in a position to command the whole view and was in touch with every part of the state. Employing a word again which John does not particularly favor, the psychology of a public mind was right. Barnstorming politicians, rough necks, slanderers, political cockroaches and other denizens of the political zoos may howl, strut, bluster and fight, but they are not indicative of public sentiment nor do their little antics carry more than the weight of a bubble. The noisy politician stands in proportion to the public as a soldier does to the civilian population, and if you wanted to know the state of mind of the nation, you wouldn't cross the waters to inquire of a soldier, therefore, I believe that fellow who is in the thick of the fight sometimes places too much importance upon the noisy conflict made by the poignant politicians. Then I received a letter, and there were many from various parts of the state, from volunteers who would say "Dear Senator:—At a school meeting yesterday politics were discussed and most of the people are with you," because this or that I felt more confident of the situation than from a disconcerting telegram from "Dear Tom", or a nervous letter from Jack or a leg pulling note from Bill, or "the other fellows got you whipped" from Sam who wanted a $100 to distribute cards.

I do not want to take part in the selection of a State Chairman and whoever you and John decide upon will be all right to me, except that I will not stand for young Sherman, as I treated him fine during the Hughes campaign and he lied about me all over Douglas County.

Yes, I like the use of reservation and believe that is a place to make bad Indians good.

Very sincerely yours,
Charles McNary, United States Senator

Opal Whiteley
1898-1992

Opal Whiteley became Oregon's and, perhaps, one of America's best-known diarists when her journal excerpts began appearing in the March 1920 issue of Boston's *Atlantic Monthly*. Opal and her publisher insisted her childhood diary had originally been written in Oregon on paper bags and scraps before a jealous Whiteley "sister" had ripped it into thousands of bits. While staying in Boston, a fey and childlike Opal Whiteley painstakingly reassembled the jigsaw puzzle-like pieces of the "lost" journal. Soon after, Atlantic Monthly Press published *The Story of Opal: The Journal of an Understanding Heart* (1920)—a book which became a record-breaking national best seller by what seemed to be a precocious and allegedly abused little girl. She claimed that the Whiteley family had adopted her and dragged her off to bucolic Wendling and Cottage Grove in Lane County.

Almost immediately after its publication, the authenticity of *The Story of Opal* was to be questioned—much to her and her publisher's humiliation. The debate concerning both Opal and her mysterious diary extends into our own era. One recent researcher, Benjamin Hoff, persevered in securing the right to reprint Opal's diary in a volume entitled *The Singing Creek Where the Willows Grow* (1986), the source of the following selection. Perhaps, Hoff posits, Opal Whiteley, in the manner of many brilliant and highly gifted persons, was afflicted with schizophrenia. Opal died in a nursing home in Great Britain. She continued to maintain that her *real* parents were royalty, and that she herself was a French princess named Françoise d'Orleans.—S.A.

The Many Things That Opal Sees When She Is Sent Straight for the Milk
CHAPTER FROM A CONTROVERSIAL BEST SELLER

The colic had the baby today, and there was no Castoria for the pains. There was none because yesterday Pearl and I climbed upon a chair and then upon the dresser, and drank up the new bottle of Castoria. But the bottle had an ache in it, and we swallowed the ache with the Castoria. That gave us queer feels. Pearl lay down on the bed. I did rub her head. But she said it wasn't her head, it was her *back* that hurt. Then she said it was her *leg* that ached. The mamma came in the house then, and she did take Pearl in a quick way to the ranch house.

It was a good time for me to go away exploring. But I didn't feel like going on an exploration trip. I just sat on the doorstep. I did sit there and hold my chin in my hand. I did have no longings to print. I only did have longings not to have those queer feels.

Brave Horatius came walking by. He did make a stop at the doorstep. He wagged his tail. That meant he wanted to go on an exploration trip. Lars Porsena of Clusium came from the oak tree. He did perch on the back of Brave Horatius. He gave two caws. That meant he wanted to go on an exploration trip. Thomas Chatterton Jupiter Zeus came from under the house. He just crawled into my lap. I gave him pats, and he cuddled his nose up under my curls. Peter Paul Rubens did squeal out in the pig-pen. He squealed the squeals he does squeal when he wants to go on an exploration trip. Brave Horatius did wait and wait, but still those queer feels wouldn't go away. Pretty soon, I got awful sick.

By-and-by, I have better feels. And today my feels are all right, and the mamma is gone a-visiting, and I am going on an exploration trip. Brave Horatius and Lars Porsena of Clusium and Thomas Chatterton Jupiter Zeus and Peter Paul Rubens are waiting while I do print this. And now we are going the way that does lead to the blue hills.

Sometimes I share my bread and jam with yellowjackets, who have a home on the bush by the road, twenty trees and one distant from the garden. Today I climbed upon the old rail fence close to their home, with a piece and a half of bread and jam—and the half piece for them, and the piece for myself. But they all wanted to be served at once, so it became necessary to turn over all bread and jam on hand. I broke it into little pieces, and they had a royal feast there on the old fence-rail. I wanted my bread and jam—but then yellowjackets are such interesting fairies, being among the world's first paper-makers; and baby yellowjackets are such chubby youngsters. Thinking of these things makes it a joy to share one's bread and jam with these wasp fairies.

When I was coming back from feeding them, I heard a loud noise. That Rob Ryder was out there by the chute, shouting at God in a very quick way. He was begging God to dam that chute right there in our back yard. Why, if God answered his prayer, we would be in an awful fix—the house we live in would be under water, if God dammed the chute! Now I think anger had Rob Ryder, or he would not pray kind God to be so unkind.

When I came again to the house we live in, the mamma was cutting out biscuits with the baking-powder can. She put the pan of biscuits on the wood-box, back of the stove. She put a most clean dish-towel over the biscuits. Then she went to gather in clothes. I got a thimble from the machine drawer. I cut little round biscuits from the big biscuits. The mamma found me. She put the thimble back in the machine drawer. She put me under the bed. Here under the bed, I now print.

By-and-by, after a long time, the mamma called me to come out from under the bed. She told me to put on my coat, and her big fascinator on my head. She fastened my coat with safety-pins. Then she gave me a lard-pail with its lid on tight. She told me to go straight to the grandpa's house for the milk, and to come straight home again.

I started to go straight for the milk. When I came near the hospital, I went over to it to get the pet mouse, Felix Mendelssohn. I thought that a walk in the fresh air would be good for his health. I took one of the safety-pins out of my coat. I pinned up a corner of the fascinator. That made a warm place next to my curls for Felix Mendelssohn to ride in. (I call this mouse Felix Mendelssohn because sometimes he makes very sweet music.)

Then I crossed to the cornfield. A cornfield is a very nice place, and some days we children make hair for our clothes-pin dolls from the silken tassels of the corn that grow in the grandpa's cornfield. Sometimes, which is quite often, we break the cornstalks in getting the silk tassels. That makes bumps on the grandpa's temper.

Tonight I walked zigzag across the field, to look for things. Into my apron pocket, I put bits of little rocks. By a fallen cornstalk, I met two of my mouse friends. I gave them nibbles of food from the other apron pocket. I went on, and saw a fat old toad by a clod. Mice and toads do have such beautiful eyes. I saw two caterpillars on an ear of corn, after I turned the tassels back. All along the way, I kept hearing voices. Little leaves were whispering, *"Come, petite Françoise,"* over in the lane. I saw another mouse with beautiful eyes.

It is such a lovely lane. I call it *our* lane. Of course, it doesn't belong to Brave Horatius and Lars Porsena of Clusium and Thomas Chatterton Jupiter Zeus and I and all the rest of us; it belongs to a big man that lives in a big house. But it is our lane more than it is *his* lane, because he doesn't know the grass and flowers that grow there, and the birds that nest there, and the lizards that run along the fence, and the caterpillars and beetles that go walking along the roads made by the wagon wheels. And he doesn't stop to talk to the trees that grow all along the lane.

All those trees are my friends. I call them by names I have given to them. I call them Hugh Capet, and Saint Louis, and Good King Edward I—and the tallest one of all is Charlemagne, and the one around where the little flowers talk most is William Wordsworth; and there are Byron, and Keats, and Shelley. When I go straight for the milk, I do so like to come around this way by the lane, and talk to these tree friends. I stopped tonight to give to each a word of greeting. When I got to the end of the lane, I climbed the gate, and thought I had better hurry straight on to get the milk.

When I went by the barn, I saw a mouse run around the corner, and a graceful bat came near unto the barn door. I got the milk. It was near dark-time, so I came again home by the lane, and along the corduroy road. When I got most home, I happened to remember the mamma wanted the milk in a hurry, so I began to hurry.

I don't think I'll print more tonight. I printed this sitting on the wood-box, where the mamma put me after she spanked me, after I got home with the milk. Now I think I shall go out the bedroom window and talk to the stars. They always smile so friendly. This is a very wonderful world to live in.

John Casteel
1903-

During the 1930s, the nation passed through a severe economic depression. Because Oregon was less dependent on such hard-hit industries as automotives, steel, and textiles, some historians believe the state may have been less afflicted than other regions of the country. Nonetheless, Oregonians suffered hardships as well—agricultural prices declined, housing starts fell, unemployment rose.

Dr. John Casteel joined the faculty of the University of Oregon as a professor of speech in 1931. He provides a graphic description of the effects of the Depression in Eugene, at the University of Oregon, and in small Willamette Valley towns. The following excerpts from his journal, which first appeared in *OHQ* 89 (1988), also include his reflections on university education and describe the beginning of World War II.—T. O'D.

Where There Is No Vision, the People Perish
A PROFESSOR'S DIARY FROM THE WILLAMETTE VALLEY

September 6, 1931. Eugene, Oregon

We left the hotel this morning, and went down to our house. By daylight we saw the setting,—a small grass plot, a few willful rose bushes and shrubs by the door, and two poled willows close to the edge of the mill race shading the house from the south. The stream runs by constantly,—four feet deep, and some twenty five across. A white bridge spans it just at the corner of our yard. Up stream and down are poplars, seventy feet tall, and weeping willows drooping to furrow the water in midstream. This is almost idyllic. . . . Our meals we have been eating at public cafes, with the usual distress to our stomachs.

September 26

Winter comes on soon, and more than 8 million people are out of work, destitute. In Eugene, these unemployed will have to depend upon charity chest gifts.

October 26

Had conversations with Dean Onthank and Dean Parsons this morning, the latter outlining his plans for program service to small community clubs in this part of the state. I want to help in it by putting the Speech division at his service. At last, I may get to do my part in stabilizing, and enriching, the small country neighborhood. I wonder whether the topography of this region doesn't encourage the solidarity of these neighborhoods. The hills shut about this or that center, the roads are few,—people are bound together.

November 9

Tonight Pres. Hall called a special faculty meeting. The state committee for unemployment relief has asked (?) all state employees to give one day's salary a month, for 5 months, to the state unemployed relief fund. There is no legislation compelling such action, but the force of public opinion, more especially political maneuvering, is such that we couldn't refuse to give on these terms.

January 10, 1932

After dinner, Audeline and I went to a concert performance of George Enescu, Roumanian Violinist. . . . I was impressed to see that a large number of students attended,—a larger proportion than would have done so at Wesleyan or Northwestern. My respect for the students here increases. They are unsophisticated, without being childish or petty in their interests, and they show an appreciation of varied values that discredits the popular caricature of college students. The concert was beautiful and inspiring, but I was a little too dull to be lifted by it. This evening I went to the Congregational Forum, to hear Rolla Reedy and Wallace Campbell speak on economic planning. The audience showed a lively interest in the discussion. One statement the boys made is most significant:—that no amount of industry, willingness, moral character, education, intelligence or ability will guarantee a young man a chance to earn a living in our present times.

January 18

Tonight I went out to Veneta, with some other people and Dean Parsons, from the University, to read at a community "Library" program. I don't know when I've enjoyed an evening more. In a clapboard pavilion had gathered about two hundred people from the farms and lumber tracts,—men, plain women, babies, impatient boys,—the stuff of humanity. Women in aprons loitered in the kitchen, waiting the time to serve up coffee (hours away, when we saw them), and girls were selling candy. Aside from our part of the program, they had items of their own, a skit by school children, old time music by a trio of lumber folk,—a stolid father, a tall son, and a younger brother who needed a haircut long ago. We left after our part of the program,—but the audience was staying on for an hour or two more. Well, here was happiness of a kind, and assurance not to be had in any place else. I am so much interested in this kind of movement that I'm reluctant to turn my effort toward debating, and its artificiality. I would much rather put time into preparing students to speak before audiences of this kind, where life is real.

April 1

My mind was full of speculations over the future of my work here. The prospects seem bright. I suppose I'm one of the few men who anticipate a better opportunity for themselves and their work as a result of the school re-organization plan. But over us all hangs the uncertainty to follow as our depression continues.—I think it significant that such straightened conditions, a hundred years ago, were called "a panic," fifty years ago, "hard times," and now, neatly, "a depression." The sophistication of our language, however, is not accompanied by a corresponding sophistication of our hardships and woes. Starvation is starvation. On my ride to Corvallis yesterday I noticed how many homeless, penniless men were camping along the tracks.

February 2, 1933

Tonight I went out to Lorane with a group to put on entertainment for a Parent-Teachers Association meeting. I enjoyed the experience, as I always do a meeting with these rural people. Wally Dahlberg said the other day that it had taken me to romanticize country life for him. I may have done so too much for myself. But this is one of the few whole-hearted pleasures that I know. I even "pinchhit" as song-leader tonight;—and then gave three little readings. I wish I had a more accurate sense of the view these people take

toward us when we come out. Trying to over-reach the distance we feel to lie between us, we may not understand that we are not so far from them as we imagine,—tho life in a university seems sometimes as artificial as that of a monastery or a Greenwich Village. On our way home we stopped by the roadside to cut some budding pussy-willows. The moon lay dimly behind a thin, shifting mist, and gave a ghostly haze to the country. All about us the meadow and the hills lay in silence,—and we heard our own voices painfully clear. For the first time I felt as tho I were at home in this country.

February 5

Met with the Sunday School class this morning. We talked of the perplexity we meet these days in trying to practice personal charity in a time of mass need. One woman told of a woman she knew, a former member of the class, who was without food or wood. Our personal impulse was to take up a collection,—to rush in at once with a basket of food and a load of wood. But in despair, we realized that these would not last long,—and they did not correct the trouble. I heard Rev. Whitesmith at the Unitarian Church, afterward. His observation, during a trip to Vancouver and back, was that people are sinking into an apathy of helplessness. They wait, he says, with a kind of millennial hope, for deliverance,—some by the Second Coming, some by Communism,—but all by cataclysmic deliverance.

September 14

I have no enthusiasm for taking up my teaching this year. So much of our routine classwork is futile,—so much of our educational procedure is designed just to keep boys and girls preoccupied for a few years longer, lest they discover what life is like. The number of graduate students swells as these hard years continue. Having nothing else to do, young people graduate from college, and go on with advanced courses, and masters degrees. In this they are encouraged by teachers who think that in training students in "research,"—mostly card-filing and bibliography checking,—they are advancing the knowledge, and therefore, the well-being of society.

September 2, 1939

England and France have announced war against Germany. The weight of this news comes to us with almost sickening force, unbelievable, yet so easily to be believed. No one really can say why the war came,—yet we have all known it would come,—it has been inevitable since Versailles,—and before that, far, far, far back into human history. It may be that after this scourge of war, we shall be rid of it,—as Berdyaev wrote, that we should finally discard war,—yet little in the attitudes & habits of men give promise to this hope.

November 17. Klamath Falls, Oregon

At K.F., I was picked up, and taken to Bonanza, 25 miles east, to judge the declamatory contest. What a weirdly desolate country,—volcanic buttes, and level primeval lake-beds, all over-grown with sage brush. This little town made up of weather-seared shacks, set at any angle, amid sagging fences and tangles of Russian thistles. Everywhere, the slate, gritty soil. I heard over thirty-five "selections" during the day,—some unbelievably terrible. But for these youngsters, the experience may mean something. Here was a boy, a sophomore in Merrill high school, whose mother had gone to the hospital for her 4th operation for cancer. He had been keeping house for his brothers and sisters, meanwhile—cooking, washing, ironing,—had kept up his school work,—and had been under the necessity of borrowing clothes for his appearance today.

Another boy was the oldest of 8 in a Norwegian family. He had never appeared before; but did well. His sister & he had alternated going to High school,—and are determined to get thru college that way, too. When I think, then, of some students at the University, I lose patience with their indolence.

March 1, 1940

It seems amazing to believe that the first of March is here. Already, we are enjoying the first blooms of spring. Behind my office, the old Japanese plum tree is full of delicate, pink bloom, and the daffodils and crocuses have blossomed up for days. The weather blusters, with alternate days of showers, and warmest sunshine. Across the valley, the low hills that prelude the Coast range, take on a deep blue-black here, entangling at times the fleece of mist and clouds that roll in from the sea. Mystery and wonder, and pleasant marvels seem to be generating. At such seasons as these, I can understand well the lure of the strange and beautifull country, as it began to infect the pioneers, when they heard the first rumors of the land.

October 7, 1941

To the library for study this morning. . . . I enjoy these quiet hours in the seclusion of my little cell. I go in thru the circulation foyer, into the stacks, slide up to the 6th tier in the little self-operating elevator, peering out thru the little glass in the door as I rise past the gray gloom of successive tiers,—and then walk into the narrow hall between cells, and into mine. The perfect day for study here is one when rain drips in the court outside the window, and the deep grey light makes it necessary to turn on the ceiling globe. If only I could have a small fire, and a little tea in late afternoon, I would be wholly content.

November 18

The public market thrills one, on these days before a holiday. The fowls hand dressed clean and creamy skinned; pickles, jams, scrubbed carrots, bulging cab-bages, jars & crocks of mince meat, pumpkins, squash, bread & pie—all manner of the fruit of the good earth are there, and the cheerful, weathered faces of the farm people in the stalls, all these give us a kind of vicarious return to the agrarian life of our grandfathers.

December 7

We came home from a quiet hour of church, to turn on the radio and hear that the Japanese had carried out a bombing attack on Hawaii, with many Ameri-can soldiers killed & wounded, and much damage. So war for us has begun irrevocably.

Ernest Haycox
1899-1950

Ernest Haycox was one of Oregon's best-known literary figures during the 1930s when he gained national recognition for writing formulaic Westerns for such famous periodicals as the *Saturday Evening Post* and *Colliers.* His popular western novels have sold millions of copies. A number of Haycox's short stories and books resulted in screenplays—among them *Canyon Passage* which was filmed in various Oregon locations in the 1940s. (See *The World Begins Here* of the Oregon Literature for a story.)

Born near Portland, Haycox attended Reed College and then transferred to the University of Oregon where he blossomed under the tutelage of W.F.G. Thacher, who taught various writing classes and later wrote a book entitled *Dear W.F.G: Letters from Ernest Haycox* (1951). Haycox wrote many lengthy and lively letters, one of which appears here for the first time. "Eddie" in the letter may refer to the poet Edgar Guest. "Bob" refers to the writer Robert Ormond Case. (The original of the following text is located in Special Collections, Knight Library, University of Oregon.)—S.A.

Pulp Hack or Enduring Artist?

A WESTERN NOVELIST IN CONFLICT WITH HIMSELF

Box 5064
Portland, Oregon
Wednesday 1933

Dear W.F.G.:

Yours is the kind of a letter that needs answering while my reactions are fresh: You are right about Eddie. I like Eddie, but greatness isn't in him. In some ways he is really a little man. It is all right to have weaknesses; the point is to know you have them— and to rise above them when the occasion calls, not to be jerked around by weaknesses and not realize it. You're right about Bob. Bob is not a little man. I know him very well and he is one of my best friends in spite of average irritations we sometimes suffer. But Bob is somewhat mentally sluggish. His perceptions are good; his emotions are sound. But his life is running more and more along a narrowing track. As for me, I really don't know. Actually I don't. I do not doubt. I am not afraid, and I have the same ambition that I had ten years ago. I have really an unlimited faith in certain aspects of my writing. I'll stack my best lines of writing, for instance, against anybody writing today. Insofar as pure style is concerned, I'm not afraid. So you see my ego isn't cramped; and that a writer must have in superabundance.

At the present moment the financial angle is most important. It may make me less of a writer, but I can't overlook the obligations I have. I can't overlook the matter of security for the family. As things now stand I should say that it will take me another five years to accomplish this much. I'll then be 38. So much for economics.

The other angle is that I doubt if I am well-enough bottomed now to sling a very heavy pen. I have seen my fundamental views modified in the last few years. Not changed greatly, but modified by the plain ordinary experiences we all pass through as we go along. In some things, my reactions at 20 were as sound as those now; but I have now what I did not have then, a reserve of knowledge to color and strengthen—and sometimes to abate—my first conclusions. I do not think any writer has a deep mind. We are not heavy thinkers. It isn't our function. We are creators and dissectors; we create illusions, we telescope time and reality into one scene which looks and sounds more truthful than anything in life—or we try to. Well, we are like painters drawing a tree that in detail doesn't look like any tree nature ever produced until the observer stands off ten feet.

I think a writer's mind is like one of these old fashioned roll-top desks, crammed with God only knows how much collected junk. I never consciously go out to seek color and characters and plots. I have never consciously tried to get "experience." But because this is my job and my mind runs that way, I cannot go anywhere without absorbing detail. The seeming confusion is extraordinary. It may be war debts, it may be the twitching of my dog when he's asleep. Well, you know all this. I'm only repeating what you were aware of when I sat under you eleven years ago, as green as ink. All normally equipped writers are sensitive to impressions. I go to the Lions club and to save my life I can't sit there and be content with the surface things. I do not mean to be unkind, but when my eye lights on a man I begin to mentally scalp him. I hear what is behind the things he is saying; I build him up as another man than he appears to be. And so on and so on. At 20 or 25 I could do very little outside of certain bloody sea and land tales. But all the while I am stretching a little. I can handle more situations, more kinds of people; and I think I can do a better job. But some of my work is still pretty pale. I'm not satisfied. I do not consider any writer to be such who is confined to one narrow field and is lost beyond it.

This isn't defense, W.F.G. This is only statement. I can say one thing: Wherever I may be now in writing, it is impossible for me to go back to what I did 3 years ago. I cannot do it. This week *Argosy* ordered a straight western, not too conventional. 3 years ago I should have had no trouble. It would have been exactly as they wanted it to be; a surface story with just enough variation to give it some spice. What am I writing? A western yarn with an old plot completely honeycombed with motive and aside-thoughts that will leave *Argosy* utterly disgusted. I think I have lost that $600. But I cannot write the surface story any more. So that's some progress, if we forget the $600, which is no simple trick.

I don't think you ever need worry about the rut getting me, or any technic capturing me. If my energy holds out—and that's *my* only worry—I shall be just as restless and unsatisfied in 1937 as I am now. And there is one more thing, though you may not believe this. You have always been more or less of a shadow behind me; a pointing finger, as it were—not accusing, but definitely demanding. And if I ever do a piece of work of which I can really be proud, you have no idea with what actual pleasure I'll ask you to read it. I think I'd get a bigger wallop from your satisfaction than from any other person's.

Well there isn't any peace. Just heavy dust and hard weather and a lot of sweating. I do not mind that—if we can go on working.

As Ever,
Erny

Fred M. Brenne
1909-?

Fred Brenne may have once aspired to be a writer in a league with his contemporaries Ernest Haycox and Albert Wetjen. Although Brenne worked briefly as a journalist and also wrote for a Portland radio station, his principal form of literary expression seemed to be writing lively letters.

As his letters (one of which is excerpted here) to his friend Doug Fox attest, Brenne did not appreciate the small-town atmosphere of Marshfield (today's Coos Bay), Oregon. Over time, however, he seems to have adjusted to his role as a promoter and Chamber of Commerce executive—vocations which occupied him for most of his working life in various western Oregon communities.

Doug Fox, in whose file Brenne's letters were uncovered (see Bibliography), seems to have been well connected to the 1930s Portland literary scene. The Fox file includes letters from several writers including Albert Wetjen, an Australian seaman who had adopted Oregon but was drinking and writing short stories in San Francisco at the time, and Eugene novelist Myron Griffin.—S.A.

A Fast Hard-Talking Progressive in Coos Bay
—a Slow and Easy Town

Marshfield Chamber of Commerce
221 N. Broadway
Marshfield, Oregon
Thursday, December 13, 1934

Dear Doug and Hec:

The promptness and interest displayed in yours of this morning, shames me to a hasty, if incomplete, acknowledgement thereof.

Things have been in bad shape here the past week—looks as though the fairhaired boy was going to run into some unprecedented trouble in the matter of next years relations with the above named civic body; as the end of the year approacheth, the sec. has been out on the streets sounding out the prospective membership for the coming year as to the support, financial and moral, that may be expected. . . . strangely enough, and yet not so strangely, when analyzed, I find that many of them have buck fever at the prospects of being asked for additional dollars to maintain this office; well, I'm not greatly worried yet, as I have several aces in the hole. One, my Federal Building deal, which hinges upon McNary's efforts in Washington at the opening of Congress, the first week in January. I sent him a rabid, yet restrained note yesterday, politely informing him that the eyes, and by that I meant the voters of 1936, were watching with bated breath, his efforts in behalf of our sadly aborted appropriation . . . in other words, I gave him to understand, under the letter head of this body, that his work was being watched, and, if he expected votes here during the next campaign, 1936, a Roosevelt year when Republican votes will be harder to get than ever before, he'd better try and secure a satisfactory consummation of this here Postoffice and Federal Building, AND, in the amount of at least 140,000 dollars, the original amount appropriated (and since cut to 72,000) . . . well, sir, if this thing goes over, I can assure you that little Fred will lose no time in shouting from the hill tops that the Chamber of Commerce CAN, and DID get "something done", contrary to the protests and complaints of the majority of fishbenders here. . . .

When I said rain, I perhaps gave the impression that it was entirely unpleasant—a correction; namely, that while it does rain, plenty and persistently, at the same time, the temperature is very mild . . . fact of the matter is, it's warmer here in the winter than it is in the summer. No fooling. The mercury has a mean low of fifty degrees average, yet . . . so, with the discomforts of rain, we do have the compensating asset of warmth. Shucks, I'm getting used to the rain now—kinda tough for a while, but it's just like dandruff, coldsores, or blondes, after a while they become more or less of a permanent fixation and therefore unnoticed. . . .

Interlude of coupla hours—been out walking around in the rain, talking to several friends over coffee—oh yez, I still maintain the custom, even though in less metropolitan surroundings than of yore; we have several comfy spots for this diversion—Mel's Community Center, secluded booths, good service, good coffee, and nice smattering of local townsfolk to discuss the time of day with. Another, the Seafood Grille—long, narrow room, with a row of booths with high backs (a discreet feature) where a fellow can sit for two hours if he wishes, talkingsoftly and sincerely upon the more speculative features of life; the coffee is not so good here, but this is compensated for in the more subdued atmosphere of dark and quiet, then, there is the College Inn, the town's most enterprising restaurant—the advantage lies in the comfortable, almost luxurious leather upholstered booths—another likely spot, the Jack O'Lantern—has a balcony, with eight or ten booths, flowery, but not too brilliant wallpaper, and black and red decorations thruought; this spot is a favorite of the more genteel element, such as young barristers, doctors and dentists, as well as the pseudo-social strata, the wives and sweethearts of the logging officials, the deep-sea operators and the white-collar millworkers' wives . . . all in all, these few coffee centers afford me a certain necessary release, as I am finding that I can always depend upon finding some individual or other to buy me the brew in exchange for the privilege of presenting his own private axe for the Chamber of Commerce to grind. . . .

This morning, after writing the introductory squabs to this note, I made an appointment with the town's leading, and most obstinate banker—Ben Chandler, one of the leading figures in the codfish social ring . . .; I was granted the audience I sought, and boldly, but a bit timorously, I started my salestalk—"I want your bank to increase its support of the Chamber of Commerce—you're paying only $6.00 monthly now, and there is no reason why this should not be increased to $12.00—" Well, with that glazed eye of his, and with a tightening of his lips, he turned towards me and asked why, why did I think this was justified—well, I talked, hard and fast for nearly half an hour, and I think I made my point clear—I mention this just to show you some of the angles a fellow's got to work down here; it's screwy, I know it, but it's a job.

Oh, hell, this town isn't so bad—it's just the people in it. They've lived here so long, they've been forced upon each other's company so much that they almost doubt that an outside world exists. . . . it's a fact, until just a few years ago Marshfield was completely isolated from the coast and inland, except by train and boat, and few people ever left home. Now, with good roads, reaching every point along the coast, they are beginning to realize that the sun doesn't rise and set within a twenty mile radius of their bedroom window.

All of these things have a very definite bearing upon my job—they force me to use different angles than I could use elsewhere, they make it necessary to be tolerant and patient, to learn to speak quietly and slowly, even deliberately, in order that their laggard minds may clearly grasp the things that can and will be done down here . . . they can't realize that 1929 has passed, many of them are still basking in the pre-drop prosperity days when lumber possession meant power—today, they can't get a thing for their logs; many of them seem to wander about in a daze, almost as though they were expecting the stagecoach to rumble in from Roseburg—oh man, this IS potent country!

There are a lot of colorful figures in Coos Bay—many of them have made much money, spent it wildly, and are starting to make more—there are many has-beens here, far too many. There are a few cultured people in town, a few who do understand and appreciate music, art, and drama, and a few of those things that I doubted the very existence of, after having been here a few weeks. But sadly enough, they too, are resigned—they do not feel that anything can be done along these lines, owing to the presence of an overwhelming substrata mass mind. If there is any expression given these things, it must be given quietly and unobtrusively, for fear that one's neighbor will ridicule. . . . I met a fellow over coffee the other day who is a marvellous sculptor, yet, he admitted that he didn't say anything about it to anyone, unless he saw they were truly interested—said that he'd been laughed at so much, that he didn't care much whether he worked at his hobby or not. I visited his home, and actually, men, he *is* good—several busts of historic figures, several nudes, all graceful and perfectly proportioned, a few modernistic figures I couldn't understand, but which, nevertheless, would certainly elicit praise from competent critics. I asked "Why don't you leave town and work where these things would be appreciated?" He replied, dolefully, "Aw shucks, I've got to stay here with the family, their relatives have lived here forty years, and they sorta feel as though they'd like to live along, quietly, making what they can, and just taking it easy—anyway, I can't stand crowds. . . ." And there you are—maybe he's happy, maybe he isn't, but, can you or I say which? . . .

sorry, gotta go now, the evening train is about to leave—please write soonest, and I'll reply in kind. . . best as always, and don't forget . . .

fogbound fred

A.J. Tittinger
?-?

It was to be a survey "unique in the annals of the Survey of Federal Archives and the National Archives," wrote A. J. Tittinger in a 1937 letter to his supervisor. The destination of archivist Tittinger and photographer David H. Ellis was the barely accessible, storm-blown, sea-battered Tillamook Rock Light Station often described as the loneliest beacon on the Pacific Coast. The following excerpts from his 3-page letter give a detailed description of the adventures of Tittinger and Ellis on their harrowing and, in retrospect, humorous journey via the U.S. Lighthouse Tender *Manzanita* to "The Rock."

Tittinger's account does not exaggerate the tumultuous seas typical of parts of the Oregon coast, particularly in the vicinity of Astoria. In 1912, during a fierce gale, a huge wave struck Tillamook Rock, tearing away part of the rock itself, and smashing a lighthouse lantern-pane thought safe because it had been installed 133 feet above normal sea level.

The Historical Records Survey conducted by the Works Progress Administration, an inventory of federal, state, county, and town archives, has been a boon to ensuing generations of researchers and historians.—S.A.

Seasick All Day

A FEDERAL LANDLUBBER REPORTS HIS SHORT UNHAPPY VOYAGE TO TILLAMOOK ROCK

Room L, Post Office Bldg.
Astoria, Oregon
April 4, 1937

Mr. Paul Hartmus
Regional Director
Survey of Federal Archives
Portland Oregon

Dear Sir,

I hereby respectfully submit a supplementary report on the survey of Federal Archives at Tillamook Rock Light Station, made on April 2, 1937, by the undersigned and accompanied by David H. Ellis, photographer for the survey. This particular survey is probably unique in the annals of the survey of Federal Archives and the National Archives because of the difficulties attendant after leaving the mainland until the destination was reached. The humor of the situation and the point at issue will be more obvious when one considers an archivist to be a studious and bookish person of sedentary habits.

After leaving Astoria, Oregon, on the U.S. lighthouse Tender *Manzanita*, my intentions were to survey the records of this vessel with the assistance of Mr. Ellis. This intention I was soon compelled to forget because of my own personal physical discomfort. This distraction came about through *mal de mer*, or just plain seasickness. The vessel's archives were furthest from my thoughts and so were those on Tillamook Rock. Mr. Ellis experienced the same symptoms but in a lesser degree. The Captain, Charles A. Modeer, and the mates assured us that this was fine weather, although a heavy westerly swell was going and a south wind of near gale velocity blowing. Their assurance did not fool me and I know rough water when I see it and feel it, besides it brought back memories of a similar "smooth water" on the Atlantic coming back from the AEF in France. After a bleak trip and still bleaker outlook the *Manzanita* finally arrived at its destination, a quarter mile from the rock. At this position somebody wrapped me up in a life preserver, Mr. Ellis too, and hustled us into a life boat. Before we knew what had happened were adrift in the Pacific Ocean between the good ship *Manzanita* and Tillamook Rock, wolfish waves licking at our life boat and jagged rocks beckoning our frail craft to destruction. However, under the skillful guidance of the second mate of the *Manzanita* and its gallant boat crew we managed to evade both evils, but more was in store for us.

A few feet from the rock where billowing waves surge madly into foamy spray, a crate was lowered from the boom on the lighthouse onto the bow of the boat. Expert oarwork by the men and surprisingly skillful timing by the second mate kept both boat and crate together.

The good keeper of the Tillamook Light did as is the custom, let us dangle, evidently to enjoy the three elements: land, sea, and air. Lest the cable break I tried to convince our host above the fury of the gale . . . still the boom did not move landward; finally in fear and desperation I yelled uncomplimentary remarks about his ancestry. Understanding dawned on his face as he nodded and swung the boom inland. After climbing something like eighty steps we reached the feudal castle like shelter of the lighthouse.

Our work finished the keeper summoned the *Manzanita* by phone. I saw the launching of the life boat with great misgivings. Back in the crate, high in the air, Ellis focuses camera standing up to take shot of lighthouse, myself crouching in the crate trying to keep it balanced. We go lower and swing out to sea; lifeboat tries to meet us. Some men jump on deck, mate beckons to me to jump, I jump with brief case containing serials tightly clutched in my hand; I land on deck and stumble like a spavined horse. Into the cabin, seasick again, no survey done on *Manzanita* on return trip either. Back in the Columbia River, smoother water, we land and thank the captain for a pleasant trip, say good bye to officers, wave to crew, down to office for mail, then home.

On the way home musing, this ought to be good for a medal of honor or a National Archives medal. Anyway it was some trip and you can't be a sissy working on archives. It may be a rat-infested cellar, a musty attic, a lighthouse at sea or a luxuriously appointed office. Archivists go where they send them.

In conclusion I desire to state that we were treated with utmost courtesy and kindness by Captain Modeer and his officers and crew, and would be remiss if I failed to bring this to your attention. During the dangerous part of the trip we were their sole concern and it is because of the personnel that no harm befell us under the circumstances.

Very respectfully,
A.J. Tittinger

Lee Owen
Stone
1904-1977

Father Stone was Portland's first African-American Episcopal priest. Born in Kentucky, Father Stone came to Portland in 1936 to serve at St. Philip's Episcopal Church. While there, he increased an all-African-American congregation of 45 to an inter-racial congregation of 250.

Father Stone was one of the founders of the Urban League of Portland. He also served on the boards of the National Association for the Advancement of Colored People, the Council of Churches, the Council of Social Agencies, the American Red Cross, and the YMCA. For a time he was president of the Boys and Girls Aid Society. The following letter to the *Oregonian* expresses his outrage when learning that a labor union prohibited membership to African Americans. The original letter is housed in the Oregon Historical Society Library, Portland.—T.O'D.

Make No Peace with Oppression

A PRIEST CALLS FOR UNION REFORM IN PORTLAND DURING WORLD WAR II

Portland, Oregon
January 17, 1942

The *Oregonian*

To the Editor:

Democracy is based upon the Sacredness of human personality. Every man has the inalienable right of development physically, spiritually, mentally and economically. These are the rights for which men have fought and died throughout the ages. Today the world is engaging in a conflict which will ultimately decide whether or not men shall continue to enjoy these hard-won privileges.

The A. F. of L. Boilermakers Local No. 72 and Machinists Local No. 63 has placed "a limitation upon the basic American right to work." It is excluding American born citizens from their inherent right, which "is an intolerable invasion of individual liberty." If they are not stopped by the American people, these invaders will continue to usurp individual liberties until they have denied all people of their rights. Hitler followed the same plan. First, it was the Jews. Then it was the business men of Germany. Europe was next. Now it is the world. It can "happen here" if the American people let this pass, as the German people let the first act of oppression by Hitler pass.

The American Negro is being called upon to do his duty in protecting and preserving these basic human rights. He, like all other Americans, is being called upon to give his life in whatever part of the globe his country may send him. Yet, we find in our midst a group that denies him the right to work. In denying the Negro his right to work, the A. F. of L. is no better than Hitler and his Nazi oppressors.

This attack upon the rights of the Negro is an attack upon the rights of every American. If the A. F. of L. is not checked now it will invade the rights of others. Therefore, let us make no peace with oppression at home or abroad.

Yours truly,
(Rev.) *L. O. Stone*
1216 N. Williams Ave

Adrian Wilson
1923-1988

Adrian Wilson was born Adrian Peter Wezel to Dutch emigrants in Ann Arbor, Michigan. Wezel legally changed his name to Wilson in honor of President Woodrow Wilson. Adrian Wilson was profoundly influenced by the pacifist convictions of his mother, Christine. Despite Mrs. Wezel's empathy for tiny Holland as it struggled against Germany, she warmly supported her eldest son's decision to become a Conscientious Objector (C. O.) during World War II.

Wilson left home at age eighteen to attend Wesleyan University in Connecticut and began chronicling the events in his life in highly expressive and entertaining letters. As the war began, he was inducted into the military in "alternative service" as a C.O. He served briefly in a camp in North Dakota, participated in medical experiments in Minneapolis, then was assigned to Camp Angel, Waldport, Oregon. At Waldport, one of three C.O. internment sites in Oregon (the others were Cascade Locks and Elkton), the men worked as foresters by day and spent their evenings as poets, artists, writers and musicians—printing books of poetry, editing literary magazines, staging plays, and producing concerts.

Many of Waldport's artists contributed significantly to the San Francisco Renaissance of arts and letters beginning in the 1950s. (See *Varieties of Hope* for an essay on this subject and *From Here We Speak* for poems by Glen Coffield and William Everson, the "Bill" in the September 17 entry.) Adrian Wilson eventually became an internationally known printer, typographer, and teacher, and he received many prestigious awards. He learned much about his craft at Waldport, where he did his first experimental designing and printing of playbills and programs. The following selections come from his collected letters, *Two Against the Tide* (1990), edited by his wife Joyce Lancaster Wilson. Addressees, addresses, and closings were removed in that publication to create the impression of a journal.—S.A.

All War Stinks to High Heaven

A C.O.'S DIARY FROM WORLD WAR II

August 1, 1944. Camp Angel, Waldport

Already this is my last evening at Waldport—for two weeks. About twenty of us have been assigned to the side camp at Marys Peak, the highest in the Coast Range, 4,097 feet. It will be two weeks of trail and road building and in case of a fire in the area, we will fight it. In anticipation, the Forest Service has supplied me with brand new caulked (spiked) $18 logging boots, beautiful pieces of craftsmanship. The unfortunate part of my assignment to Mary's Peak is that it was done without any consideration of the fact I transferred supposedly for the Fine Arts School, which functions at the base camp here. But along with that, it takes me away from my discovery of this afternoon—the ocean. We had the afternoon off to pack for tomorrow's journey. The bearded Dupre had been ribbing me so much about my not going to the beach, much less swimming, that I finally agreed to go with him. So after sleeping until 1:00 p.m. I dragged him out of the Untide Press room, borrowed a bathing suit, and walked across the highway to the strand. The beach here is clean white sand that blends into mist on both sides, and the surf, even on calm days like today, is as good as on that very best day after the storm at Prides. To my amazement I found the water no colder than York Beach and could have kept on being buffeted by those crashing and hissing waves much after Vladimir called me out to go to supper. Such exhilaration being catapulted on the foaming crests and then dropped behind in the swirling froth ! I can still feel it as I write. I tingled all over when I came out, full of health and warmth. Could this be C. P. S.?

August 3. Marys Peak, Philomath

I am writing under a gas lamp because the generator doesn't work, but otherwise this miniature C.C.C. camp in the midst of typically Oregonian forested hills is very nice, even flush toilets. Just now I have had a wonderful session with Steve Pith, a J.W. from Pittsburgh who plays accordion better than I play clarinet, and knows all the songs. We are already booked for a dinner concert when the base camp has its monthly banquet. But otherwise there are neither intellectuals nor artists here, unless they are keeping their lights under a bushel as much as I am. . . .

During the two weeks we are here we will, among other things, [clear the brush off] twenty miles of telephone wire land. . . . I had a fine lunching place today. Having taken off my boots and left them at the bottom like at a Dutch house because the fire tower doesn't like spikes, I toted my sandwiches up to the top. It was a gray day, completely overcast with mist hanging like moss into the valleys. A break in the velvety hills to the east revealed a broad plain stretching all the way to the foothills of the Cascades but the snow-capped peaks themselves were above the clouds. . . .

August 7

Over this tortuous asphalt ribbon the logging trailers grind all day long fairly grunting under two, three, or four fir logs two or three and a half feet thick, and occasionally one really big one four to seven feet in diameter, all thirty-two feet in length so that they will yield two batches of sixteen-foot boards.

When the trucks get over the summit they shift gears and start the joyful plunge into the valley. The brakes on the double back wheels of the trailer steam from the cooling water and leave two-inch tracks of wet on the black pavement. We wave to the drivers as they come lumbering up, and again as they come back, driving fast with the trailer wheels perched up on the back of the truck behind the cab and the beam sticking out over the windshield. The fellows say these trucks last only three months, they are driven so hard, but the drivers who own their trucks clear $40 a day, being paid percentages on the worth of the board feet they haul. It is a frightening industry, this ruthless plundering of the forests and noisy hauling of the fat logs, full of the power, wealth, and immensity of the Northwest.

Our telephone line which connects the Forest Service Ranger Stations in the area, follows the road in general but when it isn't straight enough, or when it twists over a valley, the lines go cross country. We usually walk along the side of the road in our spiked shoes, carrying axes, brush hooks, spurs, and tree saws, and sight down the line every once in a while to see if there are any Christmas trees, shrubs, or maples that threaten to touch the line within the next twenty years. If there are, we have to scramble down banks and into canyons through ferns six feet high, brambles, and veritable fishnets of under-brush. Often we can escape, however, by walking along the fallen rotting trunks of big firs, for most of the land has been logged off and many of the pieces have been too heavy or too far from the spar poles to be taken to the mills. One fellow with whom I hitch-hiked said he had been logging for awhile but when they would cut down fourteen-foot trees and then not use them because they were too heavy, he quit. . . .

August 9

I smacked a hornet's nest and they all came swarming out, giving me four stings before I had run a mile up the trail, and Carroll three and when he thought they were all gone home and he went to do a *plaschje* two more in just the worst spot. . . .

I finished Lawrence's *Sons and Lovers* tonight so that it will always be a very definite part of my memory of Mary's Peak. I think it is a very great novel in which every sentence is vital, every incident shrewdly chosen for its symbolism, and the whole a beautiful study of character, love, and home relationships.

Of the movements of the Allies I am unaware. It's insane; the arts, the forest, and the ocean here are a direct antithesis. . . . Fred Millett wrote a fine letter ordering ten copies of Bill's poems to distribute and praising them highly.

September 17

Roberts left for Cascade Locks yesterday morning. . . . In exchange, this afternoon we got the famous Glen Coffield who wrote the Untide Press's first printed publication of poems—the surrealist *Horned Moon*. For our weekly reading of creative writing tonight . . . Bill read four fine poems by an English anarchist, George Woodcock, and the best of one of three books the prolific Coffield finished in two weeks. I was positively amazed at Coffield's genius. His rhyming particularly is miraculous. He is the first poet I have met who writes systematically. . . . It is strange that for this character C.P.S. has meant a great flowering. I kick myself for not doing likewise.

This is my message to my brother:
Inwardly you know that the act of killing a man, in which you participate no matter where you are in the Army team, will never settle anything. It is very easy to forget that this is what you are doing when you are studying in v-5 at Wesleyan or cavorting in an airplane. The old argument that is always being thrown at C.O.s about letting them come over here and rape your grandmother is difficult for you to surmount. O.K. Don't bother with it. Only realize the business of war is rotten. You are not a killer. When they put a bayonet in your hands at Parris Island let it sink in that this isn't football practice anymore. Stand their taunts and long months in the guardhouse. You won't be the only one. This war and all war stinks to high heaven and I don't want a big clean loving guy like you in it.

Vance de Bar "Pinto" Colvig
1892-1967

Vance de Bar "Pinto" Colvig, whom millions of American children would eventually know as Bozo the Clown, was born in Jacksonville, Oregon. His family and friends, however, knew him as "Pinto"—a nickname that stuck because of his many freckles. "My mother covered me with a crazy quilt when I was born," Pinto liked to tell people, "and I've been clowning ever since." He first encountered the fateful smell of grease paint about 1900, when he was eight or nine years old and got a walk-on role in a touring vaudeville show. In 1911 while attending college in Corvallis and growing increasingly bored, Pinto began his clowning career during summers with the Al G. Barnes Circus.

Clever with a pencil, Pinto worked briefly as a newspaper cartoonist in Nevada and later in San Francisco. In 1922 he moved to Hollywood and did animation work and voices for the Max Sennett Co., Walter Lantz, and other studios. In the 1930s he worked for Walt Disney and created the cartoon voices of Pluto, Goofy, and other famous characters. He wrote the lyrics for "Who's Afraid of the Big Bad Wolf," the title song for the feature-length cartoon *The Three Little Pigs*. He was also the voice of Sleepy and Grumpy in *Snow White*. He claimed Grumpy was "a composite of all old codgers in Jacksonville in the early days."

Pinto always stayed in touch with his friends in Medford and Jacksonville and loved to write humorous letters, sometimes sentin elaborately illustrated envelopes. His kindness to all the children he encountered throughout his life will long be remembered. Pinto's unpublished letters, many of them illustrated, are held with this one by the Southern Oregon Historical Society, Medford.—S.A.

Bozo the Clown

A JACKSONVILLE BOY NEVER FORGETS HIS FRIENDS

2134 North Highland Avenue
Hollywood 28 California
March 10, 1948

Dear Tom:

A few weeks ago that long, lanky nephew Gordon Warner dropped in on me down here and presented me with a 1907 post card bearing the signatures of you and Harry Lewis, which brought back a lot of old time memories. Am glad to hear that you're still on top and still running the village butcher shop—which reminds me that my Ma used to send me down to Orth's Shop with two-bits and I'd bring back enough beef steak for the whole family—and a big family at that—and along with it he'd slice me off a few hunks of baloney for good luck. Those days are gone forever. Up in San Francisco a couple of weeks ago at the Sir Francis Drake Hotel I had a New York cut—size of the palm of your hand—$4.50!

How well I remember that old J'ville slaughter house—I used to play hookey, sneak down a back alley, cut through Charlie Payne's blacksmith shop, bum old Charlie for a chaw of t'bacca, hop in the back end of the butcher-wagon and lie flat (so gossipy neighbors wouldn't see me) and hideout at the slaughter house while Oscar Dunford and Hine Orth would do their butchering. Do the present J'ville kids do that sort of thing with you? And do they bum you for the beef and hog bladders for footballs?

I often think of the old days when we went to school in the old white, wooden schoolhouse (which was so full of woodpecker holes it hardly stood up). And how us kids all rejoiced the night it burned down (except Fleta Ulrich and Frances Kenny, who actually cried!).

If I remember right, YOU succeeded me in becoming official mascot for Bum Neuber's Gold Bricks—and how we'd travel along with the team in the old town bandwagon (with the eagle painted on the front—and the seats were always piled high with turkey and chicken crap where they'd roost above it all winter long!)

All of the Donegan boys played on the team, played in the town band, and were on the volunteer fire department—and during a game on sunday afternoon the band was always weak, and if the fire bell rang, the Donegan boys and Lewis Ulrich and Charlie Noonan and possibly a few others would have to leave the game and run to the fire.

Yesterday I went out to visit Bailey Brothers Circus and had a good time playing in the band and smelling the elephants. How I do remember early circus days in Medford. Us kids would collect "gunny" sacks and beer bottles and whiskey flasks for weeks to get enough money to go to the circus. One time Harry Lewis and I were scouring the neighborhood for empty whiskey flasks and for a long time couldn't find any; when suddenly Harry said: "We're on the wrong trail—let's go out past your house and up the Jacksonville hill— that's where Yockey Eaton, Hine Bleecher and Shorty Swartzfigger and a lot of others like that live." We did, and all along the side of the road we picked up nearly a dozen. (Incidentally, a feller could get a damned good full pint flask of whiskey in those days for four-bits!) Little did I realize in those days that eventually I'd travel all over North America with a circus—but I did! Also, when Paul ("Scantlin'") Force and I used to waste our time in school drawing cartoons, did I ever think that some day I would be doing it seriously; however, I do very little drawing now days; just something for the fun of it. It's easier working out at Walt Disneys or other places and watching the other guys do it while I just sit by and write the gags or make the screwy voices.

Hope to be comin' up that way this Spring (it's been several years now since I've been up there, and I get mighty homesick for God's Country.) When I do, I'll drop in and we'll roll a Bull Durham, or a pine-needle, or a hunka buggy whip, or some mullen leaves, or hoss manure, or go out to the "bam" patch an talk over old times. In the meantime, take keer yourself and tell all my oldtime friends

> "HOWDY"
> From
> *Pinto Colvig*

William Nunn
1861-1956

Sometime in the early twentieth century, William and Alice Nunn of Portland purchased land near Estacada on which to erect a "camp," as they called it, for at the time the rustic style summer home was popular.

In 1921 the Nunns sold their "camp" to the Gerald Beebe family and not long thereafter removed to Florence, Italy, where they lived for some years. In 1951, Robert Beebe, Gerald Beebe's son, wrote William Nunn asking for any information he might wish to provide on the establishment of his family's summer place. By then in his nineties, Nunn replied as follows. The longer original letter is held by the Oregon Historical Society, Mss 485.—T. O'D.

Building Our Summer Place above Eagle Creek

2347 N.W. Flanders St.
Portland, Oregon
October 4, 1951

My dear Beebe,

I must apologize for this unconscionable delay and commend you for your patience in waiting so long.

One day either Alice's eye or my eye, or all four of our eyes were attracted by an advertisement reading: "*For sale*. 16 acres of wild land with the largest waterfall in Clackamas county." We took the electric car to Estacada, where Mr. Palmatier, who was afterwards to be our neighbor, met us with his team and wagon and drove us to the property, five miles east of Estacada.

It certainly was wild land. Delft creek and Eagle creek, the larger of the two, cut deep canyons through the property, but the view from the high bluff looking east to Mt. Hood was superb and the waterfall of Eagle creek, though perhaps not the largest in Clackamas county, was some fifteen feet high. When our guide took us to this waterfall a salmon was trying to get to the upper stream. As he leaped again and again in futile effort to swim up the waterfall, his silvery scales catching the sunlight, it all made a charming picture. How did the bucolic-minded Palmatier manage to have that salmon at that moment perform his part in the sale of that property? He never divulged the secret.

I did not give up my desire to make the place a farm without a struggle. A bucket of cold water dispelled this dream. "However luscious and bountiful your peaches might be, to get them to market, a road would have to be built up the canyon."

On a high bluff overlooking the canyon there were some twenty acres of level land with a number of magnificent first-growth fir trees placed as by some skilled landscapist. Under them was a low growth of salal whose pink-white blossom and dark purple fruit was most decorative. There was also a quantity of the red American currant and solomon's seal.

On this spur formed by the two streams, and some three hundred feet above water level, we planned a house, or rather camp.

From the spot where the house was to be there was a wonderful prospect, bold grey rocks in the foreground, till the sides of the canyon met, then wave after wave of mountain and forest, distance beyond distance folding one into the other, each receding plane increasing in mass and density of colour tone, but ever losing more of its detail till lost in the bulky base of Mount Hood.

With men and lumber on the ground, we drew plans for our house, following the uneven contour of the land and taking advantage of a forest giant, that had been felled a generation ago, on which to rest the main veranda running the full length of the structure.

Our house was built of overlapping rough lumber, stained brown per se to tone into the trunks of the grand fir trees which formed a background.

When our house was partly constructed, ominous rainclouds were gathering, and the roof of the building was not completed, so all hands were ordered aloft. Alice, who never could sit idly on the sidelines when any activity was afoot, soon joined us on the roof, hammer in hand. She had never had occasion to handle shingles but was soon doing yeoman service in getting the roof on the house.

When we were all on the ground admiring our handiwork, a big Swede carpenter, some six feet two, said to me: "Mr. Nunn, you have the fine wife, she like to work. If I had a wife like that I would soon be a rich man. The women, all they want to do is ride around in a streetcar." Arise, ye women, arise! and in your might, smite these six foot two Swede carpenters, your traducers!

I had with much labor collected rocks as big as a man's head for the construction of a fireplace that would take a six-foot log. We engaged a stone mason from town, and I acted as his helper, handing him each stone and supplying him with cement. To solace himself during his temporary exile he had provided himself with a bottle of whiskey. This he consumed the first day, which made him the more anxious to return to his home and a further supply. We paused from our labors as the chimney was just peeping above the roof, when with a loud crash our whole structure crumbled, leaving two or three tons of assorted rocks in the middle of our drawing room. In his haste to be gone he had not allowed sufficient time for the cement to set. At our invitation the "master mason" made a hurried exit from the scene of our activities. I was with difficulty restrained from accelerating his departure by means of pedal propulsion.

Our problem now was to convert this mass of rock into some semblance of a fireplace and chimney. Our boss carpenter said he would arrange with a stone-mason who was an expert builder of chimneys to go out with us and do the work. Nearing Estacada on our way out, we spoke to him about the work to be done. Listening to us politely, he then said: "My brother is the stone-mason. I am a painter." When we had recovered our breath, we explained that we had made arrangements to stay for two or three days for the purpose of building the fireplace, that it was not our fault that he was a painter, and that a fireplace had to be built. He agreed that with our assistance he would do his best.

My practical partner, who was as much at home at one end of a sixteen foot crosscut saw, shingling a roof, entertaining her friends in her own drawing room, or at the bridge table, soon solved this problem. She remembered that in an old copy of *Country Life in America* there were instructions for building fireplaces. We three went into a huddle over this article.

We went to work with a good will, and with Alice to keep us in line with the directions. I tried to select the larger stones for the base, but most of them were at the bottom of the heap, therefore we had to use indiscriminately large and small stones. When the chimney was finished, this irregularity gave a pleasing spontaneous effect to the whole structure.

Prompted by curiosity to see what it looked like inside, I stuck my head into the chimney, expecting it to be dark with a gleam of light from the top. What I saw was a sleasily woven wicker basket with little shafts of light sifting through about a million little holes and cracks in the masonry. That damned painter brother of a stone-mason had not used enough "marter". I said nothing to dampen the ardor of the other two. When they started a fire on our hearthstone, I expected to see squirts of smoke coming through every little hole. To my surprise the fire crackled merrily, and the smoke went up the chimney straight and true as did the smoke from Abel's sacrificial fire.

Our telephone being a party line, kept the whole neighborhood posted on the movements of one another. If we were disappointed when we telephoned Mrs. Jones asking if she had any eggs, Mrs. Brown would kindly advise us that she had eggs. If the telephone called from town, all our neighbors were fully informed who was coming out to see us, or why we had to leave for Portland. This was very convenient for had our house caught fire one phone call would have brought assistance from a dozen willing neighbors.

This cleared land we planted into a small mixed orchard, and . . . we enjoyed watching the maturing of our trees. The first to bear was a red Hungarian plum. We were so pleased that we kept it to show to friends from Portland. The morning they came, birds had arrived earlier and not finding the promised worm, had eated the ripe side of every plum on the tree. During our absence in town a friendly neighbor's pig harvested our potatoes. He did a fine job. With the devastation caused by the weather, birds, and pigs, a "farmer's life is not a happy one."

In 1921, having determined to remove our residence from Portland on the banks of the Willamette to Florence on the banks of the Arno, we sold The Wilderness, lock, stock, and barrel to Gerald Beebe, an old resident of Portland, who with his family still enjoys this hundred and sixty acres of wild land and "the biggest waterfall in Clackamas county."

Yours Sincerely
W.H. Nunn

Shizue Iwatsuki
1897-1984

In 1965, the Tokyo journalist Kauzo Ito began collecting reminiscences of Japanese immigrants to Northwest America. One of his correspondents was Shizue Iwatsuki. Born in Okayama Prefecture, Japan, she left her home at age nineteen to settle with her husband, Kamegoro, in the Hood River Valley. After years of hard work, Shizue and her husband eventually owned their own orchard. During that time, she also raised a family and wrote nearly 1,500 traditional Japanese tanka. (See *From Here We Speak* of the Oregon Literature Series for examples.)

Like most other Americans of Japanese ancestry, she and her family were forced into relocation camps in the interior West as a result of President Franklin Roosevelt's order on February 19, 1942—an order justified then as a military necessity, but later recognized as a violation of constitutional guarantees. Written between 1965 and 1968, the following portion of her letter to Ito appeared in *Issei: A History of Japanese Immigrants in North America* (1973). She here describes her early experience as an Oregon pioneer.—T. O'D.

How Many Nights Did I Cry

AN ISSEI SETTLER REMEMBERS HER EARLY LIFE IN HOOD RIVER

Hood River, Oregon
ca. 1965

Dear Mr. Ito,

In June of 1916 I landed at Seattle accompanied by my husband, Kamegoro Iwatsuki, who was from Okayama Prefecture. Graduated from Ashimori Entle Girls' High School, while I was taking a pre-marriage course in flower-arrangement, sewing and other domestic arts, he had happened to come back to Japan from Hood River and was looking for a bride. We had an interview marriage, our go-between being a person close to my father. I was nineteen years old and my husband was twenty-nine. He said, "I am a farmer growing apples." I only knew America through books, and I had a picture in my mind that America was a place where even the farmers wore shirts and ties when they worked in the fields. We sailed in a third class cabin on the *Mexico Maru* . . .

Landing at Seattle, we went by train to Hood River. At Portland we changed trains, and after that we travelled through the middle of a wasteland. While I was still marvelling that even in "flowery America" there was such an out-of-the-way place, four hours later we arrived at our destination. We were to stay at the Yasui Company nearby. Though it was called a company, it was actually a store displaying bits and dabs of Japanese goods on the first floor. On the second floor were two or three bedrooms. Next to Yasui Company was a small Japanese restaurant named Niguma Company. In those days people came by buggy from the country into town for shopping. They were served Japanese meals at the restaurant, stayed overnight on the second floor of Yasui Company, and then returned home the next day. We, too, stayed there. At the time I wondered why we stayed in such a place and didn't go to our home directly. I felt a little strange about it but didn't worry too much, and as it turned out we stayed there for three or four days.

Then my husband said, "I'll take you strawberry-picking." Thinking that it was going to be some kind of picnic, I went along, only to find that I was completely wrong. The fact was that my husband was an employee of a strawberry farmer. The farm was about ten acres, and there were many pickers. My husband's job was to direct them. Mr. Kasaishi, the owner, looked over the rim of his glasses at my hands and said, "Mr. Iwazuki, your Missus (Okamisan) can't pick strawberries with those hands! If she has time after we eat, ask her to collect the boxes of picked strawberries." Being called "your Missus" made me feel insulted somehow, and I blushed.

One day I asked my husband, "Where is your apple orchard?" upon which he answered, "I'll take you there soon." Since he had said that in the orchard the trees were loaded with apples, I was waiting with anticipation. But when we actually went there, I found that the trees had only been planted four or five years ago. I asked him, "Where is our house?" and he pointed in a certain direction. I looked and there was a small, isolated shack. He said, "Kozaemon Takenaka, who owns this apple orchard jointly with me, is now living in the shack. He will stay till the end of this year, and after that we will live there." Realizing that this was one of the things which my husband had said would break my heart, I just gave up and swallowed my disappointment.

As expected, I had trouble with English. Since they said that if I worked in some American household, I could learn English faster, I also began doing that. The place was the residence of Parke Davison, the owner of a large acreage of apple orchards, and it was a mansion where they had put the whole skin of a lion, with the head attached, on the floor for a rug. Japanese men were working around there too. Since the lady of the house was very nice to me, I worked happily enough.

But then one morning, after taking the ashes out of the stove, I was walking along behind the nine-year-old son of the house, and since I was lagging behind him, he beckoned me with his forefinger. I felt somewhat like I was a maid, and when I went home I asked my husband. He said, "Yes, sort of . . . you are . . . sort of a maid." So I said, "I didn't come all the way to America to be somebody's maid!" and I quit. Thus I completely lost my chance to learn English.

The days were a continuing series of hardships. Getting all tired out, how many nights did I cry, longing for home in Japan, looking up at the moon and stars! Also, I wanted to tell my sadness to my mother, so I wrote letters. But, thinking twice, even if I worried my mother it wouldn't help the situation at all, so ten times or more I threw the letters into the stove.

Kenneth Reber
1950-1970

Kenneth Reber served on a personnel carrier in Vietnam in 1969. Before being drafted, "Kenny," as his Douglas County family and friends called him, enjoyed hunting, camping, riding motorcycles and playing the mandolin. "He didn't want to go at first. But after he thought about it a while, he wouldn't turn his back on it," his older brother Don remembers.

PFC Kenneth Reber was sent to an area in Vietnam where heavy combat was a fact of life—or death. In Chu Lai, personnel carriers were hulking targets rolling across heavily mined terrain. On July 7, 1970, Reber died under "friendly fire" when an American bullet hit him in the chest. He had been scheduled to come home in a few months. The following are letters Kenny wrote during his stint in Vietnam, originally published in the *News-Review*, Roseburg, March 13, 1988. "Duke" in the November 9 letter refers to Reber's dog, "Robyn" to his girlfriend.—S.A.

It's Great Here Except I'm Lonely, Homesick, and Going Crazy
LETTERS FROM AN ARMY PRIVATE IN VIETNAM

Chu Lai, South Vietnam
November 9, 1969

Dear Folks,

So far, we've been out for seven days. Tonight when I got back, I found that everything I have was stolen.

The first day out, I earned a CIB. It's a medal you get for action in a fire fight.

We got hit by a V.C. There was three of 'em in a village that was in a wooded area. They had AK-47 automatic rifles and ChiKon machine guns. They managed to seriously wound five of our men but finally we killed two of 'em and took the other one as prisoner of war.

We also got their weapons as war souvenirs and burned down their village, also we burned down seven other enemy villages that day. The next morning, we had six enemy V.C. walk into our camp, they wanted to come over to our side like I told ya. There was some in Chu Lai. They call them Ghu Hoys.

They are valuable to the Army cause they know enemy positions and methods. Also they are good at finding their own type mines and booby traps.

The following three nights we got hit with rockets and mortars, however, no one was hurt. The rest of the time, we just lay around, sleep, rest, eat, write, tell stories, jokes, etc.

We sleep in the tracks. We eat hot food cause we heat it with C-4, an explosive demolition charge. However, it makes a good, safe fuel. It won't blow up without a blasting cap. Our tracks have built-in stoves to cook on, we have lots of fresh water and supplies.

We got the biggest gun on our track, in F Troop. It's called a (105) the barrel is approximately 9 feet long and 8-inches diameter. Each shell or bullet is 5-feet long and 7-inches in diameter. We also have a 50-caliber machine gun, a M-60 machine gun (mine), a grenade launcher, six M-16 machine guns and about 78 frag-grenades, 20 CS gas grenades and lots of Ammo.

O yea, each night I set out two Claymore mines in front of our track then we take turns guarding our position from on top the track. We have a starlite

scope, you can see enemy at night with it and we use a radio to call in enemy sightings while on guard.

For your information, Hawk Hill is about 40 miles north of Chu Lai. It's pretty close to the DMZ. The heaviest enemy contact in NAM is in this area. Up here, it's not just Viet Cong and Viet Cong sympathizers, it's hard core NVA well-trained Sappers. All Sappers have at least 10-20 years of hard-core training behind them. They are experts on sneaking into perimeters and sniper techniques, etc. But ya just don't run into them that often, so (NO SWEAT).

Well I've been in Nam a month now and I haven't been hurt yet! I've never polished my boots yet and I won't have to either. No belts or brass buckles, no standards for uniform. You don't have to call an officer (Sir) or a sergeant (sergeant). They're just like one of the guys. When I first met my platoon sergeant he shook my hand (very unmilitary like) like a civilian does. It's just great here, except lonely, homesick and miss people, you, Dad, family, Duke, Robyn, car, etc.

March 1, 1970

Wow! I'm about to go crazy, I've never felt so useless, lost, empty, tired, etc. in my whole life. I was doing OK till about two, three weeks ago and all of a sudden I just feel like I'm losing my head. I've gotta find a way out of the field. I've had it.

March 7, 1970

Did you know that there are FOUR different ways to make every chord on a guitar? Yeah, I only thought there were three different ways. But now I discovered that I can play anything. I really know the keyboard!

Well, it sure is getting hot and dusty here, rather miserable too.

Wow! I'm so filthy I can't believe it. I guess I'll have to get used to it, cause it's gonna be so dusty this summer, along with being sweaty.

Oh yeah, could ya send me a couple bags of black licorice, the kind that is in pieces, sometimes different shapes. But I want the kind that's soft, chewy and shiny, smooth black.

I remember how I used to be so tickled when I got to go fishing and hunting with Dad and Don, even though I didn't show it.

Actually I never did show my feelings much. But I'll tell ya right now that I know I've got the best Mom and Dad in the whole world! Of all the people I know over here, I'm the only one who gets a letter or two every day from my parents!

Also I never really realized it before, but I now know you and Dad did everything possible to get me everything I ever wanted, and usually ya succeeded too!

I just want ya to know that I do appreciate it more than you'll ever know. I guess it just took me being away that brought me to realize how great of parents I really have.

Well, I'll close till next time. I'll write when I can so take care and I'll be home soon. I'm almost halfway there now!

Love
Kenny

Miriam Murphy
1904-1983

"In the Fall of '77," wrote Sister Miriam Murphy in her journal, "my creativity was at a low and I felt the need of help." Those who knew and had been influenced by art historian, painter, and teacher Sr. Miriam were delighted by her renewed vigor as she began working on an Intensive Journal at a Marylhurst College workshop. She believed that "the non judgmental, non analytical, free flowing" writing in her journal counteracted other more constrictive impulses and reinforced her memory of early years, especially in relationship to her family. She wrote about the discipline of journal keeping and noted, "It is a self-discovery tool and has softened the ground of my being so that I am painting again and even though I am still struggling with self judgment, the work is moving along."

Her long tenure at Marylhurst College was marked by her explorations as a teacher, counselor, and artist, by numerous exhibitions of her work, and the founding of Closeline Studios. Her paintings are treasured by many friends and collectors. Permission to use portions of Sr. Miriam's journal is given by the owner, who wishes to remain anonymous.—S.A.

A Marylhurst Nun's Diary, or Exploring the Sacred Mainland Within

Fall 1977: "The Roots"

My father's reaction to my becoming a nun was such that it took two years before he could speak to me. He bro't the family to the convent and spent his time speaking French to the French nuns who came [from eastern Canada where he derived]

His ignoring of his daughter was an indication of his pain and lack of understanding. I think now, I did very little to explain my step to him and prepare him for the separation. He was noble not to have opposed me openly. Finally he accepted this choice I had made when he saw I was serious about it.

However, when the time came for my final decision, he put me to the test. He came alone, knowing it to be a time of freedom to change, he offered to set me up wherever I wanted to be if I wanted to leave the convent and start another way of life. When I expressed my determination to go on this way since at that time there was religious persecution in many countries—he asked me if I'd be willing to stand up to risk my life for my belief. He cautioned, nuns priests are the first to be liquidated. Does your vocation mean that much? That sobering question had already crossed my mind and my decision had already been made in that context. My father seemed satisfied with my seriousness & accepted my determination to persevere in my initial decision.

This account has revealed to me the influence of my father in my life—He is the tree & the root.

This experience is the latest in a long history of inner healing relative to my own self worth and relative to my father. The amazing revelation is that in this writing I have accepted him as my root. In finding him I have found my real self; I have resisted being his daughter.

This resistance has forced me not to accept myself not to feel real nor authentic I inwardly did not accept his love I do now whole-heartedly & I am me.

February 22, 1980

Daffodils—I'm walking thru 3 ft daffodils their upturned skirts rustle as I wade thru their petticoats—The sky is blue solid Dutch blue. My feet find difficulty in footing lest I crush the thick growth, I part the flowers to find footing —Oh my feet are so big so clumsy. I feel like an elephant I bend over trying to be gentle—I can't help crushing some plants. The liquid of their fragile leaves is spurting its life under my footfall.

October 10

NOW, time of renewed energy and well being. physically, BUT spiritually—I feel a bit DULL searching time for meaning—what will I do with this energy—can I count on it? Will it last? What is the prospect of continuance at age 77? Where will I go from here—I am at a stand still WHY because I doubt if I have a future. What am I doing relative to the future—getting my house in order DISPOSING, simplifing my life. Am I getting ready to die or to live. What role does contemplation play?

Am holding my breath—as if I have an urgency to complete these preparations for a finality.

February 21, 1981

The aging process is such that it puts a great demand on my endurance to keep it up is a full time job for me. I feel so much better getting the morale of the place "up." I see how the dinginess of things is a real problem to my well being. I have to have a certain order to feel free as a person. Material environment needs to be cleaned. I have to be clean—have clean drawers—mended clothes etc. This afternoon—I should fix my skirt—that would free me a lot to feel I could be ready to go places and do things because they are ready.

July 3

I feel like a tortoise. I have a hard shell to protect myself. I pull my neck in and hide thinking no one can see me when I can't see out. When I move this slowly—and uncertainly because I am never sure of my situation—I must guess at what is going on due to hearing loss. I often guess wrong so I proceed constantly in fear and insecurity or I don't proceed at all & just sit still. I lack direction—I lack enthusiasm—I'm filled with heaviness loggy & burdened by existence. Is this depression? I fear it may be. If so how do I deal with it? How [this is] the question.

Depression is clay so that it cakes & bakes in the sun. One must moisten & work the soil over but if no humus is added it will harden again.

William L. Sullivan
1953-

Backpacking 1,361 miles in 1985, writer William L. Sullivan realized a long-held dream—to walk across Oregon. In a 64-day solo trek from Oregon's westernmost point at Cape Blanco to the easternmost point in Hells Canyon, Sullivan recorded his adventures in tiny script in four spiral-bound notebooks. His journal, later published as *Listening for Coyote* (1988), was an Oregon Book Award finalist in 1989.

His adventurous spirit also led Sullivan to bicycle 3,000 miles through Europe and to build a log cabin by hand on the Oregon coast. He is the author of several books including *Oregon's Wild Areas* and is currently completing a novel about another adventuresome Oregonian—poet Joaquin Miller.—S.A.

Not Likely to Cut Corners

ONE DAY IN A SOLO WALK ACROSS OREGON

August 22,1985. 7:07 P.M.
Kalmiopsis Wilderness. 78°F. Day's mileage: 19.9. Total: 119.4

Len Ramp is a lean bantam of a man with dark eyes and a trim black mustache. His weathered face is older than I had expected. A dozen pockets in his red canvas vest bulge mysteriously. A geologist's pick, the tool of his trade, hangs from a loop on his belt.

He smiles, but waits for me to speak.

"Len Ramp? I'm Bill."

He shakes my hand with a firm grip, and gives a signal to the driver of the pickup. The pickup growls back up the dusty road. Finally Len speaks. "He'll meet us ten miles up the road, at the edge of the Kalmiopsis. You didn't want to toss your pack in the truck, did you?"

I look at the dust cloud left by the truck. How could I have failed to think of it myself? The pack's straps have worn searing red grooves into my shoulders. But now I just shake my head.

"I didn't think you would. Anybody backpacking all the way across Oregon's not likely to cut corners. Well?" Len flashes another smile. "Ready?"

He leads the way up the road at an amazingly brisk pace. I don't want to criticize—after all, he's taken a day off from his office work in Grants Pass to hike and talk with me—so I jolt my pack along, trying to keep up.

While I try to pretend this semijogging is my normal gait, Len does most of the talking. He says he usually runs five miles before breakfast, but he didn't today, knowing he'd get in some hiking with me. He is fifty-nine, and each summer he competes in marathons. In the winters he climbs the peaks of the Cascade Range wearing crampons, and skis down. "Had a close call climbing a glacier on Shasta not long back," he says. "Fell through the snow into a deep crevasse."

"Len Ramp!" a harsh voice shouts.

I turn and see an overweight man hustling up from a barbed-wire gate. He wears a very clean and very taut white T-shirt over his great, jolting stomach.

"Well howdy, Sam," Len says, smiling.

The man puffs a moment, then says, "I just been out checkin' cabins for the Bar Sixty-six—you got any more of them eight-dollar maps?"

"You mean the geologic quadrangles?" Len asks. "Sure, I've got a few." He unzips a hidden pocket inside the back of his red vest and pulls out a large manila envelope.

The overweight man opens the multicolored map on top of his stomach. "Goddam! Looks like a baby spit up on it, all the colors. Fella's got to have it, though. It tells where there's gold." He shakes his head. "What are you up to today?"

Len waves his hand toward me. "I'm hiking with Bill. He's just come down the trail from Bald Mountain."

I smile and nod.

"Goddam!" the man says. "Had a coupla Mexicans wanted to go up that trail not long back, let 'em borrow Willy for the trip. Now, Willy, he's OK, you understand, but he's a donkey—that's all there is to it, he's a donkey. So the fellas load up Willy with all their stuff and start out fine, 'cause they brought along some apples as donkey incentive, you know? Well, when they run out of apples they have a disagreement. Willy takes a bite out of one of 'em and hightails it home, scattering their gear all down the trail."

The man wheezes—is it a laugh?—and asks, "Where you headed next, kid?"

"The Kalmiopsis."

"Up *there*? Goddam!" He jerks his head back to stare at me. His crewcut seems to bristle. "Had a coupla young prospectors head up there last year. They had it all figgered out how they was going to get rich. Took along back-packs like you're doing, too. They wandered around lost for ten days before I went in and dragged 'em back out. They'd been down to eatin' toothpaste."

The man gives me a meaningful look. Then he nods to the geologist beside me. "Well, see ya, Len." And he leaves.

As I continue down the road with Len, I comment, "You seem to be well known around here."

Len shrugs. "Almost everybody in these parts is a prospector, at least part time. And I'm the only state geologist south of Salem. So everybody talks to me sooner or later. They all want to know where to find gold."

Len pulls a quart bottle from a pocket inside his red vest, and takes a drink. Then he takes a bandanna from another pocket and mops his brow. I am beginning to marvel at this vest of his, which easily conceals a supply of large maps and bottles. Then he spots a screwdriver and two empty beer cans in the ditch and stashes them somewhere in the vest, too.

"How many pockets do you have in that vest?" I ask.

"My vest?" He looks down at it, as though he were just discovering it. "Well, I don't know. This pocket's got rock specimen bags. Here's a first-aid kit. This little zippered thing's got an altimeter and a barometer. This pouch has my transit compass and mirror. Here I've got my hand lenses. My lunch is in this back compartment. And there's—let's see—seven pens and pencils in these loops, including a magnetic one to check ferrous samples."

My marvel has turned to awe. The vest's an entire geologic field station. It must contain twenty pounds of gear.

"Oh, and there's this hidden pocket," Len adds, "with my Sasquatch weapon."

"Your *what*?" I had not known defense was necessary—or possible—against the mythic apeman of the Klamath wilderness.

"Well, it's a sling, actually." He pulls out a long thong attached to a small patch of leather. Then he loads a peach-pit-sized piece of gravel in the leather patch, whirls it fiercely over his head, and lets go of one end of the thong. The rock crashes into the forest one hundred yards across the river.

"It'd stop Bigfoot, if I met him. I've put rocks through a three-quarter-inch board. I worry a whole lot more about meeting marijuana growers, though."

Eastside

Thomas Farnham
1804-1848

Thomas Farnham, a New England-born attorney, attended an 1839 lecture given by famous Oregon missionary Jason Lee in Peoria, Illinois. Lee was attempting to raise funds for the Willamette Valley Methodist Mission. Fired by the Reverend Lee's boosterism, Farnham helped establish an emigration society that formed the "Peoria Party," one of the earliest overland migrations to Oregon. Farnham served as captain of this party of nineteen men who attempted the tough trail to Oregon in 1839. With the aid of a Shoshone guide, Farnham and his party reached the Grande Ronde Valley in September. While crossing the Blue Mountains, Farnham encountered a Cayuse family—described in the following entry. Of the original nineteen men in the "Peoria Party," only Farnham and four others—one of them wounded—survived the journey to the Willamette Valley.

After visiting the Sandwich Islands and California, Farnham returned to Illinois, where he lived for a few years. During the California gold rush era, he returned to the Pacific Slope and died in San Francisco in 1848, his fortune still unmade. His diary, *Travels in the Great Western Prairie* (1843), the source of the following selection, was an important contribution to the literature of western expansion, but to a large extent his writing was based on earlier diary commentaries. As his writing shows, Farnham was a somewhat self-assured optimist, an enthusiast who believed that all Native Americans desired Christian instruction.—S.A.

Observing Instead of Disturbing

A PEACEFUL MEETING IN THE BLUE MOUNTAINS

September 22, 1839

We saddled early, and ascending for two hours a line of gentle grassy elevations, came to the beginning of the north-western declivities of the Blue Mountains. The trail ran down the ravines of small brooks flowing northwest, and occasionally over high swells which stretched down the plain that lies about the south-western branches of the Wallawalla River: we halted to dine. In the afternoon we struck off north-westerly over the rolling plain. The soil in the depressions was a light and loose compound of sand and clay, and thinly covered with bunch grass. The swells were of gravel, and generally barren; trees on the brooks only, and these few, small and of little value.

About three o'clock we came into the camp of a middle-aged Skyuse Indian, who was on his onward march from the buffalo hunt in the mountain valleys east and north-east of Fort Hall. He was a spare man of five feet eight inches, dressed in a green camlet frock-coat, a black vest, striped cotton shirt, leather pants, moccasins, and a white felt hat. There were two children, boys, neatly clad in deerskin. His camp equipage was very comfortable—four or five camp-kettles with tin covers, a number of pails with covers, a leathern tent, and an assortment of fine buffalo robes. He had had a very successful hunt. Of the seventeen horses in his caravan, six were loaded with the best flesh of the buffalo cow, cured in the best manner; two others bore his tent, utensils, clothing, robes, &c.; four others were ridden by himself and family; the five remaining were used to relieve those that, from time to time, might tire. These were splendid animals, as large as the best horses of the States, well knit, deep and wide at the shoulders; a broad loin, and very small lower limbs and feet; of extreme activity and capacity for endurance.

Learning that this Indian was proceeding to Dr. Whitman's mission establishment, where a considerable number of his tribe had pitched their tents for the approaching winter, I determined to leave the cavalcade and accompany him there. My guide Carbo, therefore having explained my intentions to my new acquaintance, departed with the remainder of his charge for Fort Wallawalla. Crickie (in English "poor crane,") was a very kind man.

The weather was so pleasant that no tent was pitched. The willows were beat, and buffalo robes spread over them. Underneath were laid other robes, on which my Indian host seated himself with his wife and children on one side, and myself on the other. A fire burned brightly in front. Water was brought, and the evening ablutions having been performed, the wife presented a dish of meat to her husband, and one to myself. There was a pause. The woman seated herself between her children. The Indian then bowed his head and prayed to God! a wandering savage in Oregon calling upon Jehovah in the name of Jesus Christ! After the prayer, he gave meat to his children, and passed the dish to his wife.

While eating, the frequent repetition of the words, Jehovah and Jesus Christ, in the most reverential manner, led me to suppose they were conversing on religious topics; and thus they passed an hour. Meanwhile, the exceeding weariness of a long day's travel admonished me to seek rest.

I had slumbered, I know not how long, when a strain of music awoke me. I was about rising to ascertain whether the sweet notes of Tallis's Chant came to these solitudes from earth or sky, when a full recollection of my situation, and of the religious habits of my host, easily solved the rising inquiry, and induced me to observe instead of disturbing. The Indian family was engaged in its evening devotions. They were singing a hymn in the Nez Perces language. Having finished it they all knelt and bowed their faces upon the buffalo robes, and Crickie prayed long and fervently. Afterwards they sang another hymn and retired.

This was the first breathing of religious feelings that I had seen since leaving the States. A pleasant evidence that the Oregon wilderness was beginning to bear the rose of Sharon on its thousand hills, and that on the barren soil of the Skyuse heart was beginning to bud and blossom and ripen the golden fruits of faith in Jehovah, and hope in an afterstate.

William Chinook
1827-1890

Robert Hull
1805-?

Joel Palmer
1810-1881

Joel Palmer

With the Donation Land Law of 1850, Congress offered free land to the immigrants before the Federal Government had purchased it from the Native Oregonians. The following letters illustrate the conflicts this created.

Written in 1853 to Joel Palmer, Superintendent of Indian Affairs in Oregon, the first letter is from William Chinook, a Native Oregonian living at The Dalles. His land was being usurped by whites. Chinook had been a guide for John Charles Fremont, who later arranged for him to attend school in Washington, D.C.

The second letter is from Robert Hull, a settler whose land claim at Mollala was disputed by Native Oregonians.

Palmer replies to Hull in the third letter urging patience in his dealings with the Native Oregonians. The Indians, he wrote, "have the greatest cause of complaint," while "on the part of the whites, a little forbearance should be exercised." These letters are taken from *An Arrow in the Earth* (1991) by Terence O'Donnell.

In 1859, Chinook moved to the Warm Springs Reservation where he served as an interpreter and a scout. His tombstone reads: "A faithful and true friend of the white man." Lake Billy Chinook, a Deschutes River reservoir, was named for him. Joel Palmer was discharged from his office of Superintendent of Indian Affairs in 1856 for opposing a clique of the Democratic Party and for his generally sympathetic attitude toward Native Oregonians.—T. O'D.

Selling What You Don't Own
AN EARLY FEDERAL FIASCO WITH NO FAST FIX

The Dalles, Oregon Territory
November 3, 1853

Dear General Palmer:

We are tormented almost every day by the white people who desire to settle on our land and although we have built houses and opened gardens they wish in spite of us to take possession of the very spots we occupy. We remonstrate and tell them that this is our land, they reply that Government gives them to settle in any part of Oregon Territory and they desire to take land in this very spot.

Now we wish to know whether this is the land of the white man or the Indians. If it is our land the whites must not trouble us. If it is the land of the white man when did he buy it?

Now if we as Indians have no power to defend our right against the whites; will you inform us how we are to do. . . soon all the good land will be taken. Where will we go, where will we make our homes. If we lose our country what shall we do. I know that the whites are strong, that they have ammunition and guns and power; we cannot resist them, but we ask them to leave us our homes for we are poor and have no power. Be so kind as to answer us and tell us what you think.

William Chinook

Molala
November 14, 1853

Dear General Palmer:

I emigrated to Oregon in the fall of 1848 under the Territorial Government which gave to each settler one section of land. I made me a claim on the Molala some time before the land bill was passed in Congress. When I heard of the land bill I was perfectly satisfied with the same; it stipulates that the Indians should be removed beyond the Cascade Mountains. I was on my claim some-time before I knew that I was on the Indians' camping ground, but the land bill requiring them to be removed I remained satisfied thinking that Govern-ment would soon take them away. I have continued to suffer from them ever since, every fall they have stolen some of my cabbage and potatoes. They would tell me I have stollen their lands. A number of times they have thrown down my fence. Year after year has passed and they are still among us. When we got a change of government, I thought then surely they will be taken away but they are still among us. I am not the only individual that has suffered from them. A few days ago an Indian that is well known among the settlers by the name of old man Yelkir came to my house. I had just been geting supper. He had the ribs of a side of venison. He said he wanted to swap for some flour. I did not like the look of his meat. I told him I did not want to buy it; he said I must either buy it or give him some flour. I told him I would do neither. He came towards me; he took my hat from my head and struck me. I got my gun as quick as possible, thinking to shoot him down; but I did not know whether I would be justified or not. I want to know of you whether I should be justified or not. I want to know of you whether I shall take the law into my own hands, and shoot them down or not, or shall I wait a little longer expecting to have them moved? I want you to write and let me know.

Robert Hull

Office of the Superintendent of Indian Affairs
Dayton, Oregon Territory
December 20, 1853

Robert Hull, Esq.
Upper Molalla

Sir,
Your letter of the 14th informing me of the difficulty with an Indian and asking my advice has been received. I am far from advising you to take the law into your own hands "and shooting them down," as you suggest. To the contrary, I would advise giving them no cause to commit acts of retaliation but to treat them kindly.

It must be admitted that the Indians have the greatest cause of complaint and when the aggression is on the part of the whites a little forbearance should be exercised until means be devised to remove them. It is true that by an act of congress all citizens of the United States are permitted to claim and occupy a tract of land upon conditions therein named but I don't conceive that by that act whites have any right to displace Indians who are already in possession of a particular tract of land.

The act of Congress approved August 14, 1848, organizing the Territory of Oregon provided "that nothing in this act contains what shall be construed to impair the rights of persons or property now pertaining to the indians in said Territory, so long as such rights shall remain unextinguished by treaty between the United States and such Indians." No rights pertaining to indians in this Territory has as yet been extinguished by treaty; it must therefor be conceded that they have rights in that land upon which their villages, camping grounds and fisheries are situated. . . .

At present there are no persons in this Territory who have been designated by the President as provided by law to enter into negotiations with these Indian tribes, only insofar as may be deemed necessary to maintain peace. How long this state of affairs may be allowed to exist, I am unable to say but if power be conferred and means provided, it will be remedied at the earliest possible moment. . . .In the meantime I hope all citizens will use forbearance in their conduct towards this unfortunate class of beings, use them kindly and instead of abuse to arouse their savage passion, try and inculcate a desire for peace and encourage good acts, and if danger be apprehended, the civil law is ample to protect the rights of our citizens and punish wrong doers. . . .

I am, Sir, your obedient servant,
Joel Palmer,
Superintendent

George Irving Hazeltine
1836-1918

"If I had my apparatus for pictures, and my dear little wife here, I could make an easy thing of money-making." So wrote frustrated gold seeker Irving Hazeltine in an 1862 love letter to Emmeline, his new bride. Along with brother Martin, Irving eventually became one of the West's best-known photographers. But in the early 1860s, in the rough-and-tumble mining town of Canyon City, Oregon, Irving Hazeltine taught dancing and did other kinds of work to raise enough cash to send for his bride. Occasionally, he frequented the saloons where "hurdy-gurdy dancing and gambling and Corn Whiskey" with "no bet too big to call" helped Irving and other men feel less lonely.

When Emmeline died at age ninety-three in Canyon City, her husband's love letters were discovered neatly tied up in a small flour sack. Hazeltine's descriptive power lingers in words as well as in the photographic images so prized by collectors. The following selection is taken from *Whiskey Gulch: Letters of G.I. Hazeltine and Wife Emmeline, Cañon Creek, Oregon 1862-1863 and Later History* (1981).— S. A.

A New Husband—Alone in John Day—Learns How Not to Make His Bread

Cañon City, Oregon
Monday Eve. April 6, 1863

Little One,

The express does not leave until tomorrow at twelve, so having nothing to do in particular, I tho't best to sit down and have a chat with "mine leetel frow."

Oh! I have forgotten, I said I had nothing to do. I'll take that back. I ought to be making bread, but then bread-making is not so much of a job for me now as I have been taking lessons in that line. I can make a kind of "chemunch" in the shape of bread that I'll bet you never heard of, that is, you might have heard of it but I mean never saw it.

I'll tell you how I came to learn the new "kink". You remember writing me a bit of a lecture with a letter in it, I mean a bit of a letter with a short lecture in it, about staying home all the time and so forth and how you never got jealous and so forth. Well, I did not know what to do about it, but finally came to the conclusion that I was not a very good cook and that I would get the widow to board with me. Oh dear what a mistake, I mean that I would try and get to board with the young widow. She keeps boarders, you know. So I shut up Bachelors hall and went to tea. Arrived at the house, rapped at the door, widow came to open, widow very glad to see me, smiled splendidly, widow is very pretty when she smiles, four teeth out in front. Could I get to board with her for a week or so? Certainly, certainly, walk in tea is just ready. In a few minutes I found myself sitting "forninst" the charming relic of A. Augustus Cooper, Esq. I was soon rapt in conversation, moments flew like hours. Widow terribly interesting, never thought of you more than once or twice a minute, and then not more than a minute at a time. Conversation turned on breadmaking. Widow was sorry that I had such poor luck in the pastry line, if I would be pleased to call in the morning she would be pleased to instruct me in the bread line. Of course I would, a few more words and I took my departure. As soon as I was outside the door I looked at my watch I had been engaged with the charming relic just fifteen minutes I was surprised the time flew so quickly, I thought it as many hours. However, I thought I had done my duty to you. You said you'd much rather hear of me spending an evening in some pleasant family than to be at home all alone, so I am happy, as I know you would be, when you heard of it.

Well, in due time I went to bed. Morning came and I was on my road to the boarding house, early, as I had several men working for me, I was obliged to go early, to get my lesson as well as my breakfast.

As I passed by the window of the boarding house kitchen, of course, you know men do not have as much curiosity as women, but at the same time something whispered to me to look in the window. And as I looked in. Lo! this is what I saw, looking glass with widow's face in it, widow's back to me. Corset and petticoat, two bare arms and a comb, table between the petticoat and glass, piece of brown resin soap, wash basin, dirty towel, shoe brush, piece of charcoal, basket of chips, bread pan with flour in it, right under the charming widow's head, sitting on the table, all on the table except the widow. Ah! I thought I am too early, lady is just making her toilet, so I walked away to await my time. Not long after, not more than two hours, I heard the breakfast bell ring and off I started to breakfast. Found all the boarders assembled, and partaking of the frugal repast. Widow was very polite, very sociable, very agreeable, would I have some bread? No thank you, I am not hungry this morning. I'll take a cup of coffee and a small slice of steak. While the charming hostess was out in the kitchen this conversation passed between the boarders. I say, Bill, what is this you are holding up—a piece of bread, Bill. Why that's bread, ain't it, Sam? I'm damned if I know, it had a little too much hair in it to be bread and not quite enough for plaster. At this period widow came in so conversation turned on some other topic.

That day I was obliged to go away, of course could not board any more with the charming relic of A.A. and C. But I have learned to make bread and I can do very well for a new beginner. My bread is not like the widow's exactly and you could not expect it to be not having all the ingredients to put in it.

Dear, Dear Emma, how I would like to see you tonight. I wonder what you are doing, sitting by the fire place with the family or playing Blind Man's bluff or perhaps singing with the girls and Mr. Whittier. Oh Dear! I wish I was there. This is a miserable place without you. Dear Emma, wouldn't you rather I would stay at home than to be spending my evenings in "some pleasant family"? I'd rather stay at home, I mean in my cabin, I cannot call it home. Well, I must "shut down" as your Pa says for it is late for a working man to be up so Goodnight and please write often. The only pleasure I find in this wooden country is in your letters. Love to all kisses to you and Nora. Do you want me to see the widow any more?

Irv

Julia Gilliss
1843-1926

With the possibility of more resistance by Native Americans to settlers' land and property theft, and the possibility of more violence by both Native Americans and white settlers, federal troops continued to be stationed in the 1860s at various outposts in Oregon.

Julia Gilliss of Washington, D.C., was the wife of a young officer sent from Washington to The Dalles during this period. Her husband also served at Fort Stevens on the coast and at Camp Warner in southeast Oregon. The following excerpts from Julia's numerous letters to her family in the East are taken from *So Far from Home: An Army Bride on the Western Frontier* (1993). Her letters are among the earliest to document and protest the unconscionable slaughter of Native Oregonians in the region. (See "Ghosts" in *Varieties of Hope* of the Oregon Literature Series for an essay.) "Jim" was her husband.—T. O'D.

To Think We Are So Far Away

AN ARMY BRIDE IN EASTERN OREGON

Fort Dalles, Oregon
January 10, 1866

My dear Parents,

Here we are at the Dalles!!! The Finis and Ultimatum of all our hopes. We arrived about eight o'clock last evening and found a carriage sent from the garrison for us, merely on the supposition that we might come. The largest house burnt down two weeks ago; and there are now only two left. The one which was consumed cost ninety thousand dollars, and was the handsomest house on this coast. The two remaining are very pretty Gothic villas, but all of wood, and as they have the same kind of chimneys which caused the destruction of the other, they may possibly fall victims to the same fell destroyer. The rooms are beautiful and I expect to have a lovely little home.

Captain C of the 14th Infantry is in command of the post, and to his courtesy we are indebted for a sheltering roof. He has most kindly taken us in and really given us nearly all his quarters, reserving only two rooms for himself. I never saw such kindness to strangers! When we drove into the post it was quite dark, but we were met by the Surgeon and his wife, swinging a lighted lantern between them, and waiting to take us to their house to supper. When we arrived, we found their parlor occupied by two hospital cots, daintily made and ready for our use.

Our sleep was sweet and this morning we have moved (one valise) into what will be our future home. The rooms are pretty, but you would laugh to see our furnishing. The kitchen is sumptuously supplied already, with a stove, some pans, a wooden chair and table. The parlor has a bowed window on the front, consisting of six narrow sashes with tiny diamond shaped panes set in lead. Hung on the walls at each side are swabs, rammers, sabres and other things whose names I have not yet learned, while on the floor with its nose (J. says I must say muzzle) pointing out the window is the dearest brass gun mounted on a wooden carriage. Captain C. says it is a mountain howitzer. A large bookcase built into the wall, a very large mantlepiece and a few chairs complete this room. Our bedroom has a buffalo robe on the floor; a bedstead made by a carpenter here at the post and painted sky blue; a bed sack filled with sweet hay. That is all at present.

In point of scenic beauty, I must say a word. You can imagine yourself transported to the crater of an extinct volcano, or as a Californian graphically observes, "to the Infernal regions, after the fire has gone out." For miles nothing is visible but huge masses of rocks and stones, of every size, but of volcanic description, sown broadcast. Trees all seem to have forsaken the land, for with exception of the firs and cedars at the garrison, I don't believe there is as much as a blade of grass for miles. It will look better however when the snow melts. I would like you, Papa, if it is no trouble, please send me some seeds, flowers and vegetables, from the Patent Office, and send them by mail.

Jim sends his warmest love to all his adopted family. I could cry over every letter I send to think we are so far away. I try to be patient and think that all things are ordered for our good, but it seems very hard. I know I can't have everything my own way, and I am very thankful for my darling husband.

Your loving daughter
Julie S.G.

Camp Warner, Oregon
November 9, 1867

My Dear Parents,

We are living in slab huts. Ours has a glass window, the only one here, but I have only a dirt floor while some of the others have planking. We put our planks in a tent, which we opened from the log room so we have two rooms. We brought with us a wooden bed and a crib, and as our dirt floor is a slope we have put blocks on the legs which stand down hill. Our walls are unhewn logs with the cracks between filled with mud, the roof is a sort of thatch of young saplings with sod covering. In the tent we have a pine table made of a packing box; a long box stood on end with two shelves in it forms our sideboard; three wooden chairs; a grey blanket on the floor for a rug; a good stove, and you have before you our combined parlor and dining room.

We have given up learning billiards because the table has been moved to the Sutler Store. We have a particularly nice store, but a very limited supply of goods. My green riding dress has worn to perfect rags. I have just made one of stone colored flannel (which was the only material I could get) and trimmed it with black braid & jet buttons and it really looks quite stylish. I am trying to wait patiently for an answer to Jim's application, but I feel forlorn as each mail comes in without it.

The Indians are giving great trouble killing settlers, stealing stock, etc. They do not venture near our post in daylight, but at night they often shoot arrows into our corral and have already killed sixteen mules. Whenever the troops go after them they all hide in the stronghold of Steins Mountain. Genl. Crook with three or four companies from here & Harney have been out for several weeks on a scout he returned rather unsuccessful. They killed thirteen Indians, nearly all they could find. He is going out again. This persecution of the Indians goes against the grain with me. I think it is a wretched unholy warfare; the poor creatures are hunted down like wild beasts and shot down in cold blood. The same ball went through a mother and her baby at her breast. One poor little creature just the size of my baby was shot because he would some day grow up. Ugh! it makes me sick. And all for the few grains of gold that tempt the cupidity and avarice of grasping men. The land is wretched. The fact is acknowledged that this country will never be good for anything but its mineral resources, and therefore this race of human beings which God has created and given their place on earth must be crushed to the bitter end. I do not believe such an enterprize will ever be blessed and I think the Indian depredations are a just retribution on their persecutors. Well, I will change the subject, for this is one on which I feel strongly and I may say too much.

Julie S. Gilliss

Orson Avery Stearns
1843-1926

Orson Avery Stearns was ten years old in 1853 when he accompanied his parents and twenty-six other family members to Oregon via the Applegate Trail. Most of the Stearns family settled in Talent, a community near Ashland, but after a stint in the army at Fort Klamath during the Civil War, twenty-seven-year-old O. A. Stearns decided to file on a 120-acre homestead on the Klamath River. One of the region's earliest white settlers and dairymen, Stearns married Margaret Riggs in 1873, and became active in local and state politics.

While living alone in his "castle of hewn logs" in 1870, however, it was a lonely Stearns who wrote a lengthy letter describing his living conditions to a friend in the Middle West. In the manner of most southern Oregon settlers, Stearns was much taken with the lushness surrounding him, especially the abundance of wild grasses which provided pasturage for livestock. Because of numerous water impoundments and other factors, the landscape O.A. Stearns rhapsodized about has been forever altered. Fewer than one percent of Oregon's native grasses remain in the 1990s. The complete seven-page letter may be found in *Klamath Echoes* (1977).—S.A.

A Lonely Bachelor in His Log Castle in Paradise

Briar Springs, Oregon
January 1, 1870

Kind Friend

In looking over my old letters today I came across yours of last April which I had laid away marked "Answered." Now as I had thought all the time that it was never answered there is good reason to believe that it was so marked through mistake. I will try to answer some of the questions asked in your letter, but which you have doubtless forgotten ere this.

Since I wrote you last, great changes have taken place in my father's family.

Last February I lost one of the best of mothers. She died of smallpox, and was followed in eight days by my youngest brother, George.

My younger brother, Newel, is on my father's place, and there is talk of his being married soon. As for myself, I am about sixty five miles East of my father's on the margin of the great Klamath basin country and across the Cascade range of mountains, East of Rogue River. I have been here nearly two years and a half; ever since I was mustered out of the U.S. Service. My place was the second one taken up in this country and when I came here the indians were still occupying the country though it had already been ceded to the U.S. by treaty stipulation. The indians were subsequently removed to the reservation about thirty five miles from here on Sprague River, Upper Klamath Lake and Klamath Marsh. During the past year there have also been collected there several hundred Snakes (indians) and during the past week the tribe of Modocks numbering nearly three hundred were removed, here from Little Klamath and Modock lakes, South, and South East of here.

Some of the time I have been a lone, some of the time had hired help for company. My castle I built of hewn logs eight by ten inches in thickness and fourteen by sixteen feet in length. It fronts towards the setting sun and has a porch on the side with a ground floor. The apartments are divided into two, one below stairs and the other above.

The lower apartment has a fireplace in the North end built of volcanic rock and mother earth, large enough to admit a stick three feet in length. My floor is of sawn lumber which was rafted from the fort down the lake, thirty miles and hauled eight miles, the distance from the lake here. The boards are neither planed nor jointed, but are put down rough, leaving a few small cracks, not quite large enough to admit a persons foot between the boards, but quite large enough to admit plenty of fresh air.

An empty sugar barrel (that is emptied of its sugar) standing against the East wall and against the cupboard contains a part of a fifty pound sack of flour; the head of the barrel unlike the majority of barrel heads is on top of the barrel and has a piece of wood nailed across the top of it, projecting about an inch on either side with a scallop cut underneath it in the center to admit of being hold of. This latter piece of architecture of my own invention and took about ten minutes to complete it.

The log forming the window casing is a very nice place to keep my lamp, two empty cigar boxes (I don't use cigars, though I find the boxes convenient) containing thread, beeswax, thimbles, shot, caps, matches, etc., etc. Still nearer the southern wall and just under the joice is an empty boot box nailed with the bottom against the wall, in this box (open at the front) are several books, among them Greeleu's Conflict, "Grant & Sherman, Their Generals & Campaigns", "General Laws of Oregon", "Welles Leawyn", "Davis' Algebra," "Parker's Philosophy," "Inquire Within", "Guide to Public Business," "Hooker's Illustrated Nt. Hist.," and the "Arabian Nights", the last I have never read but kept it on hand as a last resort when other reading matter fails.

On top of the cupboard between the joice, are about a dozen numbers of "Harper's Magazine," and one copy of the Overland Monthly Justice Docket Leger, several papers and my portfolio.

From my wardrobe, along the wall towards the southwest corner of the shanty on numerous nails driven, pendant upon them several articles of wear that never get washed, my great coat, best trousers, & etc.

Resting on the floor between the foot of the bed and the west wall is my wooden trunk containing my ammunition in reserve, many old letters, new clothes (not many of the last) and other odds and ends that somehow or other will accumulate around a bachelor ranch, a sugar barrel half full of sugar, molasses keg with a gallon or two of golden syrup in it, a nail keg with a lot of nails in it and a pair of moccasins on top of it; a box containing two partly filled sacks of salt, coarse and fine, a sack with a few beans in it, several small sacks of garden seeds, two sacks of barley, one of them nearly empty, the last named my hay feed (seed).

South of the house about twelve or fifteen steps is a spring of pure water, not ice cold nor milk warm, but just about halfway between the two in temperature. A root house built of double walls of logs and in an interveneing space of two feet between the walls filled with dirt, roofed over with boards first, straw next and dirt afterwards, the floor of earth about two feet lower than the ground outside, in it about twenty bushels of potatoes (my own raising) and two hundred pounds apples brought from the valley, a plow and a few other farming tools.

Along the river at the East Side of my place are two ricks of hay, one of twelve tons, another of forty.

This is my meadow; in fact my claim is nearly all natural meadow, the remainder being so situated that the water could be made to overflow all but a few acres of it. The upper spring near where my castle stands is just where the hill ridge terminates in a gently sloping lawn facing the river.

There is also quite a heavy growth of sagebrush in places and through it, as well as where it does not grow is the most luxuriant bunch grass I ever saw. The flat lands are covered with a great variety of native grasses, prominent among which is the rye grass; this frequently grows from seven to nine feet high so that a man riding on horseback is completely hidden by it where it is thick upon the ground.

A fine variety of wild clover grows abundant near where there are springs and a native blue joint is also quite plentiful. There are no meadows of tame grass yet and everybody depends upon the natural grass for grazing and feeding all their stock. Some idea of the grazing qualities of this valley can be gained by taking into consideration the fact that there are nearly eight hundred cattle and one hundred horses owned and kept by persons residing here, besides the thousands of cattle, sheep and horses grazed by droves in passing through here. With all this amount of stock here, and the grazing in droves passing through, the grass upon the hills seems nearly as abundant as ever; and we do not think of feeding unless the snow falls a foot deep over the ground.

This valley is but one among many in this great basin, and though the first to commence settling up is by no means the only one that is becomming peopled with industrious pioneers. I suppose if I want to say that there are already more than three hundred people in this country when I was the second one, I would not exagerate. To a man of my social nature, a lover of busy active life, this pioneering is sometimes very discourageing and irksome.

I am not disposed to grumble at the decrees of fate, but, I would like to be foot loose for a few months, and try and baffle the old fellow for once. I have tried batching until I am satisfied that I was never cut out for one and to submit to what is unnatural is not part of the program I have laid down for myself.

I have made some pies, have some canned fruit, light bread, coffee, fried mush, fried pork, mashed potatoes, molasses sauce mixed and intend to make a duff. This is a pudding composed of a great variety of fruit, the more the better, boiled from one hour to two hours according to size, and eaten with a prepared sauce. Won't you feel releived when I go to gitting dinner?

Good bye. Respectfully yours
O.A. Stearns

Kate Robbins
1834-?

Eunice Robbins
1852-1917

Kate and Eunice Robbins, mother and daughter, were among the first settlers of the Ochoco country. When Kate, a native of Massachusetts, married Abner Robbins, she doubtless had no intimation of her future life in the wild West. Living thousands of miles from her family, in what the region's boosters called "the high pure atmosphere" of central Oregon, she witnessed Indian uprisings, vigilantism, lynchings, and bloody feuds between sheep men and cattle ranchers.

Her daughter Eunice became a school teacher, then married James Clinton Luckey, and together they ran a small hotel in Prineville. Between 1869 and 1886 Kate and Eunice wrote numerous unpublished letters to New England relatives vividly describing frontier life on the east side of Oregon's Cascades. The original letters are housed in the Knight Library, University of Oregon.— S.A.

Anxiety and Astonishment
A MOTHER AND DAUGHTER REPORT ON THE OCHOCOS

Ochoco, Oregon
September 8, 1871

My Dear Uncle:

I have just commenced school again and under very favorable circumstances. Expect Ma has written that Father changed his mind and went to Idaho after all. It is getting really cold. Every thing freezed solid at night and we keep a fire all day. Last week I went to the W.S. Reservation and will give you a brief account of what I saw there. I did not have time to stay as long as I wished to and most of the Indians were gone to the Cascades huckleberrying. The distance is about sixty miles from here and over a rough lonely road. We reached the Deschutes River at 3 P.M. and were ferried across by two Indians. Two miles farther drive brought us to the oldest white community and I was never more astonished than to find what a degree of elegance and refinement existed out here in that little wilderness, hundreds of miles from any town and nearly as far from any white settlement; large tasteful white dwelling houses, with gardens, croquet grounds etc. attached, while inside all the modern improvements, piles of the latest sheet music, centre tables laden with choice literature and ladies in gorgeous apparel greet the astonished vision. The government employees there now were besides the Agent, Clerk, Supt. Farms, Supt. Mills, School Teacher, Physician, Blacksmith and Minister. Most of these except the Doctor have families and very highly cultivated ones too. The evening I spent there was passing rapidly away with music, flirtations, conversation, refreshments, etc. when an alarm of fire was given and the General Office discovered to be in flames. Although much was injured it was not wholly destroyed.

As I said before all the Indians, except perhaps a dozen families were away, and the Indian Store closed. On the morning that I left, I called on John Mission, the richest and most civilized "native" on the Reserve. Before reaching the house we were met by its head who turned and walked back with us to his somewhat pretentious dwelling. Having ushered us into his parlor and seen us comfortably seated he left us in search of his squaw, Nancy, by name, whom he introduced as "Mrs. Mission." Leaving her to entertain the other guests he proceeded to inform me in broken english with a "right smart sprinkling" of jargon that he was Chief of his tribe, that he tried to live like white people, that Nancy could make pies, that he had a dance at his house once at which a white man fiddled, etc., etc. After a few minutes he left the room and soon returned to ask us out for refreshments. On following him into another apartment, I was surprised to find a table set with heavy white stone-china ware and glittering cutlery, *perfectly clean.* Having seated ourselves we ate largely of the most luscious water melon. John and Nancy seated at either end of the table but refusing to eat out of respect for their guests. Soon after lunch John left us in charge of Mrs. Mission and departed. Before leaving she displayed some of her treasure to our wondering gaze. Most noticeable among these was a buckskin so heavily beaded that I could not lift it in one hand; the waist and sleeves were of solid beadwork of an odd design, the skirt also was very much ornamented with beads, bells, and brass thimbles, fastened by a hold bored in the top. She was recently offered $40 for this dress but refused it. Besides this I noticed two pairs of buckskin pants belong to her liege lord. Both were heavily beaded, one ornamented with deer-skin fringes, six inches long, and the other with small bells like sleighbells, some three or four dozen being used on one garment. I also saw some very handsome trappings for his horse profusely ornamented with bells, beads, and "sich." This was not all I saw but time and space forbids a further description. This was the only family I visited, and is I have been informed, a very exceptional one, some live in very respectable frame houses and are quite neat and thrifty. Others live in the very extreme of filth and degradation, in huts, tents, or rude log houses. They number about 800 or 900. The "Warm Springs" are located eight miles from the Agency. About two miles in another direction is a moss agate bed. My hand trembles so that I shall be obliged to wait until another time to finish this.

E.W. Robbins
SCHOOLMARM

Ochoco, Oregon
7th January, 1883

Dear Mother:

It seems a long time since I had a letter from you. Abner is home for the winter. He has sold some cattle, but has not received the pay yet, as soon as he does I will send that money to Ira. I am very sorry that I could not have done so before.

We had another dreadful lynching affair in Prineville and it makes me very nervous. I will send you an account of it. Mr. Swarts has lived near us for the last eight years, was a well informed, smart man, and a good neighbor, but still he was a bad man and has been thought to be the ring leader of the horse theives in this section for a long time. He left a wife and three small children. I was also well acquainted with Sydney Houston (they used to live only a little ways from here) he was a kind hearted man, but got into bad company, and was getting very reckless, he was his Mother's idol and I am afraid it will nearly kill her. It is getting so that we live in constant dread of some one being killed. A man who was found a week or two ago dead in the hills, shot no one knows who did it or if any one who had any thing against him. A few days a go a man was shot at through the window, but excaped uninjured. He lives alone. The Sheriff is on the track of John and Price Thorp thinking perhaps they did it with the idea that he belongs to the Vigilance Com, but I have no idea he does. Did Ira Norton get the mittins I knit him, and the girls their wristers?

Kate L. Robbins

Jesse Applegate
1811-1888

Jesse Applegate led a portion of the Great Migration of 1843 which virtually tripled Oregon's Euro-American population. One of Oregon's best-known pioneers, Applegate was a fascinating and sometimes difficult figure who wielded considerable influence from the early days of Oregon's provisional government to the climax of the Civil War. He strongly believed in popular government, universal education, and the abolition of slavery.

In 1846, after exploring the Southern Route (now officially known as the Applegate Trail), Applegate and other trailblazers were publicly censured—many believe unfairly—in the wake of emigrant suffering along the new, untested trail. Applegate soon left the Willamette Valley in favor of southern Oregon, where he resided until the end of his life. In later years his direct involvement in state affairs was greatly diminished. Living 50 miles outside Linkville, the old name for Klamath Falls, and reduced to herding sheep, he expressed himself largely through a voluminous correspondence with many national and regional figures. "The Sage of Yoncalla" had an enduring friendship with an equally controversial figure, Dr. Bethenia Owens-Adair (1840-1926). Jesse Applegate was one of the few in Oregon who supported her decision to attend medical school, as he does in the following letter to her. (See *Many Faces* and *Varieties of Hope* of the Oregon Literature Series for selections by both).—S.A.

Should a Woman Become a Doctor?
A MAN OF DESTINY RESPONDS

Linkville, Oregon
November 20, 1873

My Very Dear Friend—

Your letter was brought to me at my sheep ranch, more than fifty miles from any postoffice. I read it sitting upon a stone, with the broad expanse of solitude spread around me, while I watched and herded another man's sheep for a living! When you also consider that I am between sixty and seventy years of age, and poor, and have won no distinction of any kind, it seems to me the oracle you consult is a frail one indeed. But as I do love you, dear, as the "bone of my bone, and flesh of flesh," my great partiality for you may lead me to hope more from your remarkable intellect than you will realize. If you had the means (and if I had them you should have them) your plan is just such a one as I would form for you, as your inclinations lead you in that direction.

You are right in deciding that your mind was not given you to be frittered away in frivolity. I was right in deciding that marriage and motherhood were not intended for you by the Creator. He designed you for a higher destiny, and you will attain it. Let your motto be "Excelsior." Avoid love, marriage and all other entanglements and relaxations until you have attained to the high distinction to which you aspire. Fame and fortune will then await you, and there will still be time to indulge in the tenderness of your heart and the warmth of your affections.

It is not probable that you and I will ever meet again. I am old and continually receding into a deeper and darker obscurity, perhaps shortly to die in some solitary desert, being, while your course will still be onward and upward, with a fame probably as wide as literature and as enduring as Time. I feel, however, that the mystic cord of affection has drawn us together; that the love and sympathy between us has been pure and chaste as the virgin snows upon the lap of Diana, and that it will endure to the end, whatever end we shall reach.

At a time of more leisure I will try to write again.

God bless and prosper you in all your undertakings.
Jesse Applegate

Eli Sheldon Glover
1845-1919

Michigan-born Eli Glover studied at the Art League in New York and later settled with his wife in Utah. In the fall of 1875, he decided to travel by horseback from Utah through Montana and Idaho, then by boat to the lower reaches of the Willamette. The following excerpts are taken from *The Diary of Eli Sheldon Glover, October-December, 1875*, as transcribed by the WPA (1940). They describe his exciting passage from the John Day Rapids to The Dalles.

Paddle-wheel steam boats began running the Columbia in the 1850s and were the main means of transporting cargo—wheat in particular—and travelers in the Columbia country. Before the time of dams, the many rapids made travel on the river hazardous—as Glover's journal vividly indicates.

Glover returned to the Pacific Coast in 1889 and earned his living doing the then-popular "bird's eye" views of cities. In return for such a view of Tacoma, he was given land in that city on which he stayed for the rest of his life.—T. O'D.

The Wreck of the *Yakima*, a Steamboat, at John Day Rapids

November 20, 1875

A still sunny morning, not a ripple on the surface of the river, except that caused by the swift current and the eddies about the rocks. The air is sharp and frosty. The shores are becoming bolder and more picturesque as we pass down the stream. Great walls of smooth Basaltic rock rise up on either bank showing many lines of stratification, and occasionally huge masses stand up in the stream and the channel crooks in and out among them. To follow its course takes the close attention of an experienced pilot. We are approaching the John Day Rapids said to be the swiftest and most difficult pass of the upper Columbia. The rocks are nearer together and the water boils and surges between them with great force. The rocky shores are more precipitous—bare and black—and the mountains rise snowcapped on either hand.

The scene was very strange and grand. I stood on the bows enjoying it. Ahead of us black rocks seemed to fill the channel, and the river rushed through, all broken up into white foam. The monster boat steers for the center of the narrow pass, the captain at the wheel. Without a quiver of her great bulk she plows through the foam. The mate stands by my side and a few passengers. Presently we hear a dull muffled sound like the tearing of a piece of flannel and there is a slight jarring of the boat. The mate says, "We've struck." We walk to the gunwale and look over; the water is rising on the side of the boat. A passenger says, "Will she sink?" The mate answers quietly, "She's bound to sink."

I looked up at the Captain, an old white headed man. He stands there at the wheel, his eyes fixed on a certain point among the rocks to the left, his face as white as his hair, and every nerve strained to the utmost tension to turn the bow of this vessel in that direction. Then I realized that the ship was really sinking. I looked over the bow again and the water had risen to the level of the deck below and was rushing in. She was full, the fires in the engines were all out, and men were wading through the water that swept the deck to reach the flight of steps that led to the deck above. With the force of the current and the steam that was left in the boilers, she was still going at a great speed. Would she reach the shore?

The banks were coming nearer rapidly. She was driving straight on the rocks. The passengers became alarmed as they realized the danger, and came rushing out of the cabin. Nearer and nearer—and now comes the crash. The men who were standing on the extreme end of the bow ready to jump ashore sprang to the rocks as soon as she struck. But there was more space than they supposed. There was a deep channel between the rock upon which the boat struck and the shore, and men went plunging into twenty feet of water. But the current proved friendly and dashed them out onto the rocks below, with only a few bruises and a good drenching.

There was a great stampede of men, women and children, many with life preservers in their hands, or buckling them about their persons as they rushed hither and thither greatly excited. Many would have thrown themselves into the river if they could, but the mate and the purser stood by and prevented them from doing so.

The bows held fast to the rock, and the stern swung round with the current. There was another crash—a straining and breaking of timber—as the stern sank and the whole boat listed over to the left. Freight and passengers were sliding down the deck and cabin floor; much of the freight went over and was carried down the stream, but the people held fast and climbed to the upper gunwale. There was cracking of timbers and breaking of glass and general confusion as the boat settled firmly on the rocks. The officers were all cool and told the passengers what to do. The two men who were in such haste to get on shore stood shivering on a rock, but some twenty feet from the shore still. They called lustily for a line to be thrown out, to "pull the hawser off" and "fasten the ship." But there was nothing there to fasten it to.

The small boat was lowered between the ship and shore, the ladies were assisted in. A few slips, a little wetting, a scream or two and the ladies were safely landed. There was more to it getting the men off. Too many of them wished to go first, but the Captain assured them that there was no hurry, that he thought the boat had settled firmly on the rock and would not move.

Men were soon engaged in gathering sage brush and flood wood for fuel, and a fire was soon kindled, boards were set up and a rope stretched across with canvas fastened over to make a shelter from the wind for the ladies. The "first men ashore" were supplied with dry clothing from the different parties and they got behind the rocks to make the change, protesting amid the laughter and jeers of the other passengers that they went on shore to "take a line and make the boat fast." Gang planks were laid from shore to rocks and rocks to the sunken boat, and the hands were engaged in transferring baggage and freight from the wreck to the shore. Several Indians were soon about with "Dug out" Canoes, picking up the flour that was floating in sacks down the stream. The wheat, being heavier, sank. In fact it was this cargo weighing 160 tons that kept the boat firm on the rocks in spite of the rapid current. While the proverbial "Artist on the spot" made a sketch of the scene from a neigh-boring rock, lunch of crackers and cheese was served on the rocks, and the passengers dispersed themselves about among the cliffs and sand banks pros-pecting for specimens. But it was a poor field for prospecting—nothing but basaltic rock and scoria with small patches of vegetation.

The river has cut a great channel or canyon some six hundred feet deep, and in many places nearly vertical, through many stratas of volcanic formation. To the West, Mt. Hood lifts its snow-clad summit like a pyramid of crystal high above the clouds, standing solitary over 14,000 ft. above the sea level.

A horse was purchased from one of the passengers, and a man dispatched over the country thirty miles to Selilo, a telegraph station, to send word back to Wallula for the steamer *Owyhee* to come to our rescue.

Our supper consisted of coffee and crackers—all that was left above water of the ship provisions. One cup of coffee and three crackers fell to my share. Blankets and bedding were transferred from the wreck to the rocks, fires were kindled at different points where best protected from the wind, and the people prepared to spend the night as pleasantly as possible.

I went on board the wreck, where the cabin stove was propped up in posi-tion and a good fire burning. A few of the passengers and crew were gathered about this fire in very grotesque attitudes, and the efforts made to walk the cabin floor without slipping into some of the staterooms on the lower side was quite amusing.

All liquor that remained in the saloon after the disaster was considered fair plunder, and many of the officers as well as the men had rescued enough of the spirits from a watery grave to raise their ideas and make their tongues and footsteps still more unsteady. All the circumstances of the affair, with the pros-pects of rescue, were freely discussed, and many anecdotes told of similar disaster. It was ascertained that on the 20th of Nov. just two years ago today, and at nearly if not quite the same hour, this steamer was wrecked on the rocks fifteen miles above this place, and the man Kinney who was the "first man ashore" today was a passenger at the time. An old German dreamed last night while we were laying at Umatilla that he was shipwrecked and that many lives were lost. He told his dream to the other passengers this morning and said he was sure the boat would be wrecked this trip.

Would it be safe to sleep on board the wreck was a question discussed in all its bearings. Would she hold fast to the rock—or would she slide off in the current during the night? The water was boiling fearfully just over the port side and the water was rushing through between the lower deck and the cabin floor—and there was depth enough just under the stern to let her sink, smoke stack and all if she did not go to pieces. Some thought it safe to stay on the boat, but others thought it safer on shore and took their blankets and left. Others decided to sit up about the cabin fire and if they should feel the ship give, they would be ready to rush off, and a few went to bed in the staterooms without fear and slept peacefully.

I was one of the few—for I know that the ship's cargo, one hundred and sixty tons of wheat that sinks like lead, would hold the wreck firmly in place. By changing about and putting my feet where my head would have been under ordinary circumstances, and bracing my feet against the cabin wall, laying or standing at an angle of forty-five degrees, well covered up in warm blankets, the music of the surging waters soon lulled me to sleep. I knew nothing more until waked by the noises about the wreck in the morning.

November 21

The campers on the rocks had used some poles for fuel that were found piled up near by. An old Indian came and claimed them as his property. Must have four sacks of flour for the poles. The Captain gave it to him and his squaws carried it off on their backs, grinning and grinning in great glee over the "big swap." It was harvest time for the natives—some miles below we saw them fishing out sacks of flour and sundry articles from the wreck and hiding them among the rocks.

The men wear hats with fringed edges on the brim. The squaw wear a cap of rushes, straw of woven like a basket, and terminating in a rounded point at the top. They use this cap for many purposes—to gather berries in, to carry flour, or to pack "chips" (the dried dung of cattle) for fuel.

A pile of rocks was erected on the point where we lay, with a board and the date inscribed, with the name "Kinneys Landing" in honor of the man who risked his life to carry a line ashore to make the boat fast.

At one o'clock the steamer *Owyhie* hove in sight around a bend in the river above. We were soon on board and seated to a good meal, to which the most ample justice was done. A part of the dry cargo of the *Yakima* was transferred and we steamed away, glad to be on our journey once more.

Just at dusk, we landed at the dock at Selilo and passed around the falls and Dalles Rapids—fifteen miles to the little town of Dalles by rail.

The night was stormy and dark. We can see but little of the place. I wished to pass a day at the wonderful Dalles of the Columbia but could not spend the time.

James McCall Sutton
1830-1878

Sutton was one of southern Oregon's best-known newspapermen. He emigrated to Oregon in 1852 and settled in the Rogue River area in 1854, where he briefly engaged in mining and operated a drug store. After editing the Jacksonville *Sentinel*, he founded a second newspaper in Ashland, the *Ashland Tidings*, which he infused with energy and humor until his death. Sutton loved his region's history and good yarns and worked hard collecting and compiling them for the Pioneer Society of Southern Oregon.

The life-teeming tule marsh of the Klamath Lake country is the subject of the letter Sutton sent to the *Ashland Tidings* when he visited Linkville (today's Klamath Falls) in August of 1876. Toads were then but one species of the region's prodigious amphibian population. Between 1869 and 1896, the banks of warm springs along the Link River also provided habitat for a prolific species of harmless black water-snakes. In springtime, writhing tangles of snakes were commonplace. One season, settlers who wished to get rid of these snakes offered a small reward for snake carcasses. Some sources believe that the destruction of thousands of snakes resulted in the short-lived invasion by the snake's prime food source: toads and frogs. Stories about the amphibians in the Klamath Falls area have become part of the region's folklore. In the Klamath Basin, only one quarter of the vast marshes remain, marshes which once extended for 185,000 acres. Sutton's letter here was first reprinted in *Klamath Echoes* (1964).—S.A.

Walking on Toads at Linkville

AN EDITOR MEETS KLAMATH MARSH

Linkville Hotel
August 10, 1876

To *The Ashland Tidings*

Dear Readers:

Were it not for my well-known reputation for truth I should hesitate to relate the following:

Some three weeks since, an incredibly large army of young toads, about one-half inch in length, made their appearance on the river shore in and above Linkville. During their stay the bridge was black with them, they daily advanced up the river, gradually becoming less numerous within the town limits, until at the present time not more than five to the square foot is found, on the average, along the river shore in town. But to my story as I saw it myself. After walking up the river about 200 yards, I began to become interested in the great number of those rusty-backed little reptiles that lined the trail. It soon became difficult to step without crushing from one to half a dozen of them. My curiosity by this time had become somewhat excited and I determined to leave the trail and go to where toads were still more plentiful. But as I proceeded through the grass I found my progress more and more impeded, as it produced the most revolting sensation to feel them crushing under my feet. By means of a small bough I made some progress with only an occasional casualty. Fully absorbed in search of the headquarters of this vast army, I found myself beset by an army of insects which in point of numbers far outstripped the mass of hopping reptiles beneath my feet. I had entered a small thicket of low wild roses, on which had settled a cloud of these harmless little gnats, so well known in the vicinity of lakes and marshes, and of an afternoon fill the air like mist. Each movement I made among these rosebushes started up the little insects in such immense numbers that they literally covered my face and clothing until I sparkled like an iceberg beneath their gauzy, glittering wings. I was impressed with a sensation of suffocation, either real or imaginary. With bated breath and closed eyes I made quick time toward the hills until I was relieved of them, crushing great numbers of the unfortunate toads at every step. The very memory of their grinding bones beneath my feet makes me

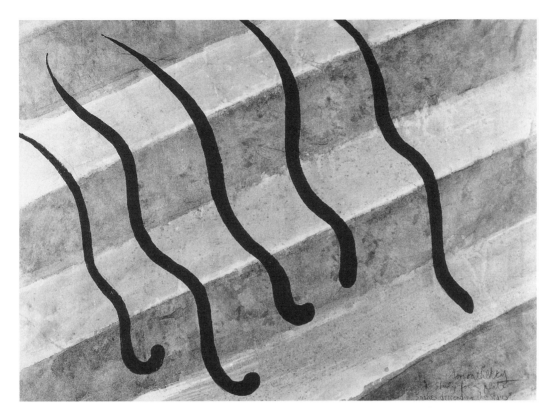

shudder till yet. Giving the rosebushes and all other bushes a wide berth, I carefully picked an open way to the river shore, in continuation of my toad investigation. I saw a great many garter snakes that had been feasting on toad, until they could scarcely crawl. They moved about among the little jumpers without apparently giving any alarm, often crawling over heaps of them. On arriving at the tule marsh that lined the river shore, I discovered the real headquarters. Toads were literally piled up in a ridge four feet wide, next to the water. On my approach they fled to the tules in a moving mass from four to six inches deep. If they had all been together along the river, I am confident that they would have filled a ditch, two feet wide, two feet deep, and a half a mile long. These toads have now grown to about one-half inch in length, and so far seem to be entirely harmless. What is most strange about them is their first appearance. How they were propagated in such vast numbers is a mystery as yet unsolved.

J. M. Sutton

Charles Erskine Scott Wood
1852-1944

Four years after graduating from West Point, Baltimore-born C.E.S. Wood came to Oregon as aide-de-camp to General Oliver O. Howard in the Nez Perce War of 1877-1878. It was then that Wood met Chief Joseph, a Native American leader he always respected. Wood also served with General Howard in the Bannock-Paiute War of 1878-1879, the last of the Oregon Indian wars. The following excerpts from the journal Wood kept while on campaign are taken from *OHQ* 70 (1969). The young woman mentioned in the June 9 excerpt was a member of a touring opera company whom Wood met while travelling by boat up the Columbia to the region of the conflict.

Wood served in the army until 1884, then settled in Portland to practice law, having earlier acquired a law degree from Columbia University. Wood remained in Oregon for many years, an establishment figure, speaker, a writer for *Pacific Monthly*, and a successful attorney for the railroads. At the same time he was friend to many of the nation's leading anarchists and artists. He was also a talented early Modernist poet, one of the first published in *The New Yorker*. His satirical work, *Heavenly Discourses* (1927), went into many editions and languages. (See *From Here We Speak* for poems and *Varieties of Hope* for prose by Wood.)
—T. O'D.

A Soldier and Poet in the Last Oregon Indian War

Friday, June 7, 1878

Left Portland 5 A.M. Through the mountain cliffs, clouds and mists of the Cascade Range to Dalles. A sunset of red tongues and crimson flakes. The Gates of the river lurid with sultry clouds. Sand dunes and driving sand. Leave Dalles at dusk. Celilo, and bed.

Sunday, June 9

I go up stairs in the hopes of seeing my Muse. Jupiter, Venus and Minerva in conjunction favor me and I meet her in the hall. She is charming. From the chrysallis of a tired wayfarer has emerged a vision of fleecy white dotted with knots of pink ribbons. So pure and fresh that it is soothing to look at her.

She says, "Oh, are you going. I thought you were to stay tonight. I have been taking a nap. If I had known you went so soon I would not have slept. Won't you come into the parlor and sit down."

I did so and she looked very pretty as she sat by the window leaning her head on her hand. Her feet were exquisite and she knew it, small blame to her. They were clad in dainty pink net work silk stockings and cased in diminutive black slippers. One resting upon the other they peeped out from their hiding place among the laced petticoats, and through the labyrinth of snowy lace could be discerned the shapely ankles whose perfect outlines gave promise of the symmetry of the hidden beauty above them. A pink ribbon was knotted in her hair and a soft mistiness of ruching nestled about her throat. A black velvet band clasped her neck and a gold cross rose and fell with the heaving of her bosom. I was enjoying her artistic posing when the inexorable Goodwin said, "The General is waiting at the stage, sir."

A clasp of the hand. "Let me hear from you. If I can be of assistance call on me. Goodby."

"Goodby," and so I left this daughter of Bohemia.

Tuesday, June 11

Heat and dust. The stage trundles wearily along. The horses cough and sneeze. Driver lays on the whip with a mechanical throw. Change horses every 15 miles. Passengers nod and sway their grimy heads as they doze through the stifling afternoon.

Wednesday, June 19

Over the rolling yellow hills to Cow Valley and down amid the blue and purple hills to Malheur City. Through the drenching rain and the deafening thunder up the turbid running stream to the little mining town. Change drenched clothes in the springy attic of the Bed Bug tavern. The blear eyed, white bearded tottering old drunkard and dotard the companion of Kit Carson, the mountaineer of seventy-odd years who disappears into the mountains and is lost to sight till given up for dead, when he celebrates his own resurrection by unlimited polutions of "whuskey."

Saturday, June 22

Malheur Agency too cold for good agricultural land. The Reservation system a good one for everyone but the Indians and the people.

Thursday, June 27

Driving Snow storm. Building fires—around which shivering groups do congregate. Lose our way and our supply train. Boyle accosts me as I ride down the line. "This is a pretty outlook, no blankets, no grub and here we are lost in the fastenings of the mountains." Boyle is the officer who reported to the General that the Indians were completely disinfected.

Wednesday, July 3

Ruminate on the character of American frontier people, content to live in a log hovel and sleep and eat and breed. No books, no education. Many cannot sign their names. "I hev a sore finger, just sign for me." "I write a powerful poor hand I tell you, you'd better sign for me."

It appears to be a greater labor to them than breaking a horse. They apologize for an unpicturesque signature as if they had spoiled a painting with "Sho' now, I spiled it here! I went too fur down," etc.

Saturday, July 6

Find a body of a herder fearfully mutilated and shot with arrows. Five sheep mutilated and left to suffer. Squandered lives of men that meet lonely and awful deaths. General character of the men rough, profane and irreligious. Are they sent to Hell?

Monday, July 8

March to the battle, sweeping over the rolling yellow and red hills. The round mountop speckled with Indians. Our gallop. Deployment. Pop, pop, zee-ee and whist! of the bullets. Riding of the bravado chiefs. They come far ahead of their followers and ride up and down, up and down our lines, throwing themselves in all manner of positions on their horses while a shower of bullets knock up the dust among their horses feet. This to give courage to their followers. The medicine men have promised them they are bullet proof—but as one tumbles off his horse they lose faith in the medicine men and keep further out of range. Charging the crest. Bandaging mortal wounds. Dead and wounded horses, camp plunder. The horde of human vultures, camp pillagers and horse thieves following in our wake. Charge of the rocky crest. The advance through the forest, cessation of the pursuit. I am sent on a night ride after Throckmorton and rations. Get rations at Pilot Rock and bring them up at sunrise to camp.

Tuesday, July 9

Arrive just at the burial of a dead soldier, shot by mistake in the dawn by Lieut. Paddock. Solemnity of the silent corpse, the simple grave, the soldier's burial clothes. The lonely mound under the mournful pines, and all the pathos of death in loneliness. How all things earthly sink into nothingness before the dread silence of the dead one.

Tuesday, July 16

Up Joseph Creek to the Imnaha, the former home of Joseph, the Nez Perce Chief. Grand view that recalled to mind Satan's temptation of Christ, for the world seemed spread at our feet. The precipice in front of us dropped in jagged battlements and terraces at least two thousand feet to the green, soft valley of the creek. Fir trees were caught and tangled in the lodgements on the rocks and in the ravines. They were twisted by the storms. Through them in middle depths of air floated hawks or eagles.

We have beautiful ride over mountains and through forests and torrents. Camping in the beautiful valley of the Wallowa. Guarded by lofty snow capped mountains that seem to mourn over the inevitable fate of the Indians who claim this country as their own. We cross the picturesque bridge over the Grand Ronde and reach Somerville on the 20th. Sarah Winnemucca becomes the object of staring for the stockaded and "forted-up" villagers, who, babes on arms, flock to see the princess. "Ain't she pretty." "Prettiest squaw I ever see." "Best lookin' Injun I ever come across." "Don't she talk purty," etc.

Sarah Jane Findley
1842-1922

Sarah Jane Findley endured many challenges and tragedies during her long life. While crossing the plains as a ten-year-old girl in 1852, she suffered the loss of her mother. At the age of fourteen, while living in southern Oregon, Sarah Jane molded bullets, nursed settlers, and narrowly escaped capture during the Rogue River Indian War. She married Alexander Findley in 1859, and the couple moved to northeastern Oregon; by 1871, the Findleys had settled in the remote Wallowa country. Among the region's first white settlers, the Findley family enjoyed good relations with the Nez Perce, whose summer camp was near their homestead. In 1878, just a year after the Nez Perce were forced to flee the Wallowa for Canada, a diphtheria epidemic swept the Wallowa country, and the Findleys lost six children. Extremely depressed but still determined to live, Sarah Jane, her husband, and a single surviving child wintered in a cave near the mouth of Joseph Creek.

The Findley family's losses resembled those of countless other nineteenth-century pioneer and Native American families who frequently died from such diseases as small pox, whooping cough, diphtheria, and tuberculosis. Findley's comment to her sister that the spread of diphtheria could be blamed on "the Indians" was inaccurate as well as ironic. The majority of contagious diseases was brought by the tide of white settlement. The Findleys eventually left the Wallowa country for the Willamette Valley. Sarah Jane Findley's letter here was first published in a series of memoirs by H. R. Findley that appeared in the *Chief Joseph Herald* (1958).—S.A.

Diphtheria Has Taken Nearly All My Children
A WALLOWA MOTHER'S LAMENT—WITH A SCAPEGOAT

Wallowa, Oregon
August 4, 1878

Mr. and Mrs. George Reeves
Cedar Mill, Oregon

My dear Brother and Sister:

I must try to write you, but it is with a sad and aching heart. I feel that life for me is over, nothing but darkness before me. Death has entered our home and all our children have been taken from us, but Florence, and she is very sick and has been for three weeks. I have been down, but am able to go around again.

Diptheria is taking nearly all the children in this and the Walla Walla country. Everett was the first to take it. He took it on the sixth of July, Sammy took it on the eleventh, Florence and Johnnie took it on the fourteenth, Emma took it on the nineteenth, and little Lora on the twenty-ninth. George was the first to go. He died on the fifteenth in the morning, and Sammy died in the evening of the same day. Johnnie died the nineteenth and Everett the twenty-first. Emma died the twenty-eighth and Lora died the first of August.

We did all that we could do to save them, but nothing seemed to do any good that we could do. We had two doctors come to see them, and some we doctored ourselves. But they are all gone, and such suffering I never saw before. Poor George's neck and face swelled until he chocked to death. The baby's neck was swollen very badly, but not as bad as George's.

The others did not appear to suffer near so much. Everett was sick seventeen days, and was able to sit up most of the time. His throat got almost well, but his stomach became diseased, either from his throat, or from some other cause. The doctors did not seem to know. Nothing would lay on his stomach for several days before he died, not even water.

Florence's throat is well, but her stomach is very much out of order. She can't sit up, but a few minutes at a time.

The disease has broken out in the Grande Ronde Valley the past month, and it is worse than ever. Mr. Russell, the blacksmith, lost four of their children. Dr. Shores lost three of their's. One of the Rhinehart's lost eight. Oh!

sister Mary, you just can't realize what desolation reigns in this country unless you were here to see. People have had to huddle together on account of the Indians who caused the disease to spread all over the land. One poor man and woman, over on Birch Creek, lost all nine of their children.

. . . one thing, I wish to say, is that we never lacked for anything in all of our affliction and trouble, which love or money could do or get. One of our neighbors came and stayed with us ten days and nights, until he got sick and had to go home. We never lacked for company. Both men and women were with us all the time. Dear kind friends who stayed and waited on my little children when I was sick and could not do it myself. May God bless them, forever, is my prayer.

Your sister,

Jane Findley

Sarah Winnemucca Hopkins
1844-1891

Sarah Winnemucca Hopkins was the daughter of the famous Chief Winnemucca, a Northern Paiute. As a young person, Sarah Winnemucca became fluent in spoken English and was employed as an interpreter and army scout during the Paiute-Bannock War of 1878-79. With the support of powerful and articulate friends such as Mrs. Horace Mann and Elizabeth Peabody, Sarah Winnemucca succeeded in establishing an Indian School near Lovelock, Nevada.

Her friends also assisted her in the writing and publishing of *Life among the Piutes: Their Wrongs and Claims* (1883)—an autobiography that drew national attention to the tragic experiences of the Paiute people whose large Malheur Reservation was dramatically reduced and then abolished to accommodate white settlement after the Paiute-Bannock War. The following letter addressed to Carl Schurz, Secretary of the Interior, was incorporated into the text of *Life among the Piutes*. Winnemucca reports that none of the letters she wrote to Washington, D.C., was ever answered. (See *Many Faces* of the Oregon Literature Series for another excerpt and C.E.S. Wood's July 9, 1878, letter in this volume for reference to her.)—S.A.

Paiute Refugees from the Malheur Need a Bit of Land
ANOTHER LETTER NEVER ANSWERED BY WASHINGTON, D.C.

Vancouver Barracks, Washington Territory
March 28, 1881

Dear Sir,

I take this matter in hand in behalf of the Indians who are prisoners here at this place. There are fifty-three (53) in all. Of this number thirteen are men, twenty-one women, eleven girls from three to fourteen years of age, and eight boys from three to sixteen. Twenty-three of the number belong to the Sheep-Eaters, thirteen belong to the Weisers' tribe, and seven from Boisé. These belong to Fort Hall. This is the second winter they have been here, and they have been provided for entirely by the military here. They receive government rations. But the only way they have to provide for the women is by what they make out of selling the savings of some of their rations, and from what castaway clothing I can collect from the employés here. I am employed here as an interpreter, and have been teaching them to read. They are learning fast. They can all read pretty well, and are desirous to learn. What I want to ask is to have them stay here. They seem to be contented. Most of them would rather stay here than to go elsewhere, but in order to make them more contented and useful it would be well to help them. If they could have a place, or a bit of land given them to use for themselves, yes, a place for their own benefit, and where they could work for themselves, I would teach them habits of industry, and it would help much in supporting them; and it is necessary that there should be, at least for the present, some appropriation made for them, in order to provide clothing for the women and children, and a proper place to live in. At present they are living in tents. The men are working for the military here in improving the post, and they all have an interest in them for their work, and I think a little help from your department, as above mentioned, would be better for them than to turn them loose again to wander in idleness or learn evil, or go back to bad habits again. I think it would be the best that could be done for them in the way of enlightening and Christianizing them. They would all rather be under the military authority. They say they are not cheated here, and they can see that the officers are doing all they can for them. Hoping you will give this a careful consideration, I am, sir, very respectfully,

Your obedient servant,
Sarah Winnemucca

Grace Elizabeth McCrary
1866-1933

Grace Elizabeth McCrary of Baker City, Oregon, lost both of her parents by the time she was fourteen years old. Continuing to live at home with an older sister and other siblings, McCrary struggled to learn independence and used her diary "to keep her company." In this schoolgirl's diary, the cycle of daily activities and holidays throughout the long and bitter winter of 1883 is darkened by illness and death. McCrary's acute awareness of the deaths in her neighborhood may possibly be attributed to the loss of her own parents. During the period of the diary, Elias, an 80-year-old neighbor, moved in with the orphaned sisters, and eventually died. Hers was an era beset by diseases for which there was no known cure. A preoccupation with physical health is typical of many diaries of the late nineteenth century. McCrary eventually was to study at the Boston Conservatory of Music.

Many well-to-do Oregon families of the era hired Chinese men who had originally come to mine or build railroads as domestic servants. Frequently the Chinese, such as the man named Chow in the following selection, formed affectionate bonds with their employer's children.

Grace McCrary's unpublished diary, from which the following has been taken, has recently been transcribed by Shirley Goodwin of Baker City.—S.A.

A Baker City Orphan Girl Endures the Worst
—With Help from a Chinese, Sisters, Teachers,
Neighbors, Friends

Wednesday, January 3, 1883

I got up at 30 past 6 o'clock and got breakfast and went to school at 47 untill 9. Sisters piano came today. I came part way from school with Adelia. Read in the Bad Boy Diary. We had fun watching them unload the new piano. It is getting late.

Saturday, January 6

Got up at 7 o'clock fixed breakfast—sewed on Myrtle's apron. Rained all day a regular January thaw. Put my bed in the hall leaked terribly in my room all day. Sent my shoe to the shop to be mended but it is Epipheny or Little Christmas and the shoe maker being a Catholic would not work on a holy day. Georgie has been sick a little all day.

Friday, January 12

Went to school early came home at noon. Andrew a little better. Gordon gave him his knife. Spider in the soup today. Dick Lawrence had a party. Examination in spelling. Mary and I went over to Mrs. Houstons. Mrs. Kellog gave an orange for Andrew. Got some apples.

Thursday, January 18

Got a letter from Crissa. Took my dinner to school today had examination in bookkeeping. Cold very. Mrs. Rheas little 3 day old baby was buried today. I came home from school done up the dishes & then we baked a jelly cake some gems 2 peach pies & some tarts. Andrew is little better today. George brought home a thermometer this evening. Claude wanted a silk handkerchief. 29 deg below zero.

Monday, January 22

Mary is so sick that I had to stay at home from school. Claude did not go this fore noon. Doctor Atwood came out this afternoon. Brought some sardines. Mixed some corn cakes for breakfast. Mary is awful sick all night.

Tuesday, January 23
I took some Gin.

Wednesday, January 24
 I staid home all day. Snowed today. Minnie P. baked some bread, it is splendid. About half past 5 I went down to Mrs. Blocks to see Chow about getting some little Chinese boy to come & help us. He did not come though Mary got up about dark.

Saturday, January 27
Want a Chinaman very bad. Claude brought a Chinaman out but he wanted $ and Mary sent him away. When George came home in the evening he said to get him anyway. So Claude went after him but he could not find him.

Sunday, January 28
I went over to see Elias this evening. It is so pitiful to see him try to talk. We received the skull caps from the east.

Thursday, February 1
I baked a lot of cookies this morning did not go to school snow is terrible deep. If mother was alive she would be 53 years old today. We commenced to reddy up the upstairs but it was so cold we had to quit for today. Terrible cold tonite.

Friday, February 2
Today Mary finished cleaning upstairs. Myrtle & I went to take our lessons at the convent. We stopped at Hatties to see how Harry was. He was real sick with a cold but not dangerous.

Saturday, February 3
Made Harry's night gowns this morning. This morning 7 o'clock mercury was 36 below zero. Myrtle and I got the morning work done when Chow came. He was nearly frozen. I practiced only a little today owing to a good deal of house work. It is terrible cold. Verdies Baby is very sick. I heard that Maggie Stack froze both her heels & the baby his toes.

Tuesday, February 6
Last night we got home about 2 o'clock. Today Chow wanted to know if he could spend his China New Year in C. town. We consented of course. Myrtle & I washed the dinner dishes. We put Elias's bed in the dining room. I prac-

ticed four (4) hours today. Harry is much better. Mary has had neuralgia in her stomach. Rev. Mr. Parker lost his only baby last nite.

Thursday, February 8
Left the dishes for Chow to do. Mary went over to Mrs. Grays. She made some butter. I cleaned the house up then dressed myself. Practiced 2 hours. Chow brought some China candy.

Friday, February 9
Myrtle got a new pair of shoes. We went to take our lessons. Sister Sup. & Victor were ready to go to town. Took part of "William Tell". Came home by the post office and got some candy. Came home by Hatties. Talking about going to California. Philly Packhaman is going to find a warmer climate. Want to go awful bad.

Monday, February 12
I started to school this morning. Came part way with Delia. I heard that Emma Thompson's mother was dead and her father very ill. That sick lad died and was buried yesterday. Practiced 2 hours and 3 quarters.

Wednesday, February 21
Elias has been worse lately. Myrtle is sick Mary is not well.

Friday, March 2
The streets were filled with carriages and sleighs for Mrs. Hindman was buried today. She died yesterday. We stopped in at Mr. Franks. The Estes girls were there buying a collar.

Saturday, March 10
Mary & I made a gingham apron for Myrtle today. Myrtle & Georgie took dinner at Hatties today. Claude is so excited for the river has overflowed & is running in Mr. Korses saloon.

Wednesday, March 21
Elias had a nervous chill. Fred Bowen and another man shot off a pistol & were arrested. Myrtle & I went up to Buchanans this evening & Mr. B. made us laught all the time. Mary is going to set up tonight with Elias.

Friday, March 23
Elias was worse today. Chow made ginger cookies today. Hattie & Baby spent the forenoon over here. Claude & I cleaned the yard & I helped trim a little.

Sunday, March 25

It is Easter today. We colored some blue, scarlet & purple   Georgie gave Harry, Willie, Andrew & Wilson & Mr. & Mrs. B. a colored egg. Harry is all broken out & think that he has the measles.

Monday, March 26

Elias is worse. He had a cold sweat and it made him very weak. Mr. B. had to come down & help to lift him out of bed.

Wednesday, March 28

We played all afternoon. Mrs. Grey came over & brought some apricots to Elias. We made kites & flew them. It rained part of the afternoon. Myrtle & I made some hats out of lace & wore them.

Wednesday, April 4

Mr. Ingerson came this morning to wait on poor Elias who is so much worse. The wind blows so strong.

Monday, April 9

Elias is awful bad. Today he pulled Mary, Hattie & me all down twice & kissed us all He said "What keeps us so long". Mary said " I don't know Elias, unless it is that we all love you so much". He is so bad now that he can't talk but a little. All that he calls for is "water."

Tuesday, April 10

The stranger across the bridge is dead.

Wednesday, April 11

Poor dear Elias died at 30 minutes past 2 last night. Oh! how awful it seems to get up in the morning to find the bed away & poor darling soul a corpse. If I was as sure of a blessed eternity as he was I don't think I would fear to die. Mary awoke me at the time but said it was best to lie still as he would not know me. He was struck with death.

Friday, April 13

How sad it is at home since Elias was buried. Its lonely & sad. It seems that the last ties of this old home were broken when we laid dear Elias in his last resting place. Mr. Maxwell preached the funeral. It was a very disagreeable day yesterday out in the burying ground. Mary nearly fell out coming back from the grave yard.

Julia Wilson
1874-?

Julia Wilson's Crook County childhood was marked by tragedy—a flash flood. It is estimated that floods, particularly flash floods, kill more people each year than hurricanes, tornadoes, wind storms, or lightning. In 1884, on a homestead near the community of Mitchell, ten-year-old Julia Wilson barely survived the onrush of waters. She witnessed the drowning of her mother and three of her four siblings.

The Mitchell disaster followed a pattern typical in semi-arid regions of the American West: hard, dry soils absorb very little water; rain, when it comes, collects in streams and rivers in an extremely brief period; the water drains downhill and overflows streams that have been dry or nearly dry for months; flood waters can rush miles downstream to places where the sun has been shining all day. Victims often have no reason to suspect that a flood is heading their way.

The following letter, written shortly after the flood, recounts Julia Wilson's experiences in a poignant manner. Mary Carroll Helms, Julia's aunt, had the sad task of explaining the deaths of her sister, Nancy Carroll Wilson, and niece and nephews, Maggie, George, and Autia. When she wrote to relatives of her bereaved brother-in-law, Sam Wilson, she enclosed Julia's eye-witness version of the disaster which took place June 2, 1884. Years later, a handwritten copy of the original letter, the source of the following, was given to the Crook County Historical Society's Bowman Museum, in Prineville, Oregon, by descendants of the Wilson and Helms families.— S.A.

I Ran for the Hills
A GIRL ESCAPES THE MITCHELL FLASH FLOOD IN 1884

Bridg Creek, Crook Co. Oregon
June 1884

Dear Grandmother and Grandfather,

What I remember about the flood. . . . Well it rained very hard then the water came right to the door   ma was whitewashing the house she had been out to the dich to let out some of the watter the ditch was raising some   then Autia went to the creek to git the tub   it was setting in creek   when he had ben back & setting in the house about 20 minutes ma went to the door & sed   oh look here Children & she got too quilts & took all us children & went through the bars   the watter was so deep she hung the quilts on the finse   we got to the dich & then ma fell down with george in hur arms & Autia helped hur up & then we went up the dich a ways we saw the flood coming down the creek 3 hundred yards above   then ma commenced praying for help & then Autia sed to ma   if we can git to the hill we will be all write and ma sed   we cant do that   then Autia commenced gitting us across the dich   he fell in with Clyde & ma helped him out   he had us all across but ma & maggie & he had gone back fore them when the watter was up to his neck   that was the last I ever saw any of them. Ma and Autia and George and Maggie was all gone under the waters   I then ran for the hills   the last word I hurd them say was Autia said   if we can git to the hills we will be all write   ma said we will never get there   maggie said oh we cant live any longer can we,   George was standing by the dich crying   the watter was up to my wast about half way to the hill

when I got thare I looked back too him waved and stoped a minut & then the house & evry thing was gone   I stade on the hill along time   I could not see eny one of them & then went up to Mrs. mires & stade all Night   dident know Clyde was alive untill the next day.

From,
Julia

John Waldo
1844-1907

John Waldo was born and grew up south of Silverton in the Waldo Hills, a range named for his pioneer father. After graduation from Willamette University he embarked on a legal career and eventually became Chief Justice of the Oregon Supreme Court. He combined his legal career with an intense interest in the Oregon landscape and was one of Oregon's first conservationists. His diaries record some thirty summers in the High Cascades. With William G. Steel and others, he secured designation of Crater Lake as a National Park.

Below is an excerpt from one of his letters, a plea to President Cleveland for protection of the Cascades. It is taken from an *OHQ* (1989) article by Jeff La Lande.—T. O'D.

Save the Cascade Mountain Reserve

April 28, 1890

President Grover Cleveland
White House, Washington, D.C.

Sir:

At the request of Judge Bellinger of the United States District Court, I address this letter to you, giving the results of my acquaintance with the Cascade Mountain Reserve as on the question of retaining this reservation as it now exists. I learned, if not with astonishment, certainly with regret, that the Oregon Delegation at Washington, or some of them, had applied to you to abrogate, in great part, this reservation . . . .

The whole of this range, at some remote period, has been deluged by a flood of lava. . . . These lava fields are, today, largely covered with a coniferous forest, although there are still some places, as for instance, in the vicinity of the peaks known as the Three Sisters and on the divide between Klamath Lake and Rogue River, where these fields of volcanic rock have wholly or partially resisted the approaches of vegetation. . . . Looking westward from the summit of the divide, the usual appearance is that of an almost uninterrupted, evergreen, coniferous forest, stretching over a wilderness of lofty blue peaks, canyons and divides. . . . There is a succession of snow peaks . . . from Mt. Hood, near the Columbia, to Mt. Pitt in the southern extremity of the reservation, beyond which the range suddenly drops away, without any prominent point, until it swells against the magnificent peak of Mt. Shasta in California.

A wise government will know that to raise men is much more important than to raise sheep, or men of the nature of sheep; and that this is a question which, ultimately immeasurably concerns even the purely material interest of men.

During the lifetime of men now living, the greater part of this inhabitable continent has been given into private hands. "The end of the land" has been reached. Yet ugly facts stare us in the face. Were another continent to rise out of the Pacific tomorrow, it would only defer the evil day. No one could say that the human race, ultimately, would be the better for it . . . an urgent need of the hour would seem to be, not more land to cultivate, but some change for the better in our ideas. As it is, we are having no manner of success in producing a happy or great people.

Sincerely,
Judge John Waldo

Kam Wah Chung letters
1892-1905

Oregon experienced a significant influx of Chinese laborers from the 1850s onward, and sizeable "Chinatowns" were located in such places as Astoria, Portland, Salem, Albany, Jacksonville, Klamath Falls, John Day, Baker City, Pendleton, Auburn, and Sumpter. In 1890, for example, over five thousand Chinese resided in the city of Portland. Oregon place names attest to the role Chinese (largely Cantonese speakers from southern China) played in the mining and railroad industries. Several Oregon locations designate hills or buttes as "China Hat." There are "China ditches" in southern, central, and eastern Oregon which were constructed to carry the water for hydraulic gold mining. "China walls" may be found in the Willamette Valley and elsewhere that were built as Chinese removed and stacked stones from potential farmland. So-called "coolies" also worked in salmon-packing plants, lumber mills, woolen mills, and in many other industries. Many well-to-do Oregonians employed Chinese domestics, as evidenced by several references to Chinese cooks and house servants in the letters and diaries contained in this volume.

But these exterior signs of the presence of Chinese men in Oregon (various federal and local laws prevented Chinese women from joining male relatives) provide virtually no insight into the interior lives of those who found themselves in the Land of Gum San, the "Gold Mountain." The following four letters written in Chinese were discovered in the 1970s in John Day when the City of John Day inherited the old Kam Wah Chung Mercantile Store. Recovered from the cool dark rooms that are even today redolent of medicinal herbs and opium smoke, these letters shed unexpected and welcome light on one of Oregon's most maligned yet influential minorities.

Now a small museum, the Kam Wah Chung was once the center of economic, social, and cultural life for the region's many Chinese from the late gold rush period to the 1940s. For more than five decades the store was owned and operated by two of Oregon's most well known and respected Chinese: herbalist Ing Hay was known as the "China Doctor" and treated Chinese as well as whites; his partner Lung On was well educated, and, when he did not gamble away the store's profits, was an enterprising businessman. Lung On frequently helped customers write letters home to China. (See *Varieties of Hope* of the Oregon Literature Series for more detail about and photographs of both men.) With the exception of the letter from the anonymous Chinese miner to his wife, translated by Chia-Lin Chen, the following letters have been newly translated by Jodi Varon and Ying-Ju Chen.—S.A.

The Invisible Men of Gold Mountain

FOUR CHINESE VOICES

The Kam Wah Chung Co.
John Day, Oregon
18??

My Beloved Wife,

It has been several autumns now since your dull husband left you for a far remote alien land. Thanks to my hearty body I am all right. Therefore stop your embroidered worries for me. Yesterday I received another of your letters. I could not keep the tears from running down my cheeks when thinking about the miserable and needy circumstances of our home, and thinking back to the time of our separation.

Because of our destitution I went out to try to make a living. Who could know that the Fate is always opposite to man's design. Because I can get no gold, I am detained in this secluded corner of a strange land. Furthermore, my beauty, you are implicated in an endless misfortune. I wish this paper would console you a little. This is all I can do for now.

Anonymous Miner

May 18, 1904

Kam Wah Chung
John Day, Oregon

Dear Lung On,
I'm sending this letter especially to you. As soon as you return to this city you should have money and the letter returned to you. The reason is when I first returned to this place someone was supposed to give something back, but he didn't promise, he only delayed the dates. I don't know why he cannot get every item on hand. We are all suffering from the barbarian's serious robbery; we Chinese suffered at the gold mine during several incidents and indirectly they took between $200 and $300. The men at the mine don't have the guts

to protest but several days in a row they have gathered to discuss what to do. We Chinese cannot do anything about it. I am not familiar with the local green shirts (police) and no one dares talk to officials about the robbery, so the miners just let it go. Besides, the barbarians here don't take care of us because no one can communicate in the barbarian's language. We would like to collect our resources to ask you, brother, to contribute your power to save the miners from their predicament. It is a very difficult matter because no one dares to do it and money is too dear. There is fear that the situation here will spread to another Chinese camp and there will be a series of violent chain reactions.

I want to borrow money from you, Lung On, and from the store as soon as possible so that some day when we see each other there will be good face between us. Because the entrance to our mine was damaged by water the gold is unattainable. The work wasn't lucky. It is so cold.

Happiness cannot be enjoyed twice but disasters never come alone. My partner Yen-teh gambled away several thousand dollars in gold in Baker City and that's why I don't have your money. I'm so ashamed that I have no place to hide. Some day when we meet I won't even know what to say to you.

I'm glad that your store earns more profit; it's not like my store which always loses money. It is a venture without potential. I hope you will think and evaluate, then make a decision. Wait another month and I will return the money without eating my words.

I thank you so much.

> Sincerely
> *Tong Yick Chuen Co.*

P.S. Yesterday on the 17th Li Chin's mine was also robbed by barbarians. I still don't know why no one stands up to sue.

P.S. Yesterday the barbarians returned every item to my store. It's all because of your favor to me.

I wish you wealth.

Lung On, the recipient of this letter

Portland, Oregon
June 6, 1905

Kam Wah Chung Co.
John Day, Oregon

Dear Ing Hay,

I am writing to extend my compliments and congratulations, sir.

I have heard about your medical skills for a long time and know you are very capable, with much knowledge at hand. Your medical practice and your kindness heal the world around you. I am also an herbalist, but I'm ashamed of my limitations and regret that I cannot learn from you.

Portland is having a festival soon and I happened to meet a gentleman who traveled here to celebrate. His son's eyes ached and he came to my store for some medicine. This man happened to know a barbarian who claimed he had been treated several years ago for arthritis in his legs. The symptoms started in the main tendons at the waist and traveled all the way down the legs to the ankles. When he had cramps he couldn't bear the pain. After receiving your treatment, which he said included cleansing, moxibustion, and taking herbs, he reported that you pierced his legs with a needle and bled five places for him. The pain in his ankles stopped immediately and afterwards he made a full recovery.

Ing Hay, the recipient of this letter

Now my partner has also contracted these symptoms. For three or four months his legs have been dry and wasted. When lying down he is comfortable, but if he moves at all his toes get cold and numb. The pain in his tendons spreads up from the ankles and when he has cramps on the outside of his left leg the pain is unbearable. You see, his problems are the same as those described by the barbarian, and I think, sir, you must be able to cure him.

I would like to invite you to come to Portland to enjoy our festival and to treat my partner. To show my gratitude, I will cover your round trip traveling expense and if you would like additional compensation, just ask. Please give me a reply. It would be best if you could come here; however, if you can't take the time to leave John Day, please draw a diagram to show me where to pierce with the needle and also enclose the herbal prescription and your bill. If you cannot come, please send word.

Words wishing you good fortune and prosperity never end.

Lao Chi-Kwang
Herbalist

February 4, 18??

Kam Wah Chung Co.
John Day, Oregon

Dear Lung On,
I'm shocked by the message from Lung-On that our friend, Mr. Lin, was shot and killed by a barbaric American. Grief came with that news. What a miserable act!

I've enclosed $30 in this letter to be used for the emergency. It's too bad my fate has suffered a setback, though my life has never been easy. I don't have much money.

I hope Mr. Lin finds peace under this earth. I feel sorry for him and wish I could have repaid him for all his kindness. When you receive the money, I'll feel a lot better.

I bow to you and wish you all well,

Kwang-chi

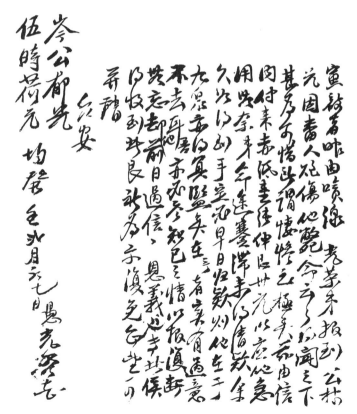

Original of letter from Kwang-chi

Henry Krieser
Miller
1827-1916

Henry Krieser Miller was German-born and, like another German immigrant with humble beginnings, John Jacob Astor, was to make a fortune in his adopted country of America. With a business acumen that some attributed to shrewdness, meanness, and parsimony, the man who began his career as Henry Krieser the meat-cutter who owned nothing became Henry Krieser Miller the rancher who owned over one million acres in five states. The Miller and Lux Ranch became the largest in the United States. In Oregon, Henry Miller constantly monitored his holdings on the Malheur (the "L.F." brand) and in Harney Valley (the "S Wrench" brand). His ranch managers were accustomed to his excruciatingly detailed letters of instruction. It was hard to ignore the advice of a man like Henry Krieser Miller who started from scratch to amass holdings worth about fifty million dollars and who was determined to survive the severe economic depression that began in 1893.

The following is one of Miller's letters to W.E. Hayes, his resident manager, published in *Tales of the I.O.N. Country* (1988). The original is housed in the Special Collections, Knight Library, University of Oregon.—S.A.

Running a Tighter Ranch in Hard Times

A BOSS'S LETTER TO HIS MANAGER IN HARNEY COUNTY

Miller and Lux
508 California St.
San Francisco
November 14, 1894

To: Mr. W. E. Hayes
Burns, Oregon

Dear Sir:

During my trip to the ranches and different camps I found many shortcomings. Also a lack of judgement as to supplying articles most needed.

The separate table is too expensive for us to keep up. Therefore your family will hereafter eat at the second table set by the cook instead of having meals prepared at your home. This applies as well to Mr. Jones and I expect this to go into effect immediately. If the cook objects to the change, he can quit. I also request that the milk be boiled for the coffee and also that not more than one kind of meat be put on the table at one time and only one kind of fruit. Everything to be well cooked and served and nothing stale need be used. I expect the cook to make hash out of the soup meat and stew out of fresh meat. Also more light bread instead of biscuits and also corn bread for the table.

When a camp outfit returns from a trip I want the provisions that may be brought back to be used at once and not allowed to stand in the wagon.

In two different camps I found that our tools had been carried away and thus became useless from neglect, those places being Silvies and Indian Creek.

There is no need of being constantly engaged at home. There is not enough bookkeeping to keep you busy and you should make time to go to the different camps and places belonging to us, to see what supplies and merchandise are needed and you should attend to the ordering instead of Mr. Jones. He does not give the matter proper attention and therefore we are the loosers.

As the barn at the Island (Ranch) will not be covered this winter I want only the most necessary repairs made on the roof and all shingles and shakes sent to where they are needed for making shelter for our stock. There are a great many ways in which you could serve us outside of your clerical work. The firm pays more promptly than any one else and when men are discharged from other places they can well afford to wait a day or two until your return.

From this day on, no family is to be paid over $30.00 per month where they have children and no man is to bring his wife as a boarder as was done this summer at White Horse. I have written Mr. Jones a long letter stating reductions I wanted made, following of which is a list: Chas. Cronin is to work for $30.00 per month until haying time; Jas. Brandon $30.00 per month; J. C. Foley to be put in charge of the Island to do the blacksmith work and to be given such general supervision as will make him fully earn $50.00 per month; same applies also to Mr. Simmons. Mr. Beatty's wages reduced to $40.00 from the time haying ceased. Griffens wages reduced to $40.00 to take effect 15th of this month; Tremply reduced to $30.00 and Walter Dahl to $30.00. Ordinary *vaqueros* shall work this winter for $25.00 and boys and inexperienced men accordingly. If this is not satisfactory to above named men they may quit.

I am thoroughly convinced that Mr. Johnson, who does the blacksmithing, does not give us full value for the money he gets and we can do without him.

I want the stableman to sack that charcoal which is in one of the stalls where the stud horses are kept, and to put some away in some dry place.

Please send me a statement of amount of hay put up for us by contract, that is number of tons and price paid for same per ton. Also number of shares received as our portion. Also statement of what the hay cost that was put up by our own men.

I have not yet seen the statement as to number of cattle, horses, colts, etc., which we can suppose to be correct estimate. Please send it, giving full details as to where stock is located, etc., as well as different class of stock. This statement is to go before the Referees and Probate Court as my showing of what the Oregon Property consists of. Send them at once .. . .

> Yours Truly,
> *Henry Miller*

P.S.: In your statement I want included all branded stock. Also beef cattle branded exclusive of stock cattle.

Charles C. Lewis
ca. 1853-?

Charles C. Lewis and his twelve-year-old son, Don, were charter members of the Mazama Club when it was organized in 1894. Unlike its predecessor, the Alpine Club, which included "arm chair adventurers" as well as amateur botanists and geologists, the Mazama Club comprised bona fide mountaineers who actually scaled mountains such as Mount Hood in order to become members. (The word *Mazama* is from the Spanish word for *mountain goat*. The name *Mount Mazama* originated as a result of the Mazama Club's avid interest in preserving the Crater Lake caldera as a national park. Mount Mazama describes the prehistoric volcanic peak that collapsed in a cataclysmic eruption about 6,600 years ago.)

William Gladstone Steel, an early-day advocate for the founding of a national park at Crater Lake, was the Mazama's first president. He was elected in July of 1894, after he and 144 aspiring members reached the snow-blown summit of Mount Hood. They voted for club officers on the spot. At least thirty women were among the group. These women, however, were not the first Euro-American females to make a successful ascent; in 1867, Mary Robinson Gilkey and Fanny Case reached the summit and disproved the claim of a Portland surveyor who publicly stated that Mount Hood was "far too steep" for any *mere* woman to climb.

The following excerpts are about an 1895 Oregon mountain-climbing expedition initiated by C.C. Lewis, then a printer and professional photographer living in Monmouth. For reasons described in his letter, Lewis and a number of friends, including several "young ladies," set out to scale Mount Jefferson. Lewis wrote his mother a 26-page letter and obviously relished telling his tale.

Archaeological evidence suggests that both male and female Native Americans also scaled several peaks of the Cascade Range on vision quests.—S.A.

The Mazamas Ascend Mt. Jefferson

A POLK COUNTY ADVENTURE IN EQUALITY

Monmouth, Oregon
August 18, 1895

My Dear Mother:

If you can stand my new style of paper, I will try to tell you *briefly* something of our trip to Mt. Jefferson. The "Mazama Club" which we organized on Mt. Hood a year ago formed a scheme of carrying messages by the aid of Heliographs (which reflect sun light by mirrors the ordinary telegraph code), from one of these high peaks to the other, and the original scheme was to send a message from British Columbia to Old Mexico and return.

The main body of the Club met at Mt. Adams in Washington, but . . . it was necessary for parties to go to all the other high peaks *and be there on the day fixed—July 10th*. I was to form a party and take Mt. Jefferson as one link in the chain.

Mr. Burford of Salem, Mr. Kirby, also of Salem, Prof. Hutchinson and Mr. W. H. Hawley (both were at Mt . Hood last year). So far there were no ladies and but one team.

We knew it would be a hard trip but you know ladies go into the mountains here as well as men and it is much pleasanter to have them along. July 3rd three ladies were going: Mrs. Cooper and step-daughter—the wife and daughter of the President and principal owner of the bank, and Miss Essie Robinson, the Postmistress at Independence. Then Miss Ella Fisher and Miss Ella Wasson concluded to go, too. I don't know what she did to get ready but both girls were on hand at 6:30 o'clock the next morning ready to start. You see *some* girls can start on short notice,—and "get thru" when they *do* start.

In the morning—the 4th—we went to Independence and joined the others—12 altogether now. The second day we struck into the foot-hills and began to ascend into the mountains.

On the way up we found an old man who has made hunting his business nearly all his life. place was ten miles north of Fish Lake . . . beyond that there was not trail of any sort. He said we could not even get pack animals through that way for he had tried it. He had never been over to the Mountain and did not know how far it was.

Here our wagons came up to where we were talking and he discovered the ladies. "What," he said, "you haven't got women with you! You might as well turn right around . . . you can never get them women there." We told him he was not acquainted with Polk County girls.

On Saturday Noon, our third day out, we began to discover that if we reached the Mountain on the 10th, we had not a moment to lose on the way. We held a "council of war". Some years ago the Oregon Pacific Railroad had been in there and done a lot of grading and built some track in order to hold their "right of way" to the Pass through the mountains. They had built a wagon road some way in towards Mt. Jefferson to their "camp". we were told we could save over 20 miles by going this way. This was on Sunday—the 10th was Wednesday, distances and difficulties had increased wonderfully as we progressed, and it was determined that three of us should go across direct from Fish Lake—afoot—while the others were round via the railroad camps with the teams and come to the mountain later, where we would meet again.

We reached the "timber line" on Mt. Jefferson at noon on the 10th—just in time and not a moment to spare. But after all this effort and hard work we were doomed to disappointment and had nothing for it but the consciousness of having done *our* part and having conquered *every* obstacle we met. For several days the atmosphere had been thickening with smoke from fires somewhere. We hurried on up the Mountain hoping that we would still be able to see the other mountains and "flash" our messages from their lofty tops. Only one of the "peaks" in sights was the "Three Sisters" and they but *very* dimly. Set up the Heliograph and "called" but obtained no response. We have heard since there was no one there if it had been clear.

Of course we did not know when the others would reach the Mountain— we were to stay till they came—and after we found how far and rough it was, it began to be questionable whether they would reach it at all. Provisions were getting low, it was several days farther from a fresh supply than we expected. Friday we decided it would not be safe to wait longer—our appetites were *increasing* to something frightful to contemplate. We went knowing only that if we kept on south we would strike the road that crosses the range *somewhere*, probably within three or four days, knowing too, that the rest of our party were in these mountains *somewhere*—but where?

We were startled by an unusual sound, the bleating of sheep. Soon came to the two herders watching them, the first humans we had seen for nearly a week. Our first question was whether they had seen or heard of any one else in that region. "Yes," they told us . . . we knew they were our people. They had gone up the canyon we were then in. All our weariness was forgotten in a moment.

Prof. Hutchinson had the old "bull dog" revolver . . . he fired a shot. Again we strained our ears to listen as the echoes came rolling back. I really don't know how high I jumped—for with these echoes came the shouts that were sweeter than any music to me. They were far across the canyon, but plain and distinct, and above them all I could hear Don's voice, which told me he was well and all right. I don't believe that old Mountain has heard such a "whooping" since the Indians roamed around it. In ordinary life, people can form no idea of the feelings that bind people together on a trip like this, and especially in our circumstances. We shook hands *several* times all around—we did *not quite* hug them but felt like it. We had much to tell on both sides and much to plan for, before us.

Two of the boys went ahead to find a way they could get through. Here the girls showed they were just as good as men on such a trip. Of course they had long ago discarded long dresses and wore mountain suits. They each took a horse and did a man's part in leading them over logs and rocks—it is the very *hardest* kind of work to lead a horse under such circumstances. They had to guard against letting them go where the packs would be torn off by trees, and they were constantly stumbling—several times they fell down taking the girls with them.

There was snow all around us . . . we were all *extremely tired* and yet everybody was jolly and happy. We all felt that tomorrow the object of all this effort would be accomplished, though the *real climb* was to come. On the very "*tiptop*" of the Mountain are a couple of "pinnacles" . . . over 300 feet and are considered insurmountable. I had a secret desire to be the first to plant my feet on the *very* highest point and take some pictures of it. we postponed the attempt; everything is straight up and down. Possibly later in the season when the snow is off. The girls all displayed the same "pluck" and endurance that had characterized them all the way through.

We have every reason to believe *confidently* that our girls were the *first* women to *ever* reach the top. When we gathered around the camp fire that night, it was a *weary* lot but triumphant and happy. We had accomplished our object, and without any mishaps or accidents that amounted to anything. The girls particularly had done what the old mountaineers declared *impossible*—and enjoyed it just as well as men. through *everything*, all were jolly, every one was happy and did their part.

With best love,

C. C. Lewis

Loye Miller
1874-1970

Miller is on the right. His colleague, John Merriam, is on the left, standing.

Dr. Loye Miller was a member of an 1899 University of California scientific expedition that explored the John Day Basin—the same fossil-rich region made famous by Thomas Condon some forty years earlier. Acting as the expedition's photographer and expert on birds and mammals, Dr. Miller kept a detailed personal journal in which he recorded impressions, reactions, and observations. Unlike the writings left by Thomas Condon, or the official report of the same expedition compiled by its leader, Dr. John C. Merriam, Miller's journal reveals his immediate pleasure in the act of scientific discovery and his very human feelings: "I came to like little Sorex," he wrote on May 24, describing the sorrel pony he rode over dry and dusty country. " [He is]. . . a spunky little chap with lots of vim." As Miller caught birds and bats and lugged his bulky camera up talus slopes or down into box canyons, he pondered the remains of ancient species and his own place in the vast scheme of things.

Dr. Loye Miller was to have a long career of scientific distinction before dying at age ninety-six. The following selections are taken from Miller's diary that appeared in *Bulletin* No. 19 of the Museum of Natural History, University of Oregon (1972).— S.A.

A Naturalist on Bridge Creek Digs All Day, Then Dreams

Sunday, May 21, 1899. Portland

Portland a very beautiful place for location and buildings. Streets very narrow.

Train for Dalles at 2:10 beautiful ride up river but could not snap the places quick enough. Multnomah falls 800 ft. down Canyon side. Bridal veil slightly less. Timber grand. Crags and pallisades all along of imposing grandure. Came into The Dalles in a Sunday Deutscher picnic. Sons of Herman having a roaring time. Put up at Umatilla House—(!!!)

Monday, May 22. The Dalles

Started rustling rest of outfit. Team sent for out in country 18 miles. Finished up groceries in morning and go to lunch at 12:20. Davis has decided to go and is rustling like a good fellow. He is quiet and reliable man who knows what he is talking about, well acquainted with fossil fields and knows much about the different forms and systems.

The Dalles is a great town. The first impression one gets at the depot is somewhat relieved by a better acquaintance. The business is in good condition. Some excellent merchantile houses to be found and wide variety of supplies. Town is supported by back country producing wool and wheat, hides, etc. Immense ware houses of wool.

Numbers of Wasco and Warm Springs indians on the streets in fantastic red, yellow, and green blankets. They come in along the Columbia for the Salmon season. The language with the Whites is Chinook and among themselves their own dialects.

Wednesday, May 24. The Dalles

Calkins came at 11:40 last night. Left his baggage in Portland (!!).

The birds I have observed are not rare so far. Western King bird, Bullocks orioles and robins singing in the maples and poplars. The robins doubtless build here as they are in full song. Meadow larks are heard outside the town. From my window in the early morning I heard this fine fellow across the river. A fine clear greeting from the sister state, by one of her country folk. A cheery "Goodmorning" coming faintly across the wide Columbia. . . . A beautiful and majestic river this, which one must come to love deeply if he lives long in its

presence. Crows have been seen more or less common along the river. A Lewis' wood pecker was seen from the train as we came up from Portland. Magpies are said to be very abundant out in the wooded country of the Jno. Day. I await with interest the acquaintance with the small birds of the wooded canyons vireos, warblers, and finches.

We hope soon to bid adieu to the Umatilla house and its imprepossessing ways and smells, table cloths and penny wall paper. Out in the country we will rough it but without any pretense of better.

The topography is remarkably like that in Arizona. The rugged lava formations resemble those scarred buttes and peaks of the Arizona country.

Got under way at 3:15 p.m. The cavalcade files out with Dr. and me in the saddles. Calkins staid to get baggage and come later in evening. Dr. rode the black bone-yard, I the little sorrel that I called Sorex on account of his diminitive size.

We reached 8 mile creek at 6:06 and outspanned. Supper of bacon, spuds, tongue gravy, and pears. Camp stoves worked finely, economical of wood and patience. The country passed over was very dry and dusty, cut up by freight teams. Crossed 2 large creeks of good water. I came to like little Sorex as a spunky little chap with lots of vim.

Thursday, May 25. Eight Mile

Calkins came at 10:00 and we *started*? The grey mare went four feet and flew back, that was the furthest she went. We sawed and see-sawed forward and back but never a go. We tried the black-Hyparion, but she was not used to pulling. An interested indian insisted on putting in his cayuse about as large as a jack rabbit. It plunged along half way up the hill and flunked so we had to take it out and back down again. The little brute could almost crawl under the wagon tongue.

We finally got all together at 3:15 and made Nansene House (9 miles) in time to camp. All pretty well tired out with the worry and delay. The country became even more barren and rocky. Numbers of yellow headed spermophyle were seen along the road living in the rocks. Their sustenance is probably the seed of the scant grass that is found on the hillside for a season. The almost total absence of Artemisia or other brush on the hills is remarkable.

After enjoyable supper, stories around the camp fire passed the time quickly until time to roll into our blankets on the hard floor of an old deserted shack the sole inhabitants of which were a nest of young Say's Pewees in full plumage.

Friday, May 26. Nansene

During the afternoon we passed through some typical "hog wallow" land. The most niggardly soil I ever saw. Large, regularly placed mounds of fifteen feet in diameter the intervening hollows stoney and barren. From the hill top above the Deschutes River the most remarkable view of lava formation was to be seen. The junction of White river gave rise to falls of 100 ft.

Tuesday, May 30. Cherry Creek Hill

Slept rather poorly last night seemed to have gotten my head down into a hollow.

First bird note I noticed was peculiar metallic clink like that of *Guiraca cerulaca* somewhat. Investigation revealed a fine specimen of Evening Grossbeak feeding in the Juniper trees. A number of small flocks were observed later in the morning. This is an interesting acquaintance which I hope to improve. Lewis' Woodpecker was also observed again.

Wednesday, May 31. Bridge Creek

Passed good night in hayloft with Mr. H. and Davis. Raining lightly when we awoke snoozed until 7:30 then came down to breakfast. Still raining no signs of stopping. Got under way about 10:15 though there was slight sprinkle. Down Cherry Creek a mile or two to the junction with the John Day River then up the river to the mouth of Bridge Creek. Where we lunched at 1:30. On the way up the river we met the mail cart going to Antelope and held him up long enough to post our letters.

The fault was shown in the opposite side of the river gorge. The sedimentary rock stratum had slipped and the intervening fissure had been filled by a dyke. Up Bridge creek we were struck most forcibly by the absence of bridges and frequency of crossings. Little Kid-Sorex wet my shoes thoroughly floundering through. The lower part of the canyon was very steep and rugged but in the upper part the floor was more level and broad, the hills lower and rounded. We made camp at 4:10 in the midst of the fossil region of Bridge creek.

Thursday, June 1. Bridge Creek Beds Junction with Bear Creek
Several ranches along the creek grow large fields of alfalfa and some few fruit trees. On the east slope high sage scrub nearly conceals our tents. Higher up the sides are the lava capped hills looking like enormous fortifications. Under the lava are the sedimentary deposits in which the fossils occur. The trees and sage offer refuge for numerous birds.

Friday, June 2. Bridge Creek Beds
Went to the fossil beds with Mr. Hatch—at 1:00 worked all afternoon but found only chips. Dr. and Davis came at 4:30 so we dug on two skulls that were found the day before. Rock was extremely tough and refractory—showing metamorphosis around the bone where calcium salts have been given off from the bones.

Above the fossil deposits the great lava cliffs rise in immense terraces, scarred and seamed. Turned in at 8:30.

Monday, June 5. Bridge Creek Beds
Howling wind all morning. No good to hunt so loaded shells and cleaned up. In P.M. went to dig on *Entelodon* skull. Took some views of the beds. Worked all afternoon with pick and did not get the head out   came home pretty late and set traps along the creek. Back to camp at 7:00 and had to get supper as Davis was still out. Dreamed last night of Bertha Holmes as a girl of 5, in Japanese costume. Prettiest picture one could wish. I made friends with her and carried her off as my partner at games and at table.

Friday, June 9. Bridge Creek Beds
Set no traps yesterday thinking we would start today. Work seems plentiful on the skull. Dr. thinks it as fine as any specimen of the kind known.

Started out for the hills at 6:45. Up and up above the valley, above the fossil beds into the lava terraces among the junipers. Beautiful old trees rugged and grizzly sentinels around the walls they keep their everlasting watch over the remains of those animals of another world that have lain burried while generation after generation of these old prophets, each perhaps a thousand years, has sprung up and passed away at the post of their duty. Time is lost and years are but the pulse beat.

Cornelia Bernard Knox Watson
1864-1930

Cornelia Bernard Knox Watson spent most of her life in Oregon's remote, mile-high city—Lakeview. After losing two children and her first husband, Cornelia turned increasingly to photography. Beginning in the 1890s and continuing for several decades, she operated her studio in Lakeview. She captured images of local families, public and private occasions, and town and country every-day life in her beloved Chewaucan Valley. Her striking portraits of local Paiutes are reminiscent of the photographs of Col. Lee Morehouse, a well-known Pendleton photographer. She also took pictures of cowboys, sheepshearers, and many other Chewaucan Valley subjects. When Lakeview burned in 1900, Cornelia hauled by mule her heavy 4x5 camera and other equipment to a ridge above town. After taking and developing pictures all day, she nursed burn victims and billeted survivors in her studio throughout the night. The *Oregonian* bought her photos of the charred remains of Lakeview.

In the manner of many creative women, Cornelia Bernard Knox Watson knew what it meant to meet the demands of traditional "womanly" roles while pursuing a career as an artist and professional. Few of her photographs have been collected. Her unpublished diary, from which the following is taken, was photocopied by the Schminck Museum in Lakeview. The original diary burned in a house fire a few weeks after the copy was made. In an effort to preserve the work of this virtually unknown woman artist and photographer, the Schminck House and Lake County Museum are now seeking Knox Watson photographs.—S.A.

Chief Lakeview John and wife Maggie, photograph by Cornelia Knox Watson, 1901

The Photographer Who Saw Lakeview Burn Makes Her New Year's Resolution

February 4, 1900

If my father had given this book to me on the first of the year I might have written in it all my good resolutions but being now Feb. 4th I feel as if they are hardly worth recording. At present my mightiest resolution is to undertake to write a line in this each remaining day of the year, and for one somewhat lacking in continuity that is a formidable task.

1900—years ago, nearly twenty I think, four of us were looking forward to 1900 and figuring out our ages for this year, wondering how old we would seem at this time and as to what changes would have come to us. We were all good friends and are yet, but one has crossed the river—marriage, motherhood, and death were her portion. She must know what comes after but though the remaining three of us may meet and discuss past and present experiences there is no message from her. Of the other two, one is married has her husband, children and a happy home. The other has devoted her life to the care of two orphan children making a home for them. As to myself unexpected experiences came and while the suffering or pleasure that has fallen to me has filled my little existence the world has not been greatly affected thereby. One little being is of such small consequence here and grows still less when we remember that "all who tread the Earth are but a handful to the tribes that slumber in its bosom." One can almost sink in ones own insignificance, and yet when that feeling comes on it is good to remember that all are born to this existence in the same way—one man's coming is no more through his choice than another man's, but when we get here we have the feeling that we can kick or keep still just as we like. I rather like the plan of the optimist frog in the can of milk—the one that kept kicking until he had a little pat of butter to sit on. Life at the longest will be very short and a person of any courage should be able to brave it through whether it seems to him good or bad.

Anna Steinhoff
1885-1955

Anna Steinhoff and her younger sister Millie were born in Nebraska and lived with their parents on family property near Sherwood, Oregon, until they were unable to resist the promise of "FREE Government Land." Like thousands of would-be homesteaders who came to the Oregon desert between 1910 and 1912, the Steinhoff sisters imagined that the new lands granted by the Enlarged Homestead Act in 320-acre parcels could be converted into wheat fields and orchards, much as they had been in Washington state's Palouse country. Single women were entitled to claim their own piece of "agricultural paradise" around Christmas Lake or Fort Rock. Owning property which could either be farmed or sold later at a profit attracted independent females like Anna and Millie Steinhoff to attempt the difficult life of a homesteader.

However, railroad promoters luring settlers to the fertility of central Oregon's volcanic ash soils failed to mention low annual precipitation rates and a high altitude. The cold high desert made profitable farming almost impossible. Like hundreds of others, Steinhoff eventually left her property, but retained local ownership until the 1960s. She married a fellow-homesteader, Frank Anderson, and moved to Portland, where they raised their family. Steinhoff's unpublished diary, the source of the following selection, is owned by Richard Anderson, her son. Alvin, who appears in the diary, remains unidentifiable.—S.A.

Sage, Jackrabbits, Infant Death
THE LAST SETTLERS ON A HIGH DESERT HOMESTEAD

Monday, November 7, 1910

About seven o'clock we left the hotel and took the stage for Christmas Lake Valley. Stopped at Lake and View Point while they looked over the mail. It was about seven o'clock and was dark when we reached our corner. Alvin met us there and helped us carry our grips, a quilt, one length of stove pipe, and a broom, to our cabins 1 ½ miles from there. The shacks were done but nothing in them. Alvin had opened our packing box and put up the cook stove. Millie took the things out of the box and made the beds which were only put on the floor. In the meantime I got supper. Fried some bacon, boiled potatoes, and baked biscuits. We put a board over a nail-keg which answered for a table. We were very tired and hungry so we enjoyed our supper and were soon asleep.

Thursday, November 10

I spent some time grubbing sage brush and after noon we went to Mr. Beckett's after a saw and shovel. He said he would take us to Lake next day to get household supplies.

Friday, November 11

As it was raining and snowing we did not expect to go to Lake, so we were busy sawing up scraps of boards for shelves etc. At 11:30 Mr. Beckett drove up. We put on our coats and shawls and each took a bean sandwich and started for Lake. The wagon was covered but it was too small so we were right in the rain. Mr. Beckett shot several rabbits on the way and at the Lake Mr. Hillary gave us some ducks. We stopped at Lake only long enough to get warm and buy a can of oil and some sugar. While there it stopped snowing. On the way home we stopped at A.W. Long's to get hay to fill our straw ticks. Shot more rabbits and reached home about 6:30.

Monday, December 5

Did nothing important today. Emptied the buckets of dirt as Millie dug them and in the afternoon chopped wood and burned some weeds. About four o'clock Alvin left for the mail box. A little later we discovered that we needed water so

Millie and I went to Mr. Beckett's for some. He gave us a nice big rabbit. It got so dark before we reached home that we could scarcely see our way. Alvin came to meet us.

Friday, December 23

Got up at about 6:30. Set the bread and got breakfast. Then I went out to cut sage. At about 10:30 a.m. Mr. Weeks came after one of us to go to Buchanan's, Mrs. B. being sick. I quickly changed my clothes and went. I reached B.'s at 1:30 p.m. Mrs. B. was quite sick. An hour later a baby boy was born. Mrs. Remington and Mrs. Gooch washed and dressed him and I helped wherever I could. She had no shirts for the baby so we had to wrap him up until evening when we made him a shirt out of some of his mother's old ones. All went well. The doctor came at about 10:30 p.m. Had supper and then gave her the necessary attentions. Mrs. Remington stayed with me. We were busy until two o'clock. Stayed up all night.

Sunday, December 25

Was busy all day doing up the work and waiting on Mrs. B. and the baby. Cooked a chicken and made mince pies for dinner.

Monday, December 26

Did up the work as usual. Had to get dinner for the stage driver. Helped Mrs. B. dress the baby and waited on her. After supper I wrote letters until about 10:30. The baby was crying so I took him to quiet him and found that he had ruptured the navel and was bleeding. Then I helped Mrs. B. dress him and fed him and put him to sleep. Then they insisted that I should go to bed. That was at 12:30 a.m. About an hour later Mr. B. called me again. The baby was bleeding terribly. I helped them to put on a dressing of flour & alum and then took him to the stove to get warm. The sight of the blood and his pitiful crying was too much for me and I got sick. Handed the baby to Mr. B. and I went outdoors. When I came back the baby was sleeping and also Mrs. B. I sat down near the stove and watched the baby. The blood was flowing from him faster than ever and at about 2:30 his breath begun to come very slowly. Mr. B. handed him back to me, and anxiously watched until life had left. Then I put the little corpse on a chair and waited until day-light before washing him. Mr. B. went after some of the neighbors and in the meantime I washed the baby and put him into the other house. Mrs. Gooch came about nine o'clock. Then about noon Millie and Alvin came. Did some sewing for the baby and whatever else we could. Mrs. Gooch stayed all night with us.

Alice Day Pratt
1872-1963

Alice Day Pratt, an unmarried school teacher who came
to central Oregon in 1911, incorporated numerous
extended quotations from her personal journals in her
first book, *A Homesteader's Portfolio* (1922). After
teaching a few years in the towns of Post and Prineville,
Pratt concentrated on her writing and the hard, solitary
work needed to improve her homestead. "In this
primitive existence one learns not to deplore the
necessity for hard labor. . . ." On the contrary, she
learned to relish working from dawn to dusk treasuring
"three years of one's own—infinite space in which to
move, infinite freedom in which to think. . . ." She
wrote of her philosophy, her occasional loneliness, her
beloved horse, her chickens, and the enduring thrill of a
wild, open Oregon landscape. She experienced
ostracization as well as a profound sense of belonging.
Her presence and that of other homesteaders was
greatly resented by large ranch owners.

After eighteen years, she left Oregon, hoping to return
one day, but she spent the rest of her life in the vicinity
of Niagara Falls, New York, teaching school and
continuing to write. After *A Homesteader's Portfolio*, she
concentrated on books for younger readers. She never
forgot her old friends in Post, who claimed that Alice
Day Pratt's heart remained in central Oregon. Even
long years after her departure, Oregon themes and
experiences recurred in all her writing. The following
selection is taken from a new edition of *A Homesteader's
Portfolio* (1993). (Also see *Varieties of Hope* of the
Oregon Literature Series.)—S.A.

This Quiet and Harmonious State Is All in Turmoil
A TEACHER'S DIARY

ca. 1912

For a thousand years, presumably, this vast plateau which is now my home has been covered with sagebrush and bunch grass and sprinkled with juniper trees, and has supported a normal population of jack rabbits and sage rats. Then suddenly comes man with his alien stock, his dogs and his cats, his new and succulent crops, with their admixture of weed seeds and germs of insect life. And, lo, this quiet and harmonious state of nature is all in turmoil.

Sage and bunch grass give place to wheat and oats and varied vegetables. Strange creatures wander upon the ancient hills. The coyote tribe samples young lamb and thereupon begins to wax and grow fat and incidentally to prepare the way for its own extermination. Hawks become delirious over the chicken yards and neglect the young rabbits and sage rats. Rabbits and sage rats, largely relieved from the depredations of their ancient enemies, and suddenly supplied with new and luscious herbage in unlimited quantity, flourish and multiply beyond all reason.

Rabbits have become what is termed "a fearful pest" to the farmer. In my own case they ate one sixth of my crop last year, this year one third. I held converse with myself and decided that I was showing myself unfit in the struggle for existence. I bought a "twenty-two" and set about defending my rights.

The rabbits were very tame. That was the worst of it; they did not fear me. I had no trouble in knocking a few over. They looked surprised, were still a moment, then rolled over in convulsions and were still forever. It was a new and gruesome experience—being responsible for that. But in one case I broke a leg. This little victim also looked surprised and puzzled. He hopped a few paces, stopped and examined himself, and then hopped away into the brush, the ruined limb flopping and dangling behind him. I tried, but was unable to find him, to save him from the cruel fate I had visited upon him. In another instance, I broke a back. The victim tried to drag himself off the field, pawing desperately, his hind quarters entirely paralyzed. When I approached to end his sufferings with a charge of shot, he regarded me with bulging eyeballs and the trembling of hopeless terror. And I? I was filled with horror and amazement at the thing that I had done. I shall remember those two rabbits as long as life is mine. Still I use poison, a remedy that is swift and deadly, and merciful chiefly to myself.

Essie McGuire
1894-1979

Essie McGuire had a brief but memorable teaching career in the one-room school at Trail Crossing Flat near Redmond in 1914. McGuire wrote numerous informative and entertaining letters home to her mother during the single year in her life she was to "school marm." The colorful wild West of central Oregon in many ways contrasted with Portland-bred McGuire's former life.

Her letter about the Crook County fair, then called the Potato Show, casts one particular "cow boy"—the father of two of her little pupils—in a most romantic light. Even so, McGuire spent the rest of her life in the more sedate atmosphere of the Willamette Valley. The following letter was published in *Redmond: Where the Desert Blooms* (1985).—S.A.

Best Bronco and Best Rider
A REDMOND POTATO SHOW STORY

Redmond, Oregon
October 1914

Dear Mother,

The affair was called the Potato Show and was on Friday and Saturday. They had a fine exhibition of vegetables and fancy work and school work and all of the things which they usually have at such affairs. Besides this was a stock parade which consisted of a few farmers and farmers' sons leading the prize stock up the main street. Redmond is a typical frontier town consisting of a drygoods store, a couple of grocery stores, a drug store, post office, barber shop and two saloons. It reminded me of a moving picture show for there were Indian squaws with brilliant, many colored shawls with their faces painted red and streaked with black, wearing beaded moccasins and carrying papooses on wooden boards and old Indian men wearing moccasins and with broad brimmed hats over their long black hair, and Indian boys and girls dressed in every form imaginable. There were cow boys with black and red and yellow fur schaps and broad felt hats and bandana handkerchiefs instead of collars and they either rode around on their ponies or walked with their ponies following them just like dogs. There was a Domestic Science lecture at the Commercial Club room by a teacher from Oregon Agricultural College, and Mrs. Martin and I attended it. She lectured and demonstrated. She made cream of tomato soup, caramel custard, and cheese rarebit, all of which she passed around that we might taste it. In the afternoon the things of interest were the cow boy race and the bucking contest. The race was fine and the ponies ran something awful. I was almost afraid to watch the bucking contest for those men get on those awful horses that have never been broken and how they stick on is more than I can see. A man on horseback holds the wild horse's head by the ears while they saddle it, and they don't use any bridle at all—only a halter. The first horse ran straight for the trees and the poor fellow was brushed by a big juniper limb. He was badly shaken but not hurt badly for he mounted his own horse and rode around afterward. Another fellow's stirrup broke right in the midst of it and he would have been thrown only a fellow caught the rope and held the horse while he got off. He only stopped to exchange saddles with another fellow and then he rode it again and waved his hat and yelled while that horse jumped and reared and bucked acted terrible. He was successful this time and came off with honors. The thing that scared me the worst, though, was when Mr. Spencer—the father of two of my pupils—was to ride "Skyrocket," a horse that had never been ridden so far and that had thrown any number of men. He was to have fifty dollars if he could ride it so you may know that they didn't expect him to do it. It took three men to hold his ears while Mr. Spencer saddled him and then he kicked and acted awful. Everybody expected and hoped that Mr. Spencer would back out but he is the most daring man that I ever saw and is known to be the best rider in the country. It was also in the bargain that he was to ride "with one hand free." That means that he must hold with only one hand. Everyone held their breath when he put his foot in the stirrup and flopped into the saddle. I trembled from head to foot when the men let go of the horse's ears and he started bucking. He put all four feet together and jumped into the air—then he reared and kicked and tore and finally tore off toward the trees. And all this time Mr. Spencer stuck on with one hand high in the air and his hair, which is rather long and curly flying in the wind and the last we saw for a few breathless minutes was a white blouse shirt flying backward and forward and up and down among the junipers. Finally a cow boy yelled through a megaphone "Skyrocket has been ridden by Spencer" and you should have heard the cheers as they led the horse back with Spencer sitting calmly in the saddle. It was fifty dollars easily earned for him, but I heard a number of men say that they wouldn't do it for fifty thousand.

Your daughter,
Essie

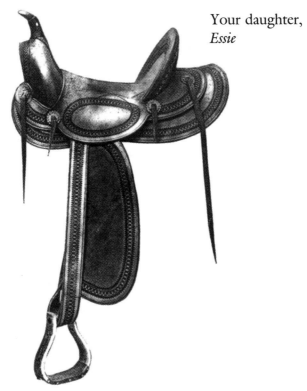

Claudia Spink Lorenz
1898-1975

Claudia Spink, student at Sacred Heart Academy

The United States attempted to remain neutral when World War I began in 1914, but Congress finally declared war on April 6, 1917, and the United States landed troops in France on June 26, 1917. The war ended on November 11, 1918, when Germany and her allies accepted defeat and agreed to a truce. The war had a serious impact on American domestic life: thousands of American soldiers were killed or wounded. Thus the end of the war was greeted with jubilation, as this letter from an elderly Klamath Falls woman reveals.

Claudia Spink Lorenz was a long-time Klamath Falls resident. The following reminiscence was published by then -*OHQ* (1970) editor Thomas Vaughn as a "Letter to the Editor," a use of the epistolary form to signal an informal, personal narrative written 52 years after the fact, rather than formal historical writing with footnotes and secondary sources. Thus, there is no salutation or close. "Not withstanding Prohibition" refers to the 18th Amendment to the Constitution which prohibited the production and consumption of intoxicating beverages.—T. O'D.

Klamath Falls Celebrates the End of War—Early

Klamath Falls, Oregon
ca. 1970

It had been reported that since August 30th, 1918, the American Army in
Europe had taken over the first American Sector on the west edge of the
Argonne Forest, in preparation for the St. Mihiel offensive, with an enormous concentration of troops, equipment and materials. We all fervently hoped
that this would be the last, great victorious drive against the German forces by
the Allies, to end World War I.

The fight, begun on Sept. 28th, was one continuous battle along the Meuse
River and through the dense Argonne Forest. Meanwhile two divisions were
sent to Belgium to help the French Army near Ypres.

War reports came in hourly and were posted on various public bulletin boards
in Klamath Falls, around which a group was always gathered those last few
days. These bulletins alternately transported us with hopeful expectation or
plunged us into discouragement. The headlines of the country newspapers
grew larger and blacker as the brilliant battles were hard fought and bitterly
won by the Allied forces and desperately resisted by the dogged Huns, who
regrouped their last best troops and renewed the counterattack, forcing the
Allies to defend every foot they had gained the days before. However, this
could not last for long, because the Germans, already drained of their best
blood, were suffering heavy losses. Their exhausted troops were losing morale.
The Americans, who were comparatively fresh and in high spirits, advanced
with their Allies, relentlessly and in increasing waves.

We sensed by Nov. 6th that the end was very near and that an armistice
would be signed most any day.

Early on Nov. 9th, the news flashed over the wire—"Firing Ceases!" "Armistice Signed!" "War is Over!"

I had graduated from Klamath County High School the year before and was
employed as the lowest clerk on the totem pole in the County Assessor's office, then occupied by that wonderful, loveable man and shrewdest of politicians,
Captain Joseph P. Lee from Tennessee. He was famous for his warm hospital-
ity and potent mint juleps. M. L. Johnson, Lee's first Deputy Assessor, has
said: "If Captain Lee had put his talents to making money instead of winning
friends and influencing people he would probably have been the richest man in

Klamath County." Upon rare occasions, such as honoring visiting VIPs, or commemorating some holidays, he would serve his guests his favorite libation in the privacy of the rear room of his office, which I think was formerly the courthouse woodshed. Nevertheless it was the meeting place for many an important gathering of prominent people, both political and social.

We young deputies (girls) were banished altogether, or if this was not practical, never permitted to enter this sanctum during these refreshment periods. We could only furtively sniff the pungent aroma of the crushed mint wafted through the closed door.

When the great news of the Germans' defeat and the Allies' triumph was received, all of the pent-up anxieties, hopes and forebodings erupted from each heavy heart and burst forth in one giant compounded geyser of relief and joy.

The town turned loose, and for a time all order broke down, but there was no vandalism. Everything that could whistle, blatt or toot was going to it. People ran out into the streets from homes, offices and stores, and proclaimed to each other: "The war is over!" "The war is over!" Overloaded autos zoomed up and down streets and whirled around corners, and no one directed traffic. Sometimes it became so congested that it would come to a complete standstill and back up for or two or three blocks. Then the shouting and honking would be redoubled. Finally the key car would break loose from the jam and the parade would begin to ooze on.

Miss Agnes Lee and Mrs. James Voye, my two superior deputies, and I, left our office around ten o'clock to join the hysterical throng. By noon we had made our way down Main Street, picking up companions, losing them, stopping here and there until we had reached the Klamath Development Office.

Not withstanding prohibition, the juice of the corn and grain was much in evidence, being resurrected from nooks and crannies, secret desk drawers and pockets. And in view of this momentous occasion, the rule was broken, the bars were let down, and Ina and I, with some other adolescents present, were permitted to be served *one* drink with a "spike" in it.

Later we directed our steps back uptown for belated lunch, again mingling with the crowd which had not decreased in size or abated in din. We had to wait in line for a table. Proprietors and employees had returned to their work, but the rural population was pouring in to confirm the grapevine reports, and join in the celebration. The hotel lobbies, restaurants, and pool halls were overflowing, and it was an open secret that informal parties were in progress all over town. A local merchant was more than a little exhilarated. He rode on the hood of an auto most of the afternoon, falling off several times, but with no seeming ill effects, for he remounted each time and continued to ride until some good Samaritan finally took him away. Back at the Assessor's office, Captain Lee was quietly going about his own business, ably assisted by his son, Will. He immediately dismissed us ladies and sent us on our way.

Amid the excitement and enthusiasm, a deep note of pathos was touched that day. Two little boys were running along the sidewalk, crying, or standing huddled against a building, forlorn and desolated. In the pandemonium, no one was giving them the slightest attention. Mrs. Voye exclaimed when she first saw them, "Why, those are the two little Bartlett boys! 'Ritchie, what is the matter? You shouldn't be crying on such a glad day.' "

Ritchie couldn't answer for his deep sobbing, but Allen, the older, turned to her and faltered, "Oh, Mrs. Voye—this might be a happy day for everybody else, but our mother just died in the hospital and our baby sister too."

Their mother had been very sick in childbirth, complicated by Spanish Influenza. She and the infant had succumbed. The father was stunned by grief and despair. Their sister was staying with neighbors. Not being noticed by anyone, they ran out in the streets, seeking solace in the crowds.

After we had seen that the little fellows had stopped crying and were feeling warm and secure in the Lees' home, and starting to play with some neighbor children in the back yard, we dispersed. The bright, early fall afternoon had faded into evening shadows, and we had to prepare for the Victory Ball that night, in the Skating Rink. Indeed, there were Victory dances in every small hamlet in the county.

The irony of it was that the next morning it was disclosed that the signing of the Armistice had been a false rumor and we had celebrated prematurely. World War I actually ceased on Nov. 11th and the Armistice was signed on that day. So we had it all to do over again, which was a very mild affair in comparison to the first one.

John Robert Keyes
1907-1971

John Robert Keyes kept a diary beginning in 1921 when he was thirteen years old. His father, general manager of a central Oregon lumber company, had died the previous year, so perhaps the younger Keyes kept the diary as a way to feel less lonely and to express his frustrations as well as successes. His descriptions of pranks, problems with authority figures, and difficulties in school are common to teenagers in any period.

Keyes served in World War II and was a timber broker and important community figure in Bend, Oregon, until his death. These excerpts from his diary first appeared in *Deschutes Pioneers' Gazette* (1990).—S.A.

A Boy in Bend—Fatherless and Thirteen—Needs to Write

March 15, 1921

It rained all day to-day. In the assembly (4 period) I went back to the teachers desk to fill my fountain-pen and when I set the ink bottle down it hit the bell and the bell made a loud ding. All the kids thought it was time to go. Miss Williams who was the teacher jawed at me for a while. I went up to the library to-night and got "The Boy With The U.S. Suvery" and "Lost With Lieutenant Pike." We had a History test to-day and it was as hard as "Old Harry." The orchestra practiced after school and I forgot to bring my Mandolin and Old Lady Grant jawed at me awhile and then made me go home and get it.

March 16

This morning in the First Period assembly I put some paper in the big tin wast paper basket and the basket dumpted over and Old Lady Umbaugh jawed at me awhile and said that if I wasn't careful I would go to the office. After school I saw a baseball game between the Sopheys and Juniors, the Juniors got beat. The score was 14-10.

March 19

Played marbels all morning. In the afternoon we played catch for a whiule and then when the men quite diging Cambell's sespool we went down in it. We took a big chain and put it over a log whitch was over the top and Skipper Cambell climed down it, it fell and broke his head oppen. We quit playing in there. We then played "Annie Over" and Cook hit me in the eye and it swelled way up. I have a bandage on it. I have a bad cold so mother is going to greese me up.

March 20

Went to Sunday School and had a lot of fun. I hit one of the Larson twins and knoked him over so the teacher made me stand up.

I played ball all after-noon until 5:30 O'clock when I went over to Blakleys where the rest of the family was. Mrs. Blakley gave us a cup of tea and some cake. Since I swore of(f) on tea during lent I couldn't drink any tea.

After supper we went down to Childers-Armstrong's and got some ice cream.

March 22

Right after dinner when we went to school they called a "General Assembly" and then all of the classes went out one at a time and had thier picture taken. At 7:30 O'clock I went up to the manual training room and we formed a Stamp Club called the Bend Stamp Club. We made a consitution and elected officers. It was eleven thirty before we got through.

March 23

We are now reading Longfellow's "Evangeline" for English. It rained and then snowed all day to-day. After school I went and saw the base-ball game between the Sophmores and Seniors.

March 24

Mrs. Sanders and Miss Kenny were both sick to-day. A teacher named Mrs. Hill is taking Mrs. Sanders place but nobody is taking Miss Kenny's place. Mr. Paulson took the rollcall and then went to the assembly and Miss Umbaugh came along and asked me why we were late. I said that Mrs. Sanders was sick and Mr. Paulson had to take the roll call.

There was a rehersal for the "Melting Pot" after school and I said I had to go to the dentist and beat it up to Ted Sathers and played baseball. I dyed some Easter eggs and so did Qupe. This noon we got a package from Seattle which had some big candy Easter eggs.

March 25

Thier was a Scout meeting to-night at 6:30. The Scouts are going to organize a baseball team to-morrow. I passed four questions for the First Class Badge to-night and gave Bones Heyburn his Tenderfoot test. Mr. Purdy would not let me take the rest of the questions or I would have.

March 27

I went to the Methodist Church this morning and saw them christen some babys. All he did was to dip his fingers in a bowl of water and put them on the babys head and say "I christen thee John Henry (or what ever his name is) in the name of the father and the son and the holy spirit. Amen." About three years ago when we were at Manchester, Washington, they christened a girl and they made (her) walk out in to the ocean with preist and then when the water was about up to her neck he ducked her and while she was half drowning he said a prair.

April 5

I put on my summer underwear and nearly froze to death. After school we had a rehearsal for the "Melting Pot." After supper the Stamp Club had a meeting and I bought some reall good stamps. We had our pictures taken after school because all other ones that they took were no good.

April 6

In the fourth period I set the alarm clock off. Bill Kribs, Mary Logan and Ruth Shepherd gave thier book reports to-day.

April 7

they had a rehersal to-night after school but I didn't stay; instead I went down town and got a hair cut. The barber stuck the scissors in my scalp and about cut my ears off. He was about the worst barber I ever had. He put some hair tonic on my hair and then rubbed my scalp about off. I bet I have a sore head for a week. After I had my hair cut I went up to Claire Paynes to invite him to my birthday party. Old Lady Grant gave us 32 problems and we got 25 sentences for English and about three pages to wright for history.

April 8

I was fourteen to-day. This morning we had to hand in a list of the subjects, the ones I took were: Latin, Algerbra, Ancient History and Manual Training. All who was in the "Melting Pot" went up to the Gym and we (had) a rehersal. I am glad I can play the mandolin because I did not have any school all afternoon. We gave the play at 8 o'clock but my (hand) was so tired I couldn't haardly play because in the afternoon Mrs. Travis kep us practicing on a piece named "Spring Spring Gentle Spring." I had Skinney and Bing Statder and Claire Payene over for supper in honor of my fourteenth birthday.

William E. Lees
1857-1942

William E. Lees was a prominent Malheur County attorney, well known for his wit and extensive knowledge of regional real-estate values. Before becoming an attorney in 1887, he pursued other interests and careers such as teaching school in Portland and prospecting for gold in Mexico, Alaska, and Idaho. For a time he was a court reporter as well as an Idaho newspaper editor.

In1921 he responded quite trenchantly to a written inquiry from a Massachusetts woman. The property noted in the letter is now owned by the federal government and is not worth much more in 1994 in dollars and cents than it was in 1921 when Lees wrote to his surely disappointed inquirer. Even so, the rough, uneven, and geologically ancient plateau in Oregon's remote, sparsely populated southeastern corner was never viewed as "worthless," useless, or barren by the Paiute people. These natives made the region their home and have understood the secrets of its complex and fragile ecological system for centuries.

A copy of this letter was forwarded to the Malheur County Historical Society by the daughter-in-law of the woman to whom it was originally addressed—Jennie F. Lyford of Wayland, Massachusetts. The letter first appeared in the *Malheur Country Review* (1987).—S.A.

Letter from Ontario to a Yankee
Who Bought 640 Acres of Hades

Office of Wm E. Lees
Ontario, Oregon
1921

Mrs. Jennie F. Lyford
Wayland, Massachusetts

Dear Madam:

Your letter of recent date in regard to Section 29, T.33 S., R. 39, EWM in Malheur County, Oregon, has been received and while this country has an area greater than the combined states of Massachusetts and Rhode Island I am sufficiently familiar with the entire county to tell you something of your land.

You ask me if I can dispose of your land. I cannot and do not think I could give it away. I am not in the real estate business, but have practiced law in Oregon for about 40 years and while lawyers are often accused of crimes and misdemeanors and practices not consistent with good morals, justly or otherwise, yet I have never known a lawyer who has been guilty of selling such land as yours, even to an enemy; this, for two reasons, first the honor that every lawyer possesses would deter him from an act of this kind, and secondly, he could not sell it.

I assume that you got this in a lottery scheme conducted by the old Southern Oregon Military Wagon Road Company, who possesses a military grant of land across the State, some 20 years ago, and, if so, it is one of the penalties of gambling and expecting something for nothing.

If the gambling microbe has entered your system and you must gamble hunt up a poker game at home and sit in but leave western land games to the people of the west for your money would be more secure and as certain of return if secured by a chattel mortgage on a school of codfish in the Atlantic Ocean.

I would like to tell you that you had a fine property; that your land was valuable; had veins of silver and gold and a fine oil prospect and grand forests of pine and fir, but being a follower of Diogenes I am unable to do so and must tell you the truth.

Your land has no present value. It lies on the west side of Crooked Creek in the southern part of the County and is without water or any hope of water. It is very high, rough, rocky and destitute of vegetation of any kind and the whole section would not support more than one jackrabbit and his wife and, if there were any children they would be compelled to go to Nevada to keep from starving to death. Your land is about 111 miles from the railroad and not more than 20 from Hades and owing to the roads and the nearness to the latter place, few people go to the railroad.

Grant said that you could deal with a surplus easier than with a deficit, but this would not be true as to your land or like land and in the lottery scheme it would have been better that you drew five acres than 640.

The old Bay State has some poor land but it has Yankees to go with it, and a Piute Indian would not camp on this section. It were better that you had a section of "Blue Sky" for then the Assessor could not reach you and blue sky is not unpleasant to the eye.

I am sorry that I have not the time to say more of your land and land schemes in general, but probably after you have read this, you will not care to go further into the subject.

I can only salute you as being a fellow free-holder of the County of Malheur and express my sorrow that you have so much of it

Yours truly,
Wm. E. Lees
Attorney at Law

L. H. Vincent
ca. 1870-?

According to his diary, Dr. L. H. Vincent served ten months and ten days as a physician during the "Great War" (World War I). While there are few available facts concerning his background and his life after 1923, the engaging personality of Dr. Vincent is vividly revealed on the pages of his lengthy diary written in Sisters, Oregon, from 1921-1923 and entitled *My Log of Life*.

The original hand-bound, typed, and colorfully illustrated diary was discovered by Helen Gillard of Palo Alto, California, when she was visiting a California garage sale in 1980. "Where was Sisters, Oregon, I wondered? I felt the diary ought to go back to the community where it originated," she recalls. A woman friend dropped off the diary some years later on a trip that took her through central Oregon. Safely tucked away in a file drawer at the Sisters Public Library, Dr. Vincent's *My Log of Life* has been largely unknown and unread until this publication.—S.A.

Commonplace Things Are Important

A DOCTOR'S LOST DIARY FROM SISTERS

Saturday, August 19, 1922

The day opened with storm; cloudy on the horison and occasionally the sun was obscured. Black Butte was wrapped in a heavy dark shroud. The wind blew in gusts and it was chillier than comfortable. I started a fire before I went to breakfast.

After breakfast I did a few chores about the house, such as sweeping, carrying a few buckets of water to flush out the toilet, scrubbing out the sink and wash basins and generally straightening up. After this I sat down to peruse a copy of the *Oregon Journal* that I snitched over at Gists.

These hum-drum affairs may seem of small consequence to record in a journal but they are not. They are the things of which life is made and it takes them together with all other things to give an accurate picture of life. If I could read now a diary kept by my ancestor Stephen Vincent telling me about cleaning out his potash kettles or feeding his dog or any of the commonplace things it would help me to understand his life better. I do not intend to record these things every time I do them. I do not mean that the times they are recorded are the only times they are done.

I intend to record from time to time such matters as will give a natural touch to the scene and enable one to vision these times. A picture is not true nor interesting that paints only the sublime. It must have its common touches to afford it a setting. It must have its contrasts to give sublimity and relief of monotony.

In Wells' "Outlines of History" there was a cut of a drawing made in the days of John Ball in England. There was a man plowing and another sowing, but the one touch that made of it a perfect rural scene was a dog chasing a bird.

It is a mistake to regard commonplace things as unimportant. They are the very things that portray life as we are living it. When Luke wrote (Acts xviii, 18) that St. Paul had his hair cut he gave us an idea of the manners and customs of the age. But we may infer that that was the first time he had had his hair cut for a long time and it was an incident to be noted.

Matters of news that I read in the paper were: Failure of a conference of railroad operators and striking trainmen to come to an agreement; funeral of Lord Northcliffe in England which took place on the 17th.

A drawing from Dr. Vincent's journal

As I was reading, an aeroplane passed over the house and cast its shadow on the street in front. It circled over the town and returning passed over the second time low down. As I saw it coming the second time it was so low down that I thought it was going to land in the street. It was marked with a green and a red diamond on the sides and stars on the wings and the number 8 on sides and wings. Mrs. Allen ran out of her house and was greatly excited as it almost touched the tree tops. It made a great roar and scared chickens and even an old cow out into the street. I heard it coming and thought it was an automobile coming up the street but soon the noise grew so loud that I knew it was an unusual motor and I looked out just in time to see the shadow and then glance up and see the machine. It disappeared over the mountains in the southwest just north of the Three Sisters mountains. It was probably one of the fire patrol planes.

Sunday, September 3, 1922

I saw the sunshine rectangle on the wall and saw it creep down and elongate on the floor until it had all left the wall before I arose. Nevertheless, in consequence of it being Sunday I was not late for breakfast.

Mrs. Dinkel is back from visiting her mother at Portland and at Gray's Harbor. The Dinkels owe me money and have owed me for six months and yet claim that they are too poor to pay anything. I couldn't afford a trip to Gray's Harbor. Mrs. Dinkel is supposed to be in a delicate condition though she doesn't appear so. I was engaged last spring to wait on her in the fall but I do not care if I do or not.

A couple of men coming over McKenzie Pass reported a woman and two girls in trouble up on the lava with a hack with a broken hind wheel. From description was decided that it was Mrs Kaylor and Leonora Kirk and Irel Harrington. Lester Gist and I procured an old wheel from a hack and started up after them. We met them about half way, having gotten their old wheel braced with poles wired on with hay wire.

I had scarcely gotten back when I was called very hastily up to Three Mile Camp on the McKenzie road to see a man who was burned with gasoline. He was a tourist. He and his wife had driven in their car over the McKenzie Pass and some thing going wrong with the car they had stopped at the road camp to fix it. He was using a gasoline blow-torch and it exploded and set his clothes on fire. Right leg burned superficially; some burned places on the back. Right arm deeply and badly burned. Left hand burned. Dressed him in Soda bicarb and waxed paper taken from loaves of bread. Shot an HMC into him and sent him to the hospital at Bend.

Barometer reads Fair. Received the promise of payment from Tyler. This would just pay my board bill and a settlement of the Wilt account and the Quiberg settlement when I get it will give me considerable southern headway. I made southage but a purchase of gas set me back to within two seconds of where I was yesterday.

February 18, 1923

Mother: Vivian Garrison, Age 32, Born in Iowa. Child not yet named.

When people are pleased they show it in their manners and actions if not always in words. They often show it in their words too, for they cannot help showing it, though their words may not always be direct to the point. This woman paid me an indirect compliment by saying how so many doctors went at this business "as if they were butchering a hog." She is now the mother of six children.

That same day I was called out to see the Hartley baby who has *cancrum oris* or *aphthous stomatitis*. It has been rather stubborn and I have been a little disposed to call it that parasitic trouble known as thrush or what the books call mycotic stomatitis. A little pearl blister appeared on the finger that the child had sucked which certainly suggests a direct infectious nature. Borax has not seemed to do much good and I have resorted to mercury. It is a bottle-fed baby and I have ordered careful sterilization of nursing bottles, nipples, and pasteurization of the milk.

I cannot now remember just how the 17th and 18th of the month passed but on one of those days I got a letter from Alex Loverenz out on the Bend road to hold myself in readiness for a call at any time from now to the tenth of

March. He had the nerve to tell me he had intended to take her to the hospital at Redmond but now feared he could not get there on account of snow. It's an ill wind that blows nobody good, but it is yet to be determined whether this wind will blow me good or ill.

I went to bed early the night of the 18th and the storm or something had put the phone line from Duckett's Mill out of commission and I was not disturbed by the telephone bell. And when Clemens's heavy footfall on my porch aroused me and I struck a light it was just ten minutes after twelve A.M.

I guess the snow is nearly three feet deep at Duckett's mill but they had opened the road with a plow or "crowder" as they called it and we got through between banks on each side.

Then at about 4-30 A.M. February 19, 1923, Helen Gertrude Clemens was born.

Father: Alma Oron Clemens, Occupation, Logger; Born in Arizona. Age 38.

Mother: Edith Matilda Butts, Age 21, Born in North Dakota. Now the mother of two living children.

This was rather a hard labor. One of those cases in which there is an urge to use chloroform before you want to use it. In such cases I like to delay the use of chloroform until the head is well engaged in the bony arch. When there is no resistance other than the soft tissues then I use chloroform.

The outcome was nevertheless gratifying and the same pleasing manifestations followed. I rather like obstetrical practice because it affords more gratification as a rule than most other branches of the medical profession. It is always romantic and like a novel with its tense moments and crises and then its happy ending.

These two cases served to lift me out of the depression occasioned by Elmer Graham's death.

Mary McKinley
1877-1934

Mary McKinley lived most of her life "out on the breaks" near the little towns of Bakeoven and Shaniko where she and her family scraped by—killing coyotes for bounty, training horses, herding sheep and cattle. "I worked all day and never got nothing done," she wrote in one entry. In reality she had been milking cows, cooking, and mending fence. The wind had been blowing dust in her eyes "all day long." She was exhausted. "When I die," she wrote in her diary in later years, "don't bury me. Jest tie my feet to the saddle-horn, slap her on the rump, and set her off running and dragging me until there's nothing left." In 1934, her life ended suddenly and violently in a car wreck.

Her family was surprised by Mary's "diary keeping all those years." It was a hard life, but her humorous bent showed itself in the quickly drawn stick figures with succinct captions she sometimes drew in her diary. One read: "The boys are looking out for the marshal and are ready to run as soon as they see a man that looks toward them." A portion of McKinley's diary is reprinted here from *Shaniko People* (1982).—S.A.

Rough and Rocky as Far as I Can See

A DIARY FROM A WASCO COUNTY RANCH

April 28, 1922

This is my birthday. I'm 45 years old.

May 1

I went to The Dalles to get my divorce. I went to two picture shows.

May 2

I didn't get nothing done today. The boys started to plow. I sent a letter to that lonesome Eldo.

May 10

This was a cold day, one inch of snow this morning. Willie got eight coyotes in the Rees place (bounty hunting). Louisa and Pink and Brother Bill all helped get the little coyotes out. A wagon wheel came off on the way home.

May 23

Last night our homestead was burnt up and the house we are in was on fire in front and in back and the barn was burnt down. This was a terrible night, a night that can never be forgotten. We found the track of a car and the car belongs to James Cooper, but he said a man stole it and run around in it all night. Reeder came, Logans came, Langs came.

May 29

Minnie and I went to The Dalles to get a warrant out for four men, and in the evening we started for home but broke down three miles out of Wasco. A man took us to Wasco, and we stayed all night. I got very sick and had the doctor to come.

May 30

We left Wasco and got to Shaniko at noon. Reeder got F. Cook and Doc and Ottis and Amiens and is taking them to The Dalles this evening. Johnnie Karlin came. Burnt on my homestead: my house and barn and all the lumber for another barn. Burnt everything in my house.

June 3
Reeder and Walter took Covey to jail for burning my house.

June 8
We went to town and bought Jones' chickens and Eddie went to Tommy Jones to haul a barn in town for Tommie. Eddie seen Pony Express riders go through Shaniko.

June 27
Mrs. R.R. Hinton was shot at five o'clock this morning. R.R. Hinton came to Shaniko early this morning and told Mr. Hoech about her death.

June 30
Leonard Armstrong got arrested the 30th of June for giving an Indian moonshine. The Indian died.

July 4
We didn't go anywhere. Was too poor to go to the 4th of July celebration at Tygh Valley.

July 7
Vannie and Eddie went up to my place and got a lot of horses. We branded six colts, Louisa came over this morning and I went back with her and tried on my riding shirt. We seen a colt in the wire on Lang's fence.

December 10
This was one more long lonesome day: nothing to do, but look at the deep snow. The house is tore up, the potatoes is frozen. This is a very cold house. My little colt got the lock-jaw and will die.

December 20
I got some meat from Ed Wilson. Willie and Ben went over to Lang's and got the turkey. Willie and Ben rode, while I washed clothes. Vannie stood around with his hands in his pockets and his pockets in his pance, in a five-cent house out of a nine o'clock town.

January 10, 1923
Well, the boys are fixing to make a lot of money. Eddie will go to town and take the Bone-Crusher (Ben Morfitt) with him. He will rassel for the gate receipts.

January 11
The boys went to town and got in a fight with the two Astons. Willie broke out the windshield in the car and he got a black eye. Al, he was there and stopped him a' fightin'.

January 12
I went to town on old Spot and Willie and Eddie went to town too, but had to leave again to keep from being arrested. Al and Elgie came home with me.

January 13
Willie and Eddie went to town and sure made a clean-up. They shot up the old town, run all the people under the sidewalks. Louisa and Hazel came out afoot.

January 14
The boys are looking for the Marshal and are ready to run as soon as they see a man that looks towards them. Al went home to Jon's Canyon, the boys went over to Langs, and layed on their porch.

January 17
The boys have gone and everything looks blue and lonely. It is a'snowing tonight and I wonder if my boys are in out of the storm. I wish I was with them. Ben Morfitt and Vannie found the horses out and the fence was cut in two places.

January 18
I and Vannie went to town to see how the shooting up the town is getting along. The boys are still out on the hills.

January 19
Vannie and Ben rode after horses way over Pine Holly. Didn't find much. The boys are staying out of sight.

February 3
Ed Wilson tried to kill Bogart, there was a dance in town and moonshine was running the whole thing. Bootleggers made money by the sack full.

Daniel Mote
1853-ca. 1932

*Mote is the tall man with white
hair second from the left*

Daniel Mote is a prime example of a type that has abounded in the American West: the bona fide eccentric. In 1902, while a lonely salesman in Montana, Mote continually experienced visions of both famous and ordinary dead persons. He permitted his itinerary to be directed by messages he received while practicing "automatic writing." Finally settling down in Joseph, Oregon, far from his Ohio origins, he lived to old age despite poor health that may have been exacerbated by quack cures. His favorite quotation was "Living is like licking honey off of a thorn" (Louis Adamic) and his favorite author was Leo Tolstoy. Despite his remote location, Mote avidly followed the stock exchange and kept himself abreast of world affairs.

He kept diaries for more than thirty-three years and no diary was ever larger than 3 inches by $1^1/_2$ inches—a size "small enough to hide from cowboys and busybodies," Mote said. Mote began his first known diary with the following instruction: "If dead, bury me quietly and decently but plainly and economically, for the love of God." Mote's unpublished diaries were transcribed by Grace Bartlett, a writer living in Joseph, Oregon. Other Mote materials are housed in the Idaho State Historical Society Library, Boise.—S.A.

Detailed to the Point of Wearisomeness
A JOSEPH ECCENTRIC'S DIARY

Friday, October 10, 1930

Very quiet. Rex Gibbs just here to see if I am still alive.—Told me Isom has not paid him rent due since last spring.—Dug potatoes. Wheat and stocks slumped to new lows. At least two more stock exchange firms have failed.

Sunday, October 12

Got mail (*Oregonian*) and read until 9 p.m. Wheat Stocks, steel, copper, cars low, if not lower. Losses, billions! Revolution in S.A. Instability in Europe; India; China,—*all Asia*. Russia threatening to undersell the world! What! Bot yesterday groceries, meat, etc. about $1.25.

Tuesday, October 14

Cloudy, gloomy, Better business "gags" fill the papers. The clean-ups are sitting on their winnings and soaking the hungry and penniless poor by promises of jobs before things get too bad. What!

Monday, October 20

Leaves motionless. Stocks slide and business "will be" better. What crust! Read Tolstoi's "Cossacks" and "Storm."

Tuesday, October 21

Now I'm glad I enjoyed the sunshine and splendor of yesterday's. Read the "Cossacks" when I should have been dancing and summersaulting under the dazzling blue. Tolstoy lets no observation contributing to sadness and gloom pass without utterance.

Tuesday, October 28

Haze of smoke lying around horizon. Paper uninteresting. Manifestly straining to find signs of prosperity—timid cowardly confesions tucked away in obscur sandwitched positions, allowing business may pick up in 1931.

Saturday, November 1

I had difficulty getting to sleep tho' I drank two cups ovaltine. Haloween! People tramping the streets. Cars whizzing, groaning; catcalls, shrills, whistles, screams, explosions. Toilets upset this morning including mine and that at Methodist church and old Roup hall. What can one do?

Monday, November 3

I had a gorgeous dream last nite. A land of mountains a mighty river that had carved its way in countless grotesque forms for millions of ages and lay far beneath, soundless, in a light miraculous and resplendent with purple, scarlet and gold. Then a palace with walls covered by marvelous landscapes, portraits, designs all done by brother Clay, who couldn't draw an elephant's ear when we were boys together. My mother proudly showing and explaining to whom I would not explain that the backgrounds had a trick of stepping into the foregrounds, lest I wound her. It was 5 a.m. when I woke. Now I must fix that old garrage!

Thursday, November 13

Spent most of the time planning, praying for a sudden and painless death— and feeling better every minute!

Monday, March 2, 1931

Breakfast Delicious apple, puffed wheat, an egg on a slice of toast, a sliver of bacon and fried potatoes, nuts, ovaltine. Had vibratory massage over stomach, colon and knees spine to 10th dorsal, face, eyes. Feeling fine physically. But weighted with apprehension. World War Vets. rushing Treasury. Hope they'll get a billion. They will not be paid then for what they did. The rulers of the world want their blood service too cheap. They should find a way of peace. Violet ray over spine, colon, liver, stomach, throat, face, etc.

Tuesday, March 3

11:00 A.M. have just finished ozone and violet ray treatment; also sinussoidal, saturation and eye.I am intensely interested in these treatments. They are bringing results I am better, stronger, more cheerful, more hopeful. I have dreaded helpless weakness and prolonged illness and suffering more than anything else This looks self-centered but any snoopy, uninvited reader doubtless can relieve his weary disgust by hope of reward for his zealous and excited curiosity. I'd like to be cheerfully well, until the final plunge, so as to smile and scintillate good humor with you, "Mr. Not me." I can appreciate your point of view if necessary.

Ella Rhoads Higginson
1860-1940

Ella Rhoads Higginson was an infant when she crossed the plains with her parents by ox-team and wagon and settled in the remote valley of the Grande Ronde. She lived in several Oregon locations, including Portland and La Grande, until 1888, when she moved with her husband, Russell Higginson, to Bellingham, Washington. Eventually she was to become Washington's poet laureate, but she began her long distinguished career at an early age as an Oregon poet, essayist, novelist, and literary commentator. Much of her earliest work was published in the *West Shore,* an important Portland literary magazine that encouraged Northwest writing and writers. In later years she achieved a modest national reputation. (See *From Here We Speak* and *The World Begins Here* of the Oregon Literature Series for other works by Higginson.)

In 1935, in the grips of a lingering debilitating illness, Higginson responded to a letter from Kate Hanley, who wanted Higginson to relate stories of her childhood days in the Grande Ronde Valley. This letter, published here for the first time, is located in the Special Collections, Knight Library, University of Oregon.— S.A.

The River Has Glimmered through My Whole Life

A WRITER REMEMBERS HER GRANDE RONDE VALLEY CHILDHOOD

Bellingham, Washington
January 12, 1935

Dear Kate Hanley,

I wish I could do all the things you ask in your lovely letter, but I have been so ill for two years that I can do almost nothing. I do not go anywhere and am not allowed to have company. They think I may recover if I live just as if I were in a hospital—where I'll never go while I am conscious!

As for my childhood the lovely Grand Ronde Valley, I do not recall much of importance. The river has glimmered through my whole life . . . the tall trees . . . the old Nesley place where we lived . . . my cats, dogs, horses, and their tragic deaths . . . a strawberry pin-cushion given to me by the eldest Nesley girl (I think her name was Mary) and she told me I "must always think of her when I sewed"—which I did for many years . . . a hired man whom my mother taught me to call "Mr. Hoover" because "working people must always be treated with respect and politeness"; he was heavenly kind to me and I loved him; Hattie Proebstel, Ada Mallory, the Slater girls, Leander Wells, who seemed quite a "grown-up" young man to me and very nice . . . and many others. I remember visiting one Sunday at your farm. The elders of the families went driving and left us youngsters alone; we got into the pantry and ate an enormous dish of corn, then were scared to death and *hid the dish*! Such foolish things to remember! The first sewing-machine in the valley, owned by Mrs. Proebstel; it stood on a table and ran by the turning of a handle! I'll never forget the big slices of snow-white "salt-rising" bread which the Proebstel children and I used to have piled half an inch thick with golden cream and brown sugar, one day at their home, the next at mine . . . the "mourning-doves" in the orchard, the night hawk sinking from the sky in the twilight and uttering his weird cry—I never hear either without a quick thrill of remembrance of summer twilights when I watched my brother and my sister milking several cows.

I remember the tall, "scary" Indians in gay blankets who traded the ravishing strings of blue, red, green, and white beads for food—but am not sure where they camped. My impression is that it was around Ora Dell. And I vividly remember *stealing* something when I was about five. We were visiting and out in the sheep-yard I found a sleigh-bell. I was too shy to ask for it, so I hid it in the pocket of my new dress. All day I went about with a burdened conscience; and that night when my mother undressed me that *darn* bell *tinkled*.

"What's that?" asked my mother. With eyes as big as saucers, I said, "I don't know."

"*You don't know*. Why, it's something in your pocket."

Her hand probed and brought it out and I had to confess. Then my mother wept; she didn't scold—she *wept* because her little girl had stolen something. I have never been even tempted to steal anything since that night! And the next morning I had to take it to our hostess and confess again. "Lord love you, child," she said, "you can have a dozen if you want them." I remember what my father called a "blooded" mare, and I was always trying to find blood on her!

Kate, you will realize that my recollections are all *personal*, and so, of no value to you. And here's my most precious one, but also personal. The Mallory drug-store in La Grande was on fire and our home directly across the street was in grave danger. I was not more than five, and while the others were packing and moving things out, I knelt by the window and prayed to God aloud, to save our home. Through all the excitement the family was profoundly moved by it, and discussed it afterward. "It's the way she did it," my father said. "As if she was sure God was right here in the room and listening. Where did she learn to pray like that?"

Well, I never learned. I was born with a faith in God that nothing can shake, and it has stayed with me all through life.

The beginning of this letter is a month old. We left the lovely valley before the Indian trouble; and I was too young to be interested in anything except hearing them say that George Coggan was killed.

Love to you and the lovely Valley—
Ella Higginson

Dave Stirewalt
1914-

Dave Stirewalt, a Wheeler County cowboy and rancher, writes letters just the way he talks—a characteristic shared with many other Oregonians. He was a baby when his father, Daniel Jackson Stirewalt, bought a homestead relinquishment in 1914 near Winlock. For most of his life, Stirewalt has lived on a family ranch on Sourdough Ridge near Spray. He is fond of telling people, "I am just a product of dem dar hills."

A well-known horseman who has furnished stock for the western rodeo circuit since the 1930s, Stirewalt is also admired for his ability to tell a good story. Although Dave Stirewalt never went to school beyond the 8th grade, his native intelligence and humorous bent have earned him the respect and affection of his region. Stirewalt's letter to neighbors—members of the Lines family—appears in print here for the first time.—S.A.

The News from Sourdough Ridge

A SPRAY COWBOY WRITES HIS FRIENDS

Winlock, Oregon
September 30, 1935

Dear Nellie and Joe,

Say I plume forgot to answer that letter I got from you all the other day till just now.

Hear it has been almost a month and you wanted to hear from us right away.

Si was home for a while but her and Ruby left the 4 of Sept they bothe left together, Matty came back by and got them.

We sold Claud Crock some stears about a month agoe Jim and I took them up to his plase he lives up by Monument had a lot of fun while we were up thear. Bought us a Percheon Stallian from a feller while we were up there he is just 4 years old weighs 1550 lbs he sure is a dandy I worked with him today with old Pat they sure make a good team.

He is registered we got the papers on him. When are you and Joe going to come up and go hunting the season is half over I have been loking for you every day putnear.

Jim and Lester left today to go hunting they went up back of the Corn Cob My arme is getting parlysed you know what I mean.

Jim and I run the horse up from whear we got them that day Branded six of them I branded that little spoted one. We sure had a lot of fun took us about a hour I gess wish you and Joe could have been thear.

Say I rode one that came un wound the other day a spoted horse Lester got from Carl Brown he sure left the earth Bucked all over the tale end of Sour Dough Rig Beleive it or not Ha Ha one on me I gess.

Dad and mom are fealing perty good for the shape ther in but they are in bad shape.

Well you will be so near blind when you get to the end of this you can't read it so better I quit.

Your Frind, as ever
Dave

P.S. my hands are dirty!

Felix Urizar
?-?

The Basques remain one of Eastern Oregon's most important ethnic groups. Arriving in Oregon's high basin and range country in the early 1880s, Basques used communities such as Burns, Jordan Valley, and Ontario as bases of operation while running sheep on the open range. Wherever water and native grass were abundant, the Basque sheepherder could be seen driving bands of sheep. His black and white dog, camp wagon, *bota* of wine, stone monuments, carved aspen trees, Fernando stories—the Basque herder became part of the high desert lore and landscape. (See *Varieties of Hope* and *The Stories We Tell* of the Oregon Literature Series for other texts.) Many herders were not proficient in spoken English; they tended to associate with other Basques from the Vizcaya region in Spain, and most spoke enough Spanish to be easily understood. As a group, herders quickly earned a reputation for toughness, frugality, and self-reliance. Basque families who lived in the new high desert towns helped their countrymen maintain their old-world traditions by establishing boarding houses, restaurants, bars, and stores in small towns throughout the arid country. These businesses predominantly catered to the needs of herders in winter, herders looking for work, herders between jobs, herders looking for bread, good wine, women, and friends.

These immigrants and their traditions seemed to be secure; there seemed to be an inexhaustible supply of grass. However, ranchers and others began decrying the destruction of the public range, not just by Basques but by too many graziers looking for free pasture. Years of overgrazing by cattle, sheep, and feral horses had resulted in severe water erosion and severely damaged most of Oregon's native bunchgrasses. Cheat grass, juniper, sage, and weeds took over. To prevent further degradation of the range, several million acres of western lands were set aside for protection by the Taylor Grazing Act of 1934—part of Roosevelt's New Deal. The Taylor Act and its administrator, Marvin Klemme of Oklahoma, required that grazing permits on the remaining public lands were only issued to "bona fide settlers, residents and other stock owners. . . ." Basques, Irish, and other "tramp" herders who wandered from range to range could not meet these standards. Immigrant herders considered the policy discriminatory, particularly in light of the 1924 Native Origins Act, which limited the influx of southern Europeans and others. As a result of overgrazing and the Taylor Act, many Basques left the region for western Oregon and northern California during the mid-1930s or went to established Basque communities in Idaho and Nevada. The following letter from Felix Urizar, a Basque businessman in Harney County, was written to his local newspaper in Burns in 1937.—S.A.

The Closing of the Range
ANGRY BASQUE SHEEPMEN LEAVE THE HIGH DESERT

Burns, Oregon
November 16, 1937

Burns *Times-Herald*

Dear Editor,

O n today's stage from the Star Hotel Teles Zavala, Joe Zarraonandia and Thomas Sabala left Burns. Joe Abasolo left last week. They left Harney County seeking a new location to live and run sheep as they have been driven out of Harney County by Mr. Klemme and his unjust administration of the Taylor Grazing Act. Teles Zavala has been in Harney County (since 1904.) All this time these men have either worked for sheepmen or have themselves, particularly in the last ten years, run from 2500 to 7000 of their own sheep.

They are going from Burns, first to Eugene, looking that country over and then to Roseburg, and then over to the coast and possibly into California, seeking a new place to run sheep and invest their money where Mr. Klemme can't run them over because of his racial prejudice and hatred against sheep.

Last year, Daniel Subiaurre, Domingo Sabala and Isidora Ynda and Andy Uquiri left Harney County. These and Zavala, Zarraonandia and Thomas Sabala took out of Harney County at least $125,000 in money, personal property and livestock. In their sheep operations they spent in Harney County a good many dollars which they produced themselves. More (Basques) will soon go, taking their property and productive enterprise with them.

Yet the County Court, who it appears seems to think they have nothing to do but make budgets and spend money, not caring where the taxes are coming from . . . sits idly by while Mr. Klemme destroys the county.

I was asked by these (Basque) men to write the newspapers as above.

Respectfully,
Felix Urizar

Giles French
1894-1976

Born in Cottonwood Canyon, Sherman County, Giles French became publisher and editor of the *Sherman County Journal* in Moro in 1931 and remained in those positions for nearly fifty years. During those years, his paper was one of the most widely quoted weeklies in the state. A collection of his editorials was published in *These Things We Note* (1966). French was also the author of histories of Sherman and Morrow counties as well as *The Golden Land* and *Cattle Country of Peter French*. He served in the legislature for eighteen years, and is generally considered one of eastern Oregon's most distinguished citizens.

The following excerpts are from letters written to his daughter, Jane French Frees, over a period of forty years. They first appeared in *Dear Dad, Love, Jane* (1980). At that time, most of the specific dates, salutations, and closings were removed. Thus they seem to appear here as a journal.—T.O'D.

Rambling Around inside My Head
A MORO FATHER'S LETTERS TO HIS DAUGHTER

August 1945

It has been hot here, a news note that has surely been played regularly. Some people have gotten married, occasionally one has died, although the ill have been very forebearing about dying in the midst of our busy harvest season; gardens have grown, wheat has matured, tires have blown out, houses have been bought—and of course, sold; the earth, I am confident, has made its daily pilgrimage around itself and also pursued its weary way one-three hundred and sixty fifth of its annual journey around the sun. Wives have been mad at husbands and husbands have been disgusted at wives, harsh words have been spoken, and either forgotten or tucked away in the folds of the minds to be hauled out at the divorce court, the girls have looked longingly at the boys and boys have been busy harvesting, liquor has been drunk and the imbibers have been likewise, money has been lost at poker—and won, shoes have worn out, cakes have fallen, food has been burned, corn gotten ripe, bearings have burned out; in fact, nothing has happened. Except, that is, the ceaseless round of little things that make up the lives of little people. Big people are the few to whom if little things happen, they are big things anyhow. Mr. Truman gets up early, for instance.

1962

Retirement is a dream of the middle-aged, not the elderly, who know better.

There isn't anything wrong with me that can't be laid to 67 damned active years, some stiffness in the joints and a fading memory for the name I want to remember; and your mother is fine too, but is a worrier. Her back hurts, her legs ache, her stomach won't work right and her hair won't stay combed, but she does anything she really wants to. I won't believe there is anything wrong with her until a reputable doctor tells her so.

I'm doing some cooking; too cold to garden, too early to fish, so cooking is a good way to pass the time while I'm waiting for Binfords and Mort to do some re-writing on my Pete French book. Yesterday I baked bread, baked a pot of beans and concocted a dish for left over roast beef. I have some new cook books and like to experiment the second time on a recipe. I do not wash the dishes.

I keep busy and if I do sell the newspaper I am not going to quit working, so if you find me lying on the davenport in the daytime it means I'm tired and if I stay there very long you can call the undertaker—I'll be dead.

Maybe this will straighten you out about us and it is a good thing for you to worry about someone else now and then. Worrying about yourself makes you a hypochondriac and none of them have any friends or even listeners.

1966

Let's talk awhile; don't know as I have anything to say, least wise, nothing helpful, but, you never know, rambling around almost any head, what useful thought might be uncovered.

Folks never talk much about their growing up, becoming an adult, shucking the silliness of adolescence. Reckon most are ashamed of it and don't want it brought up. Some do things that put them behind the 8 ball for life; especially girls who marry the boy with the longest hair and the loudest guitar and find out after five years and three kids that he had no saleable skills and no intention of acquiring any and maybe no ability to do it anyhow. Boys have a better chance to recover from adolescent ills, but it is difficult at best. There was a cartoon printed recently wherein a young man was apparently leaving home and his father was saying: "You might as well go tackle the world now when you're smarter than you'll ever be again."

How does one grow up? Kids are pretty well bossed; tie your shoes, mow the lawn, study your lesson, change your shirt. And they get damn tired of it whether they show it or not. The thing they want to do worst when they get a little freedom is to let their shoe strings dangle, the lawn grow, disdain books and wear the same shirt. Youthful rebellion comes from parental discipline and attempts at training. Lack of discipline creates its problems too—probably worse.

I'm sure you realize that if I were vindictive this would be an excellent opportunity to point out that your predicament as regards your family would be a perfect time for me to express a certain contentment and perhaps pleasure that you were undergoing some of the same miseries you one time caused. But it is so universal. Kids are all damn fools. Why shouldn't they be? We protect our children as long as we can, but there comes a time when they must face the problems of adulthood almost entirely unprepared by training or responsibility. In the days when boys worked with fathers at wood chopping or plowing, and girls learned canning and sewing from mothers there was a more useful companionship and more learning of how to live in a society and even the society was simpler. In those days a boy was often a man, emotionally, at 14; now he has to finish college and perhaps get a PhD before he is fit for the world.

Earl Russell Bush
1886-1970

Dr. Earl Russell Bush was a young physician who had never sculpted in his life until reaching remote and beautiful Crater Lake National Park in southern Oregon's Cascade Range. Between October 14 and 19, 1917, Dr. Bush, then employed as the park's medical officer, secretly carved the side of a large boulder into a generously proportioned female nude later known as the mysterious "Lady of the Woods." Many fanciful and romantic stories concerning the "Lady's" origin were told as years passed. Among others, author Anne Shannon Monroe (see *Varieties of Hope* of the Oregon Literature Series) waxed imaginative over the motives of the anonymous sculptor. The first "discovery" of the "Lady of the Woods" was made by a party of workmen in 1919, who claimed the nude sculpture was evidence of an ancient culture "perhaps earlier than that of Egypt." Others were certain that Native Americans were responsible for the unfinished carving "nestled in a moody bower of grandfather hemlocks."

After his stint at Crater Lake, Dr. Bush served in World War I. He enjoyed a long and successful career as a physician in Ohio until he retired and moved to Florida, where he lived until his death in 1970. This unpublished letter is in the Crater Lake National Park Archives.—S.A.

The Naked Truth about the Mysterious Lady of the Woods

P.O. Box 184
Lake Worth, Florida
August 24, 1953

Richard M. Brown
Assistant Park Naturalist
Crater Lake National Park
Oregon

Dear Mr. Brown,

My friend Claude Shafer made good his promise to visit Crater Lake and call upon the "Lady of the Woods." I was very happy indeed to receive your letter and learn of his safe arrival and also your interest in the details surrounding her creation.

Your letter was a voice out of the past. It has been so long—36 years in fact—that I have forgotten many names and details.

My position as Surgeon for the US Engineers was merely by transfer from the mouth of the Columbia where I had been serving in a similar capacity on the Jetty work. Being natives of the middle West neither my wife or I had any acquaintance with the ocean or the mountains. We were deeply impressed by both. Our entry into the mountain country was thru Ft. Klamath. The R. R. ran only to Chiloquin with a spur track as far as the Engineer's storage point called Werk or Wirt. Arriving in Chiloquin alone with our four year old son we found only a fly infested lunch counter. Inquiry brought us the information that we could get on to Ft. Klamath by "taxi" if we cared to wait until the Indian who drove it returned. Having no place else to go and no means of transportation anyway, we waited. In due time the taxi appeared. It was a Model T Ford, touring car with no top and rather dilapidated. The Indian driver answered our request for a transfer to the Agency and motioned for us to get in. The drive thru virgin forest on a trail over pine needles which I could not follow was a hair-raiser to us. Eventually we arrived in the little town of Ft. Klamath, filled with Indians and cowboys all in full regalia. We entered the National Park, a matter of three weeks later, since our arrival was early in July, the snow was still too deep for travel into the Park or to the Lake.

One cannot really appreciate Crater Lake unless you stay long enough to experience it's changes in color and mood. We grew to love it. One evening Francis Parkhurst and her brother Asa proposed an overnight trip to Wizard Island, the purpose being to enjoy some fish cooked over the open fire and in the morning see the sunrise from the lake level. We had noted how long the island remained dark after the sun was bright on the upper cliffs. Winning consent from their father for the trip under our chaperonage, we laid our plans, selected a moonlight night, and set out in the motor launch.

It was cold but we had a good time and the sight of the sun creeping down into the crater was worth the trip. Insofar as anyone knew we were the first ever to spend a night on the island. The natives said no one was that bold and the Indians were too superstitious. There was some hazard, of course, because of the quick storms which sometimes came.

The Hotel closed Sept 30 and Mrs. Bush and our son went out to Medford. Our workmen were released with the exception of the staff and those of the maintenance group whose job it was to prepare tools and equipment for the next season. I had practically nothing to do. It was then that I decided to do what had been in my mind all summer. Bill Ivy had made tools for the monument cutters and knew just what I needed to carve in stone. I was wholly unacquainted with the techniques of sculpturing and had no model. I must have had some sort of inspiration. Be that as it may, I began work, after selecting a boulder of proper shape. My selection was also influenced somewhat by the fact that two fallen pines had crossed each other so as to form a natural scaffolding about the boulder. I should say it was a half mile or more from the HQS camp. None of the others knew just what I was doing all day for about a week. Curiosity got the better of them however and one day they trailed me by the tap-tap of my hammer. It embarrassed me for I suddenly felt rather ridiculous. . . . I pledged them to secrecy.

I have never been back to see the Lady of the Woods, a name given by someone else, Mr. Kiser the photographer I think. It is one of my ambitions to return and if the opportunity affords we hope to make the trip next summer. I should like to travel the road and the many trails and see how well you have developed this glorious spot. Since those days we have traveled far but have never found another Crater Lake.

My hope is that the bit of sculptory I left behind has been an asset rather than a liability.

Hoping to have the pleasure of meeting you next year and with best wishes, I am

Yours truly
E. R. Bush M.D.

Brooks Hawley
1902-1991

Brooks Hawley felt so strongly about his connection to his corner of Baker County that he once wrote: "For better or worse, I have been wedded to Sumpter Valley. When I tried breaking home ties, I couldn't make a go of it, even though I have gone to college and once wintered in Seattle, during the Depression, in low spirits." Hawley was a local historian who wrote many articles concerning gold mines with picturesque names such as North Pole, Red Boy, and Bonanza. Born in the town of Sumpter at the height of its short-lived boom, he noted that his parents, Walter and Ida Brooks Hawley, had decided "not to trust the gold in these hills and in 1908 we moved to the old Duckworth place four miles down the valley to put our trust in cattle to keep us. We have hung on." Hawley always said that he was "as shy of women as Lil' Abner," but in 1949 he married Tyyne James, who was born in Finland and had immigrated to Canada. Together, they lived on the old Hawley ranch until his death.

In the 1960s, in a series of annual Christmas letters to Masonic Lodge brothers, Brooks commented upon the coming of Mason Dam and Phillips Reservoir that changed life in his valley forever. He considered that his best "writing effort" was a book: *Gold Dredging in the Sumpter Valley* (1977). "Sumpter Valley," he wrote, "is a big world in a small place to me, the center of the universe."—S.A.

Doubting the Coming of Dam Civilization

CHRISTMAS LETTERS FROM A BAKER COUNTY RANCH

Sumpter Valley 1962

Mason dam was authorized by congress this fall, . . . Sumpter declines as usual. There were 19 pupils last spring in the six grades. There are 7 pupils now. . . . The Jim Jacksons continue with the Buffalo mine, the only active gold mine in the state. The mill runs, and they should do good for several years on the new lower tunnel. . . . Logging is from two sections in Sumpter valley that have never been logged before. . . . That makes a lot of virgin pretty country torn up by rough logging that is not supposed to make much of a profit, considering the extra expensive road building. . . . We hope 250 cow elk tags for hunting in this area this fall will make less elk nuisance next year. The wild life has decided to live with civilization, or else it has decided there is no civilization here any more for elk, deer, coyotes, beaver, and porcupines are about taking over. It is developing troubles on its own front for it may be that the coyotes are taking deer.

The Columbus day blow didn't even put our lights out. . . .

The open house at the radar station in September convinced everyone that it contains more gadgets than is comprehensible to the mind of man. . . .

Sumpter Valley 1963

The lower end of Sumpter Valley nears its final destiny as storage for 100,000 acre feet of water. . . . The elk hunting score in this district included three human beings. . . . Baker Hotel is now Baker Motor Inn and intends to increase parking and tourist attractions. . . . There are as many as three vacant stores in a row on Main street at Baker, and three stores now are in the process of closing out: . . . A new postoffice is promised, not that it is needed, . . . the state employment-unemployment office is about as futuristic as anything in town.

Sumpter Valley 1964

Take a picture of the lower meadows before they are flooded! . . . The sentiment at the county seat is to call it Phillips reservoir, not even leaving us a local name. However the present Mason name has no special meaning. Why not keep a good name like Sumpter Valley?. . . During spring and summer Tony Brandenthaler continues the placer at the old Parkerville diggings in the Greenhorns. The remains of the last Northwest doodlebug here, including the pontoons and screen, were this month sent to French Guiana for gold dredging there. From break of day until after dark the busy logging trucks go by hardly 15 minutes apart from beyond Larch and Granite summits to Burnt River Lumber Co. at Baker. . . . Last winter had two feet of snow and no outstanding cold snaps. The spring was backward. June never rained so much before. October was never nicer, sunny, dry, and warm. . . .

The wedding Sept. 5 in the Episcopal church was likely the first wedding in Sumpter in 50 years. Not so rare is a shooting. We hear that the country is prosperous, but cattle prices makes strong men weep. One beneficial result could be to stop the trend for cattle barons and California buyers to want and get all the ranch and hay land in Oregon.

Sumpter Valley 1965

For the future Mason dam the J. N. Conley Co. of Portland is in the midst of relocating 6.35 miles of road. . . . The farmers have been paid for their land, something around three quarters of a million dollars. . . . Truck loads of logs, almost 50 a day continue to hurry by from the Granite country. . . . The Buffalo mine was sold to the Union Pacific Railroad but Jacksons still run the mine.

This is the roll of inhabited valley farms before the dam makes even less: Warnock, Hudspeth, Perrine, Defrees, Rasmussen, Miller, Hansen, Dennis, Simpson, Holland, Roda, Hawley, Howard. Hardly more than four, Warnocks, Hudspeths, Defreeses, and Rasmussens put all their effort into farming. Hansens, Perrines, Hollands, Howards do logging too, and some of us do little more than stay put. We can hardly guess what the next changes will be.

Sumpter Valley 1966

Sumpter Valley is in the midst of the biggest going over since the Sumpter fire or the dredging of the 30s. . . . About ten buildings have been moved and considerable of barns, corrals, and smaller buildings have made bonfires. . . . Logging from the Granite country has been as active as any year. Sumpter again lacks enough children for a primary school. Cattle are a good price, but range was poor, hay is high, and it was the driest summer ever.

Sumpter Valley 1967

After all the years of uncertainty and slow results, the actual fill for Mason dam swiftly went into place through June to October 13th. . . . The quarter million dollar Union creek camp ground is nearly finished. The Rex Kimsey Company put it in for the forest service. It has paved roads, a boat ramp, 58 camping spots with power, water, and sewage lines, but is nothing to brag about for natural beauty as there is neither view of the water nor the Elkhorns. . . . Log hauling is as busy as usual.

On the main drag, the highway now misses Huntington. The slow train from Huntington to Portland quit. Baker Hotel and the Antlers are now the same ownership. . . . A Standard Oil truck with no brakes killed nine cows when Warnocks were moving cattle.

Sumpter Valley 1968

This will speak more for Baker county than for Sumpter valley, intimating that Mason dam has blotted out so much of the valley there there is not so much news around here.

"Paint Your Wagon" dominated the year. Paramount sure did sling money around. Newspapers are still taking stock of what happened. With the movie came the hippies. A year ago the first face flies arrived. The face flies are bound to come back each year when winter is over, but we hope the hippies don't return, come spring. Some factions complain we are lacking in appreciating this finest flowering of our civilization. We sure are lacking in appreciation. Now we hear less of lice, venereal disease, marijuana, LSD and some public buildings are getting fumigated. No kidding. All we really saw was the hippies standing around, decorating Main street. The nicest sight was seeing the live-stock being trained in the old Oregon Lumber Co. ground in south Baker: mule freight teams, covered wagons, oxen. . . .

Sumpter Valley 1969

This second year of water in the reservoir the water rose to lap over the dredge tailings opposite the old Yantis place. The new Union creek camp ground had capacity crowds with over 100,000 for the season. Camping is mostly moti-vated by fishing and is city style with all the conveniences and fancy boats, carefully wrapped in softness to avoid direct contact with nature. The planted trout are good sized but not too anxious to bite. I have been over our old hay meadows in a boat with mixed feelings, but the city people claim catching a fish is far superior to haying. . . .

John Scharff
1901-

John Scharff, the Malheur Wildlife Refuge's first manager, retired in 1971 after thirty-six years of service in that capacity. In an effort to protect about two hundred and twenty species of birds found on and adjacent to the Malheur Range, the original refuge was established within the meander lines of Mud, Harney, and Malheur lakes where several ranches already existed. These included the famous "P" Ranch that once belonged to Peter French. See *Steens Mountain* (1967) for Scharff's description of the refuge. Born in Monument, Oregon, Scharff grew to know a great deal about the people of neighboring Harney County and their history.

The African-American ranchers mentioned in the following letter share some similarities with rural African-American Oregonians in other historical eras. Open racism has existed in Oregon's metropolitan and rural areas since the 1840s; however, while rural African Americans, such as railroad workers, experienced loneliness because of the smallness of their numbers, they sometimes were far more likely to find social acceptance and economic prosperity. In eastern Oregon, particularly in Harney and Malheur counties, a number of African-American families owned ranches and enjoyed a measure of respect from their neighbors. Much of the documentation of the lives of such families is missing. That African Americans made their homes in various localities is evidenced by some colloquial place names. Near the town of Drewsy in Harney County, for example, is a site known locally as Nigger Flat. Similar racist names exist in other parts of Oregon, for even when African Americans were apparently accepted, racial epithets were still in common use.

The following 1970 unpublished letter to University of Oregon professor Kenneth Porter was discovered in the basement files of Malheur National Wildlife Refuge, Burns.—S.A.

Just the Same as White People

AFRICAN AMERICANS EAST OF THE CASCADES

Malheur Wildlife Refuge
Burns, Oregon
March 30, 1970

Mr. Kenneth Wiggins Porter
Professor of History
University of Oregon
Eugene, Oregon 97403

Dear Mr. Porter:

Thirty-five years ago, when I first came to the Malheur Refuge, there were two Negro ranchers, brothers, by the name of Anderson, one having the ranch on Juniper Lake and the other on Trout Creek— both east of the Steens Mountain. Subsequent to that time, both of these men have died, one of them selling out and moving to Portland before he passed away.

Actually, I do not know very much about these folks other than they were well respected, nice people and it didn't seem to occur to anyone that they were black. They attended public dances, rodeos, and other public entertainment, just the same as did the white people. However, I am sure that a letter addressed to Mrs. Calderwood at Fields, Oregon would provide you with a considerable amount of information regarding these folks. Mr. Fred Pollock, Princeton, Oregon would also be a good contact to make for information about the Andersons as he lived next-door-neighbors to one of them.

I well remember Jesse Stahl, who, as you mentioned, was a legendary bronc rider during the 1920s and 1930s. The only thing that kept Jesse from getting into big money was the fact that he was a colored man. Jesse had a keen sense of humor and was liked and respected by everyone that knew him, and he always had a pleasant greeting for visitors.

I recall one incident at John Day, sometime during the 1920s, when there was a horse there that hadn't been ridden successfully by any of the cowboys present and, as the show was over, and Jesse received second money, he put on an exhibition by riding this horse backwards with a suitcase in one hand.

At that time there was another Negro rider, much younger than Jesse, whose name I cannot recall. I believe that bronc riders had an organization known as

The Turtles and, if a person could locate the whereabouts of these records, probably one could find out a lot about Jesse Stahl and other colored riders.

I'm sorry that I cannot give you more information about these folks but will endeavor to run down additional facts and if successful, will send them all on to you. As a youngster, raised in a cattle country during the horse period, I had a great deal of respect for a good bronc rider and especially Jesse Stahl.

Sincerely
John C. Scharff
Refuge Manager

Nora Longoria
1958-1973

"Dear Diary," wrote Nora Longoria in 1970 before her cancer was diagnosed, "I never did tell you about my family did I?" Born to Julia Del Valle and Rodolfo Longoria in Harlingen, Texas, Nora moved to Nyssa, Oregon, with her parents in the late 1960s. "I am a girl. I'm eleven years old, have brown eyes and brownish-black hair, it's curly. I wear glasses and have a loud voice." As the oldest of five living siblings, it was fortunate that in addition to enjoying singing and reading, "Norita," as she was sometimes called, also liked caring for little children. As she faced unrelenting cycles of cancer and related illnesses between 1970 and 1973, Nora's diaries reveal her attempt to live a life appropriate to her age while traveling back and forth to hospitals and doctors in Boise, Idaho. The following extracts are published here for the first time, courtesy of the Longoria family.

Nyssa, Oregon, near the Idaho border, has been home to a large Hispanic community since the late 1950s when many farm workers and their families migrated from Mexico—often via Texas and California—to the sugar beet, fruit, and potato-growing regions of the Snake River plain. It is estimated that between thirty and fifty thousand Spanish-speaking persons currently reside in and contribute to the region. Mexican Americans and other Hispanics have played an important role in Oregon's history since Vinzcaino's sea explorations in 1602-1603. In the pioneer period, Mexican Americans were among southern Oregon's first miners and packers. Various waves of migration during the twentieth century brought many Hispanics to Oregon. (Also see "Oregon's Hispanic Heritage" in *Varieties of Hope* of the Oregon Literature Series.)—S.A.

Grace in the Year before Death

A HISPANIC GIRL'S DIARY FROM NYSSA

Sunday, August 27, 1972

Today as usually we went to Boise. Joyce is still at camp and hasn't written. On the way to Boise before we left Nyssa, we passed by Billy's house. He was riding his bike and I don't know if he saw me or not. His hair is getting longer. He looks great I am very eager to go back to school! It is getting very boring!!!

Tuesday, August 29

Initition is fun!I was told to do lots of weird things! Dad's clothes are hot! Lori told me the party is going to be Sept. [1]st! Billy is going too! All the boys are dressed like girls some really look like them! Billy is in World Geo. with me— thats all! Had homework. Tomorrow have to wear clothes inside out!

Wednesday, August 30

I wore some pants and a sweatshirt. I had to carry a peanut all day and sometimes roll it with my nose. At noon we played leapfrog! Man, I was tired! When I went to Boise my lungs were hurting. My right leg is killing me. I can't put any weight on it! They told me to take it easy for the next few days! I don't think I'll go to school tomorrow. P.S. Billy doesnt like me. He is going with Daylene.

Thursday, August 31

I stayed home from school. My leg (right) hurts a lot. I can't walk on it. When I went to Boise Dr. Koones said he didn't know why it did. If it still hurt they might treat it also. At home I hurt all over so I went to bed early. P.S. I'm starting to like Jerry Baker

Friday, September 1

Last night I had a weird dream. Someone kept saying I had to have a couple of more years treatments to go, and I kept yelling "No!" My leg doesn't hurt very much now. By noon it was fine. I felt sick going home from Boise.

Sunday, September 3

It's been a boring weekend. Dad has been on my nerves about keeping our feet on the floor and not on the sofa. We have to sit straight! No one can enjoy and relax in their own home! He cares for the furniture more. He keeps warning us with his nod and shaking the belt. Just do it and don't talk so much! Pick up every grain of dirt off the floor

Thursday, September 6
Today was the first day I went to school at 10:27 and came home at 2:30. It was strange. But I'd better get used to it! Alma, Vilma, and Deanna Flores were tied for cheerleader. . . . I think I do like Billy. He is so nice.

Saturday, September 9
I went to Lori and Shelley's party tonight. It was a little disorganized but fun. Almost every dance I danced with Billy was slow!

Thursday, September 13
I stayed home from school today because yesterday and today I had some pain in my lower left side of my rib. I also had some bleeding.

Thursday, September 14
I stayed home from school today. Yesterday I had pain in right side. Bleeding. Doctor Koones and Dr. Luce stopped cobalt treatments. Think that might have caused pain. Lst. nite couldn't go to bed. Terry seems to like me but I'm not sure. Joyce likes him too. I told her maybe I shouldn't like him. She said go ahead. I think she doesn't think much of the competition.

Saturday, October 7
My fever keeps going up & down. My cough is no better. tonight I slept with Mom again. I was shaking so hard! It took 5 blankets to get me warm! On Fri. they said if my fever was over 101.6 to give me aspirin and cold baths. The aspirin helps my fever goes from 100 to 102.

Sunday, October 8
Sunday morn. Early 3:00 Mom took me to the hosp. my temp. is 104. When we got there it was 106. Gave me anti-biotics. Mom started giving me baths (cold) all day but my temp. goes from 102 to 104.

Monday, October 9
Father Simard gave the anointing of the sick to me. Hope it works. Mom called Dr. Luce. Have to go to the hospital in Boise. On our way. Dad, Mom, me.

Cindy Donnelly Fairchild
1955-

Cindy Donnelly Fairchild spent much of her childhood in the John Day River country on a third-generation family ranch whose founders helped establish today's Wheeler County. During her La Grande college years from 1974 to 1979, Donnelly was a seasonal employee of the U.S. Forest Service (U.S.F.S.). In her first year of service, while a lookout on Mt. Emily in the Blue Mountains, Donnelly kept a personal journal as well as an official daily log for the Wallowa-Whitman National Forest.

Donnelly struggled, as had many women from 1908 onward, to be accepted in the Northwest Region of the U.S.F.S. as a field worker doing "men's work." Women's opportunities increased because of manpower shortages during World Wars I and II. For instance, Gale Burwell, a former employee of the Forest Service, served as a lookout during World War II. She related that in the 1940s she had specific instructions to call in a fire to the ranger station so that a male "smoke-chaser" could put it out, even though the fire was nearby and threatening her own lookout. More than thirty years later, U.S.F.S. women like Cindy Donnelly achieved greater acceptance in many field positions including fire fighting. Excerpts from Donnelly Fairchild's journal first appeared in the Eastern Oregon State College publication, *Underpass* (1974).—S.A.

Trying Hard Not to Become Extremely Religious
A FIRE LOOKOUT DIARY FROM THE BLUE MOUNTAINS

June 10, 1974. Fire School, La Grande Ranger District

Had a lot of anticipation for this summer. Walking up on the mountains, smelling the trees and hearing the wind whistle through them, drinking clear, cold spring water, and just doing what I pleased without having somebody telling me what I was doing wrong, or how to do it different. But the first day of work just about ended all of that excitement.

Got up, and it was a clear and sunny day. Stubbed my toe going out the door. Had trouble getting my damn motorcycle going. Met down at the U.S.F.S. warehouse and tumbled into trucks. Traveled up the river for chain-saw school; Jim Garity ran the school. Tall, shaved-head, beer-bellied, chew running out of the mouth—Jim Garity. Jim kept one hand curled and tucked up against his chest, and with one leg shorter than the other, he walked with a definite limp. I decided he had been hired on the "Equal Opportunity" basis. There was only one other girl out of the twenty new employees that were there. She was the other girl lookout. Her name was Connie.

"Now we're going to tear down these chain saws so you boys will know how to take care of them. You girls better just sit where you are so you don't get any dirt on ya." Just watched most of the morning. Lunch break. Connie and I ate together. Had a seedless orange full of seeds. Heard Jim talking to the boys in the background, asking why they weren't over at the "Girls" table trying to make a little time. After all, that's the only reason we were working for the Forest Service, to meet boys.

I knew how to run a chain-saw, so I grabbed a pair of chaps and started off. "Hell, god-damned women think nobody knows what's best for them, better get out of the way fellows!"

June 19. Fire School, La Grande

Fire school over. This hillside looks like a group of giant gophers have been turned loose for all the fire line we had to dig. Connie goes up on her tower tomorrow.

Garity came over and said, "Well, this is the start of a lot of trouble, poor old heli-tach crew will be chasing fog pockets and dust clouds all summer cause of you damn women." "Go to hell Garity," I retorted.

June 29. Mt. Emily Lookout

My tower was at the narrow end of the tear-shaped district, so only two people were needed on the mountain.

Tower stood 85 feet from the ground to the floor. It was a 5 x 5 box on stilts. No cat-walk, and no room inside for my guitar. Cold, no heat, and warped windows. Rusted fire-finder and warped map. Dead trees surrounding the area. Water dripping from tops of windows, wind blowing on metal sides causing them to pop. But the view: you could see at least 50 miles in all directions. Wallowa and Elkhorn mountains on the horizon. The Grande Ronde Valley below. Connie's tower, 35 air miles away. Whats that mountain? Hood? There's Adams, and St. Helens, and over there Rainier! Fantastic! ! ! Suddenly I felt like a very small part in the picture. Insignificant.

July 13. Mt. Emily Lookout

Good to be back to the old damp cabin after a week riding in the pumper truck again. Once again I'm getting my exercise stomping on ants. The rain last week left the road in a mess again, my poor motorcycle just about didn't make it through the big mud hole. It doesn't even resemble a motorcycle now. It looks like I'm trying to make a mud sculpture in my spare time, and all the mud is sitting in a lump outside the front door just waiting to be carved. I'll go out tomorrow and try to chip some of the brown plaster off.

Had a false fire report on the district today. 801 is still trying to get even with me. Sitting in the tower trying to polish up the brass on my fire finder I heard her report over the radio about a fire on the La Grande District. I listened to the report and looked at the reported area. Nothing. Sure didn't want to be caught off guard, looked harder. 801 has rocks in her head. The only thing burning over there is the Boise Cascade wigwam. I refuse to give a cross azimuth to a wigwam burner!

I have begun to get a mental picture of 801. She must be large-mouthed, stand at about 5'5", weigh about 135 pounds, and she either has a large nose, or wears a clothes pin on the one she has. Her voice is nasal and shrill, like the sound of chalk squeaking in a large, empty room. At this particular time I must admit some doubts I have about her intelligence. She must come from somewhere down in the valley, maybe even Portland itself. I'll give her a mirror flash tomorrow morning so she can find where the tower is.

July 15. Mt. Emily Lookout

Wind came up about 4:00. Tower felt like someone was shaking the guy-wires. Took a wind reading . . . 27 mph. I've heard it can get up to 40 mph during the summer months, I can hardly wait! Strange sounds and feelings, like a herd of elephants running up the stairs. Huffing, puffing, and violent shaking at times. Felt like I was on a giant roller coaster, when you're scared the whole thing will break, but know it's safe at the same time. Haze set in soon afterwards, visibility, zero. I came down early and worked on dinner. Finally got the draft working, had biscuits, lettuce and steak.

Cooling off tonight, wind coming up again, trip to the front porch for some wood. Sitting back, picking my guitar, hearing the wood pop, and the wind blow outside. Comfortable.

Talked to Connie about breeze, she reports the wind is blowing up there, and the report is for lightning down in Southern Oregon. Mt. Ireland recites original proverbs on radio for anyone interested. Temporary replacement for Mule Peak is a girl from Seattle. Start of true fire season, nobody is going to get their days off this week, or probably for the rest of the summer.

August 15. Mt. Emily Lookout

Crawled out of bed at 4:30 this morning to check on a storm headed for the district and plot any possible lightning strikes. I saw a few, then about six, the storm was headed right at me. The wind came up to 40 mph., rain was coming down so hard I couldn't see out the windows, and lightning was popping all around. I couldn't come down the tower safely with the wind and rain, so I knew I would have to 10-7 until the lightning passed and hope the tower wouldn't get hit. I didn't want to turn off the radio any sooner than I'd have to because I don't want people to think I'm scared of a little electricity, so I waited until I thought it was a couple of miles away. Just as I pushed the button down to talk lightning hit the microwave tower and thunder was all that the office could hear. They figured I had waited a sufficient amount of time. I sat on my table trying hard not to become extremely religious, as I remembered what an ex-601 had told me about the time he was in the tower when it took a direct hit. His radio, even though it was unhooked, got blown up, two windows were shattered, and the strike was so hot it couldn't get grounded all at once so it rebounded off the metal inside the tower until it became totally grounded. He was really lucky that he wasn't fried in the deal. You can really tell when lightning is going to strike close. I got this feeling of static electricity building up inside of me till the point I thought I might pop, then there was a lightning strike, and everything was back to normal until the electricity started to build in the air for another strike to occur.

Soon the storm had passed and I was back on the radio. The lightning had come right across the mountain and I started to see smoke coming up every which way. The air was filled with observation planes, smoke-jumpers, and smoke. I couldn't turn in the fires fast enough. I guess there were about 12 or

13 fires on the mountain today, and the heli-tach crew is still on one tonight over on Green Mountain, about eight miles from here.

At one point when the chopper was bringing in crew we had a temporary radio blackout. Damn radio never seems to work when I am the busiest. Most of the fires are out tonight.

October 4. Eastern Oregon State College, La Grande

Seems I've been dragging trees around with me since I came off the tower and started back to school. It has only been four days. Tomorrow is Friday. What a way to live. In a crowded house, with seven other people, going to school, meeting demands—papers, reading assignments, housework—and having to get along. I can't believe I ever liked school and all the things that go with it. I feel lost, like I don't belong here anymore. I would like to quit, but I won't, I'm not a quitter. Still . . . just today I was opening the car door with one hand and dropping my books out of the other I glanced up to see my tower sticking its head out of the trees, and knowing that it is there and how different my life can be, I think I can hold out till summer comes around again.

Jane Bachman Tippett
1933-

Jane Bachman Tippett has known ranching life since she was a child. Born in California, she came to northeastern Oregon and the beautiful high country of the Wallowas in 1968. Writing journals, letters, poems, and short stories is a habit she developed as a teenager. The writing style that has emerged serves her well in her capacity as a highly regarded columnist for *Agri-Times N.W.* As a freelance photographer and journalist, she draws extensively on her ranch experience near Joseph.

In October of 1975, she was divorced, forty-two years old, and challenged by a new job in the rugged Imnaha River country. She worked as a "deluxe deer camp" cook and chronicled her experiences on a brown paper bag which she sent to her mother in the form of a letter. An excerpt from the work appears here for the first time.—S.A.

Packing in the Dudes

A WALLOWA COUNTY HUNTING CAMP LETTER

Isley's Deer Camp
North Fork, Upper Imnaha River
Friday, October 4, 1975

Dear Mother

Here is me on this 4th day of October, 1975 on the upper reaches of the Imnaha, 7 miles by horseback from Indian Crossing. I just finished my solitary lunch and am enjoying an apple. The little sheepherder stove gulps wood but puts forth a cheery heat. The huge cook shack tent is equipped with two small propane stoves (each with three burners) a hand hewn log table and benches, Coleman lantern, a stocked woodpile and (finally organized) the pack boxes of every description carried in by no less than 8 mules! I still can't believe anyone short of Sacajawea would have survived the last 24 hours as I did. Me at 42, divorced, a grandmother, and then things like this. When I accepted the job I thought everything would be quite simple. The Packer would let me ride with him to Indian Crossing whereupon I would receive a saddled well trained horse, ride in, cook, and enjoy my free days fishing the Imnaha, resting and reading, etc. These latter activities will still take place I am sure, but I was a little doubtful yesterday.

We arrived around noon to find the remainder of the hunters waiting to be packed in. They had this unbelievable stock of equipment to be packed, loaded on mules tied down with diamond hitches. We also had to pack in feed for the horses and pack animals, all the cooking utensils and the perishables. I made lunch in the cook tent at the Crossing. Little did we know it was the last bit of food we'd eat until midnite.

I went through cooking pots, pans, silverware, coffee pots, etc. and selected what to bring on into camp. It had started to sprinkle and was cloudy but nice as otherwise it would have been a dusty trail. We've had such lovely Indian Summer weather. Anyway, to make a long story short, the pack train led by a rather new guide didn't show. It was 6:00 P.M. and we had a 7 mile ride before us. Manford had me catch every available animal left in the corrals which included 2 green-broke 3 yr. old colts, a young mule, a white mule named

Snowball which he had to rope to catch and stood quivering like he would shoot off to Mars any moment while we packed him.

While the dude hunters (doctors, lawyers and you name it) watched, we worked as fast as we could. Darkness descended and we still had more gear left on the ground.

I put on a heavy jacket and slicker, we held horses for the dudes to get mounted and were just taking off when the pack train led by Larry came into view. 9:30 P.M. We were finally mounted and Manford led off into a black void that was the trail, the 9 hunters following on their horses.

We could hear the rushing sound of the Imnaha the whole way as the trail led in and out of timbered places that were black as black could *ever* be. Manford in the lead would holler out every so often "Is everyone OK?" "Just let your horse have his head and let him follow the one in front."

We rode on and on in the endless night. I kept a tight hold on my 3 head and tailed mules and gave up on the mare, she knew the trail so well I just trusted to blind faith, what else. We broke out on a rocky ledge that appeared terribly narrow. The remarks from the dudes were so funny that scared as I was I laughed. Far below you could see white water flowing in the river and our horses hooves would strike on the rock slide above. The fellow ahead of me (who I was responsible for) wouldn't look down, he said his fingernails were permanently embedded in the saddle horn. Another time he said he was sure we were riding out on a limb and soon would drop off forever!

We finally got into camp, a warm tent, and at midnite I opened stew and fed all of us. Then made Saturday's lunches and did dishes at 1:30 A.M. We crawled into our sleeping bags and died.

Up at 4:30 A.M. on Saturday to feed my hungry crew and see them off at 6:00 for the *big* hunt on Bonner Flat.

A lovely fall day. The Upper Imnaha country has a rare beauty all its own. Here you have canyon sides exposed only with timber instead of bare Lower Imnaha, Snake River terrain. The tamarack up here are just beginning to turn and the huckleberry bushes are yellow and there is a brilliant red bush also that jumps out with vivid color. Along the river bank, Indian Paintbrush and blue daisies wave in the breeze amid the lush high grasses. This upriver is wild and then will eddy around a big rock and make a clear pool where you can see the bull trout and salmon.

Saturday's opening day hunt only resulted in 2 bucks being brought into camp. That night, I fed the men steaks, potatoes, tossed salad and peas.

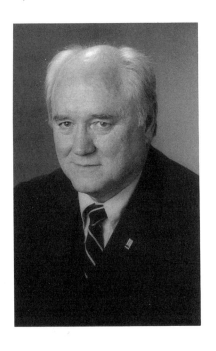

Jack Ward Thomas
1934-

U. S. Forest Service (U.S.F.S.) Chief and wildlife biologist Jack Ward Thomas started his career in 1957. Born in Fort Worth, Texas, he spent his childhood and adolescence in the small rural community of Hanley, Texas, far from the lush forests and deep river gorges of northeastern Oregon that would affect so much of his later life. For nearly twenty years Thomas lived in La Grande where he eventually served as Chief Research Wildlife Biologist in the U.S.F.S. Forestry and Range Sciences Laboratory. His stature as an innovative researcher probing the interactions among deer, elk, cattle, and timber management placed him at the center of a historic debate: the allocations of old-growth forest in the Pacific Northwest. Thomas was team leader for the Interagency Scientific Committee to Address the Conservation of the Northern Spotted Owl and later served as a member of the much publicized "Gang of Four"—a quartet of scientists appointed by the House Agriculture Committee to devise and evaluate management alternatives for the old-growth forests of the Pacific Northwest. His research in such diverse locations as Pakistan, Canada, and Poland, his award-winning publications about wildlife management issues, and a national reputation for integrity and excellence have resulted in numerous professional honors, and led him to the pinnacle of his profession. In 1993, he was appointed Chief of the United States Forest Service. With Margaret, his wife and beloved companion of thirty-five years, he left Oregon for Washington, D. C.

A student of history, an avid reader, and an engaging storyteller, Thomas has always been an acute observer. He has kept periodic journals in which he explores themes and questions and describes aspects of his private and professional life. Hunting, fishing, horse packing, and white-water rafting are among his favorite pastimes. Some of these activities are described in the following excerpts from his unpublished journals—the record of a horse-packing trip in the Hells Canyon National Recreation Area and a second trip in the Eagle Cap Wilderness.—S.A.

Whispers in the Night
REFLECTIONS OF A WILDLIFE BIOLOGIST

August 26, 1986. Hells Canyon NRA

We made camp at the site of the Kneeland Place an old homestead that was abandoned in 1916 when the bank in Enterprise failed. When I first came by this place in 1974, the old house was still standing—two-story with a basement. There was a large old barn. Those structures are gone now—the house in a grass fire in 1983 and the barn in a second fire in 1984. All that remains to mark the Kneeland's efforts are a rock-walled basement and a rapidly decaying spring house.

We camped above the old home site in the edge of the Ponderosa pine forest. After camp was set up and the wood was in, I laid on my back and studied the trees. The area had burned over several years ago—probably in the fire that destroyed the old homestead buildings. The Ponderosa pine had been scorched but in the way of that species had survived the fire the better for the experience. The Douglas fir that had started to encroach on the area were killed by the fire and the Ponderosa pine stands alone.

The twenty or so trees in the immediate vicinity of our camp all have forked tops and all at about the same height above the ground. These "school marms" were due to a well-fed porcupine some 30 or 40 years ago. The porky placidly gnawed away the bark of the trees 20 feet above the ground where it was tender and easy chewing. The tops dried, branching limbs turned upward toward the light thus forming the fork.

Strangely enough, the porcupine's mark may still be evident when all signs of the Kneeland's homestead are gone.

August 27

Old homesteads whether in Texas, the Appalachians or New England always cause the same strange feelings in me. Somehow, if you are alone, listening with your "being," you can hear the people who lived here. You see, among the rubble, the remains of a young girl's shoe, hear her laughter or, maybe, her tears? What happened to her? Did she grow and marry, have children and grandchildren, or grow old and full of life? Did she die young? Is she buried nearby?

But that is such a short time ago—1924. Down Somers Creek along the Snake, archaeologists have dug up Indian dwellings they say are 5,000 years old.

The Snake River is a good place to contemplate such things. The Snake River Canyon is, by Act of Congress, a National Recreation Area—protected from the hand and acts of man. A natural and, now, national treasure. Only a very few travel through the area except along the river and on the river.

The jet boats come upstream against the current, their engines screaming against the canyon walls. Sit back and sip your liquid refreshment while your "captain" yells out the landmarks and local history. Up stream, though there is some real white water.

Downstream come the rafters looking for quiet and the thrill of white water. They pass, the jet boater and the rafter, two kinds of beings, almost. They do not regard each other kindly—they both love the river but they want different things. . . . Really, they live in an uneasy compromise each waiting for an advantage. There are too many suitors and fewer and fewer rivers to court.

Thursday, July 28, 1987. Eagle Cap Wilderness

We decide to jump off from East Eagle Meadows because it is a relatively short 6 mile ride into some alpine lakes. The only drawback to this decision is that it is a 3 hour haul over gravel roads to the trail head. This drive, along the road to a now closed mountain resort and outfitter's headquarters called Boulder Park, has been through "back country." That condition is obviously in the process of being changed and rapidly. The road way is festooned in plastic ribbons of orange and blue and red tied to the wooden stakes that are the means that engineers use to announce roads to be. Further along the road to E. Eagle Meadows the construction of the network of logging roads is well underway. The first timber sales have been laid out and sold and logging will follow hard on the heels of the road construction. The *de facto* wilderness shrinks by another increment. Good, or bad? That is not so clear—but there is no doubt that the change in this piece of the earth is irrevocable. What has been for many centuries will be no longer. Man asserts his god-like ability to manipulate this forest betting that his knowledge is great enough to maintain that forest in a viable and productive state. Most forest managers seem fully confident that we have the knowledge and wisdom, and the technology to do just that. Others, I am among them, hear whispers in the night that cautions that we know really very little about long-term forest ecosystems and the experience is very brief. We speak readily about fully regulated forests and second, fifth, or tenth rotation. Those things lie in the future—untested and purely hypothetical.

This does not mean that we should forego exploitation of our environment—we couldn't if we wanted to. We, as a species, were condemned to that when we moved from hunters and gathers to agriculturists and learned to manufacture and buy and sell. That released the controlling mechanisms on our population numbers. Now we are firmly committed to a race between technological development, increased environmental exploitation, and disaster.

The question is not one of whether to exploit natural resources but of how and at what rate. The trick to survival is to make sure that "renewable" (if they are indeed renewable in the long run) natural resources are indeed renewable over the centuries. As we pack up at the trail head we can hear the logging machinery at work and with that logging the "buffer" between the wilderness and managed forest disappears. Even several miles up the trail we can still hear the loggers at work down below.

Friday, July 29

We are moving today over the ridge above us and then down into Trout Creek and on down to the Minam River. But there is no hurry. Bill and I sit around the fire and wait for the sun to come over the ridge and take away the frost. We watch the sun creep down the rock bluffs, talus slopes, and snow patches that tower 2,000 feet above Echo Lake. It is a symphony of light and shadow. No words pass between us. The only sound is the soft rattle of newly poured coffee. When Meg comes from the tent, she asks "What have you been up to?" I answer, "Taking communion." She looks at me. . . .

Bibliography

BL—Bancroft Library, University of California, Berkeley.
KL/UO—Special Collections, Knight Library, University of Oregon, Eugene.
LCHM—Lane County Historical Museum Library, Eugene.
OHS/MS—Oregon Historical Society, Manuscripts Collection, Portland.
SOHS—Reference Library, Southern Oregon Historical Society, Medford.
OHQ—Oregon Historical Quarterly, Oregon Historical Society Quarterly, and *The Quarterly of the Oregon Historical Society*

I. General and Statewide: Published Sources

Arksey, Laura, Nancy Pries, and Marcia Reed. *American Diaries: Annotated Bibliography of Published American Diaries and Journals (1492-1980).* Vols 1-2. Detroit: Gale Research, 1983 and 1986.

Boyd, Anne Morris. *United States Government Publication.* New York: H.W. Wilson Company, 1949.

Brandt, Patricia, and Nancy Guilford. *Oregon Biography Index.* Bibliographic Series Number 11. Corvallis: Oregon State University Press, 1976.

Constitution and Quotations from the Register of the Oregon Pioneer Association. 5 vols. Salem: E.M. Wait, Book and Job Printer, 1875.

Cullen, Matthew F. *Oregon Historical Society Manuscript Collection.* Portland: Oregon Historical Society, 1971.

Echoes of Oregon 1837-1859. 2 vols. Salem: Oregon State Archives, 1987.

Engeman, Richard, ed. *A Preliminary Guide to Local History Materials: Jacksonville Museum Library.* Jacksonville: Southern Oregon Historical Society, 1978.

Hardt, Ulrich H., ed., Regionalism: Literature of Oregon issue of *Oregon English Journal,* Vol. XIII, No. 1 (Spring 1991).

Hewitt, Randall Henry. *Across the Plains and Over the Divide.* New York: Argosy-Antiquarian, 1964.

History of the Expedition under the Command of Captains Lewis & Clarke. 3 vols. New York: Biddle, 1814. Repr. New York: Allerton Book Co., 1922.

Hollingshead, Anne Huston, ed. *The Cornwall Family's Trek to Oregon.* Ketchum, ID: By the Editor, 1992.

Holmes, Kenneth L., ed. *Covered Wagon Women: Diaries and Letters from the Western Trails 1840-1890.* 10 vols. Glendale, CA: Arthur Clark Company, 1983.

Jackson, Donald, ed. *Letters of the Lewis and Clark Expedition with Related Documents.* Urbana: University of Illinois Press, 1962.

Johansen, Dorothy O. *Empire of the Columbia.* New York: Harper & Row, 1967.

Kagle, Steven E. *American Diary Literature: 1620-1799.* Boston: Twayne, 1979. (Note: later bibliographies revise the inclusive dates for this book.)

———. *Early Nineteenth-Century American Diary Literature.* Boston: Twayne, 1986.

———. *Late Nineteenth-Century American Diary Literature.* Boston,: Twayne, 1988.

Maxwell, William. *The Outermost Dream: Essays and Reviews.* New York: Alfred Knopf, 1989.

McLagan, Elizabeth. *A Peculiar Paradise: A History of Blacks in Oregon, 1788-1940.* Portland: Georgian Press, 1980.

Moffat, Mary Jane, and Charlotte Painter, eds. *Revelations: Diaries of Women.* New York: Random House, 1974.

Morgan, Dale. *Overland in 1846: Diaries and Letters of the California-Oregon Trail.* Georgetown, CA: Talisman Press, 1963.

Munnick, Harriet Duncan. *Catholic Church Records of the Pacific Northwest.* Portland: Binfords & Mort, 1984.

Nelson, Herbert B. *The Literary Impulse in Pioneer Oregon.* Corvallis: Oregon State College Press, 1948.

O'Donnell, Terence. *An Arrow in the Earth.* Portland: Oregon Historical Society Press, 1991.

Peffer, E. Louise. *The Closing of the Public Domain: Disposal and Reservation Policies, 1900-1950.* Stanford, CA: Stanford University Press, 1951.

Sawyer, Layne. *Guide to Oregon Provisional and Territorial Government Records.* Salem: Oregon State Archives, 1990.

Schlissel, Lillian. *Women's Diaries of the Westward Journey.* New York: Schocken Books, 1982.

Schmidt, Martin. *Catalog of Manuscripts in the University of Oregon Library.* Eugene: University of Oregon, 1971.

Smith, Helen Krebs. *With Her Own Wings. Historical Sketches. . . Pioneer Women.* Portland: Beattie and Company, 1948.

Thwaites, Reuben G., ed. *Early Western Travels, 1748-1846.* 33 vols. Cleveland, OH: A.H. Clark Co., 1904-07.

West, Terry L. *Centennial Mini-Histories of the Forest Service.* U.S. Department of Agriculture, Forest Service FS-518, Forest History Unit, Washington, DC, 1992.

White, Kris and Mary Katherine Cuthill, eds. *Overland Passages: A Guide to Overland Documents in the Oregon Historical Society.* Portland: Oregon Historical Society Press, 1993.

Withington, Mary C. *A Catalogue of Manuscripts in the Collection of Western Americana Founded by William Roberston Coe.* New Haven, CT: Yale University Press, 1952.

Witte, John. "Pioneer Letters as Literature." *Northwest Review* 19, No. 1-2: 2-28.

II. General and Statewide: Unpublished Sources

Eells, Cushing. Letters. TS, 1838. MSS# 1218. OHS/MS.

Eells, Myra F. Journal. MS, 1838. MSS# 1218. OHS/MS.

Frost, Joseph H. Journal. MS, 1839 - 1863. MSS# 1214. OHS/MS.

Gray, Mary August. Diary. TS, 1840. MSS# 1202. OHS/MS.

Gray, William Henry. Journal. MS, 28 Dec 1836 - 15 Oct 1837. MSS# 1202. OHS/MS.

Judson, Lewis H. Letters. MS, 1829-1877. MSS# 976. OHS/MS.

Hulin, Lester. Diary. MF, 1847. MF# 56. OHS/MS.

Parker, Samuel. Diary. TS, 1845. MSS# 1508. OHS/MS.

Walker, Elkanah. Diary. TS, 16 Apr 1838-27 Sep 1838. MSS# 1204. OHS/MS.

Walker, Mary R. Diary. TS, 23 Apr 1838-29 Aug 1838. MSS# 1204. OHS/MS.

Whitman, Marcus. Letters. MS, 1834-1847. MSS# 1203. OHS/MS.

Whitman, Narcissa. Diary. MS, 1836-1838. MSS# 1203. OHS/MS.

III. Westside: Published Sources

Allen, Eleanor. *Canvas Caravans.* Portland: Binfords & Mort, 1946.

Anonymous Soldier. Letter. *See* Terence O'Donnell, Section I.

Applegate, Alex M., et al. "Ventures and Adventures of a Party of Webfoot Miners on Their Way to and in the Poly Region of the Northern Mines." University of Oregon Library, *Call Number* 27 (Fall 1965): 1-24.

Applegate, Harriet, and Gertrude Applegate. *See* Shannon Applegate, *Skookum.*

Applegate, Shannon. "Die Schulfrau of the Valley Willamette: The Journals of Teacher Elizabeth Trimberger." *Oregon English Journal* Vol. 13, No. 1 (Spring 1991): 38-40.

————. *Skookum: An Oregon Pioneer Family's History and Lore.* New York: William Morrow Publishers, 1988.

————. "Unexpected Texts and Contexts: Oregon's Ethnic Diaries and Letters." *Oregon English Journal* Vol. 14, No. 1 (Spring 1992): 73-77.

Atwood, Kay. "Minorities of Early Jackson County, Oregon." Jackson County Intermediate Education District, 1976.

Ball, John. "Across the Continent Seventy Years Ago." Ed. Kate N.B. Powers (his daughter). *OHQ* 3, No. 1 (March 1902): 82-106.

Bates, Bertram. *Journal of Army Life in Oregon with Illustrations by the Author 1917.* Eugene: Bates, Ray. 1989.

Beaglehole, J.C., ed. *The Journals of Captain James Cook on His Voyages of Discovery: The Voyage of the* Resolution *and* Discovery, *1776-1780.* Cambridge, England: Cambridge University Press, 1967.

Beals, Herbert K. "Spanish Explorers in the Oregon Country." *Oregon Humanities* (Summer 1992): 9-12.

Bede, Elbert E. *Fabulous Opal Whiteley.* Portland: Binfords & Mort, 1954.

Benjamin, I.J. *Three Years in America, 1859-1862.* Trans. Charles Reznikoff. Philadelphia, PA: The Jewish Publication Society of America, 1956.

Bensell, Royal A. *All Quiet on the Yamhill: The Journal of Corporal Royal A. Bensell.* Ed. Gunther Barth. Eugene: University of Oregon Books, 1959.

Blanchet, A.M.A. *Journal of a Catholic Bishop.* Ed. Edward J. Kowrach. Fairfield, WA: Ye Galleon Press, 1978.

Boit, John. *Log of the* Union: *John Boit's Remarkable Voyage to the Northwest Coast and around the World.* North Pacific Studies Series. Ed. Edmund Hayes. Portland: Oregon Historical Society Press, 1981.

Boulton, Jane. *Opal Whiteley.* New York: Macmillan Publishing Co., 1976.

Boas, Franz. *The Ethnography of Franz Boas: Letters and Diaries Written on the Northwest Coast from 1886-1931.* Ed. Ronald R. Rohner. Chicago: University of Chicago Press, 1969.

Burnett, Peter H. "Letter from Peter H. Burnett, Esq." *OHQ* 24, No. 1 (March 1923): 105-108.

Casteel, Dr. John L. *See* Betty Lawson Walters.

Chinook, William. *See* Terence O'Donnell in Section I.

Cline, Robert Scott. "Creation of an Ethnic Community: Portland Jewry, 1851-1866." *Pacific Northwest Quarterly* (April 1985): 52.

Coke, Henry John. *A Ride over the Rocky Mountains to Oregon and California.* London: R. Bentley, 1852.

Crawford, Medorem. *Journal of Medorem Crawford.* Fairfield, WA: Ye Galleon Press, 1967.

Deady, Matthew P. *Pharisee among Philistines: The Diary of Judge Matthew P. Deady 1871-1892.* 2 vols. Ed. Malcolm Clark, Jr. Portland: Oregon Historical Society Press, 1975.

de Hezeta, Bruno. *For Honor and Country: The Diary of Bruno de Hezeta.* Ed. and trans. Herbert K. Beals. Portland: Oregon Historical Society Press, 1985.

Dodds, Gordon B. *The Salmon King of Oregon*. Chapel Hill: University of North Carolina, 1959.

Dodge, Orvil. *Pioneer History of Coos and Curry Counties, Oregon*. Salem: Capital Printing Co., 1898.

Douglas, David. *Journals Kept by David Douglas during His Travels in North America 1823-27*. New York: Antiquarian Press Ltd., 1959.

Douthit, Nathan. *The Coos Bay Region 1890-1944*. Coos Bay: River West Books, 1981.

Duniway, Abigail Scott. *Pathbreaking: An Autobiographical History of the Equal Suffrage Movement in Pacific Coast States*. Portland: James, Kerns & Abbott, 1914.

Easterwood, Thomas Jefferson. "Henry Cummins, Constant Reader." University of Oregon Library *Call Number* 23, 1 (Fall 1961).

Edwards, Philip L. *Diary of Col. Philip L. Edwards: An Account of a Trip to the Pacific Coast in 1837*. Sacramento, CA: A.J. Johnston & Co. Printers, 1890.

Elliott, Thompson Coit, ed. "Oregon Coast as Seen by Vancouver in 1792." *OHQ* 30, No. 1 (March 1929): 33-42.

Feinman, Ronald L. *Twilight of Progressivism: The Western Republican Senators and the New Deal*. Baltimore: John Hopkins University Press, 1981.

Franchere, Gabriel. *Adventure at Astoria, 1810-1814*. Norman: University of Oklahoma Press, 1967.

Fremont, John Charles. *Narratives of Exploration and Adventure*. Ed. Allan Nevins. New York: Longmans, Green, 1956.

Gamboa, Erasmo. "Oregon's Hispanic Heritage." *Oregon Humanities* (Summer 1992): 2-7.

Gass, Patrick. *A Journal of the Voyages and Travels of a Corps of Discovery under the Command of Captain Lewis and Captain Clark. . . .* Minneapolis: Ross and Haines, 1958.

Glover, Eli Sheldon. *The Diary of Eli Sheldon Glover, October-December 1875*. WPA. Portland: Historical Records Survey, 1940.

Handsacker, Samuel. *Pioneer Life by "Uncle Sam" Handsacker*. Eugene: By the Author, 1908.

Harris, Mary. Oct 1855. Document 23 in *Echoes of Oregon 1837-1859*. Salem: Oregon State Archives, 1987.

Haswell, Robert. "Haswell's Log of a Voyage round the World on the Ship *Columbia Rediviva* and the Sloop *Washington*." Intro. and notes T.G. Elliott. *OHQ* 29, No. 2 (June 1928): 162-188.

Haycox, Ernest James. *See* William Franklin Godwin Thacher.

Hilleary, William M. *A Webfoot Volunteer: The Diary of William M. Hilleary, 1864-1866*. Ed. H.B. Nelson and P.E. Onstad. Corvallis: Oregon State University Press, 1965.

Howay, Frederic W., ed. *Voyages of the* Columbia *to the Northwest Coast, 1787-1790 & 1790-1793*. Portland: Oregon Historical Society Press, 1990.

Hull, Robert. *See* Terence O'Donnell in Section I.

Humphrey, Ellen Hemenway. *Diary of Ellen Hemenway Humphrey*. Ed. Edwin A. Simpson. Saratoga, CA: Edwin A. Simpson, 1978.

Ito, Kazuo. *Issei: A History of Japanese Immigrants in North America*. Trans. Shinichiro Nakamura and Jean S. Gerard. Seattle: Japanese Community Service, 1973.

Iwatsuki, Shizue. *See* Kazuo Ito.

Judson, Nancy. *Echoes of Oregon 1837-1859*. Salem: Oregon State Archives, 1987.

Kambouris, Haralambos. "Oregon Experiences: Haralambos K. Kambouris." Ed. Helen Papanikolas, trans. C.V. Vasilopulos. *OHQ* 80, No. 2 (Spring 1981): 5-39.

La Lande, Jeff. "A Wilderness Journey with Judge John B. Waldo, Oregon's First 'Preservationist'." *OHQ* 90, No. 2 (Summer 1989): 116-166.

Longworth, Basil N. *The Diary of Basil N. Longworth, Oregon Pioneer.* WPA. Portland: The Historical Records Survey, 1938.

McArthur, Polly Hewitt. *Letters to a Doll.* Portland: By the Author, 1928.

McCall, Dorothy. *Ranch Under the Rimrock.* Portland: Binford & Mort, 1968.

McCall, Thomas. *Tom McCall:Maverick.* Edited by Steve Neal. Portland:Binford & Mort, 1977.

McClay, Oelo. "My Trip to the Fair." *OHQ* 80, No. 1 (Spring 1979): 51-65.

McNary, Charles L. *See* Steve Neal.

Meacham, A.B. *Wigwam and War Path or the Royal Chief in Chains.* Boston: Rockwell and Churchill, 1875.

Merriam, Paul G. "The 'Other Portland': A Statistical Note on the Foreign Born, 1860-1910." *OHQ* 80, No. 3 (Fall 1979): 258-268.

Morse, Wayne. *See* Lee Wilkins.

Neal, Steve. *McNary of Oregon: A Political Biography.* Portland: Western Imprints Press of Oregon Historical Society, 1985.

Newsom, David. *David Newsom: The Western Observer, 1805-1882.* Portland: Oregon Historical Society Press, 1972.

Noah, Catherine. "Land of Hope and Heartache." *Table Rock Sentinel* 13 (Jan-Feb 1993).

Nolan, Frederick W. "Ernest Haycox—Writer." University of Oregon Library *The Call Number* 1 & 2 (Fall 1963/Spring 1964): n.p.

Ogden, Peter Skene. *First over the Siskiyous: The Journals of Peter Skene Ogden.* Ed. Jeff La Lande. Portland: Oregon Historical Society Press, 1987.

Ord, Edward Otho Cresap. *Diary in Curry County, Oregon, 1856.* Transcribed by Louis L. Knapp. N.p.: 1970.

Owens-Adair, Bethenia A. *Dr. Owens-Adair: Some of Her Life's Experiences.* Portland: Mann & Beach, Printers, 1906.

Owens, Kenneth L., ed. *The Wreck of the SV* Nikolai*: Two Narratives of the First Russian Expedition to the Oregon Country, 1808-1810.* Trans. Alton S. Donnelly. Portland: Oregon Historical Society Press, 1985.

Peale, Titian Ramsay. *Diary of Titian Ramsay Peale.* Ed. Clifford Merrill Drury. Los Angeles: G. Dawson, 1957.

Perez, Juan. *Juan Perez on the Northwest Coast: Six Documents of His Expedition in 1774.* Trans. and ed. Herbert K. Beals. Portland: Oregon Historical Society Press, 1990.

Pierce, Walter M. *Oregon Cattleman/Governor/Congressman: Memoirs and Times of Walter M. Pierce.* Ed. A. H. Bone. Portland: Oregon Historical Society Press, 1981.

Pomeroy, Earl, ed. "Five Early Letters of Herbert Hoover." University of Oregon Library *Call Number* 27 (Spring 1966): 2-12.

Putnam, George R. *Beacons of the Sea.* Washington, D.C.: Press of Judd & Deteweiler Inc., 1913.

Putnam, Rozelle. *This Was a Man.* Ed. Wilfred Brown. Hollywood, CA: Wilfred Brown, 1971.

Riddle, Jeff C. *The Indian History of the Modoc War.* San Jose: Urion Press, 1974.

Robbins, Harvey. "Journal of Rogue River War, 1855." *OHQ* 34, No. 4 (December 1933): 345-358.

Robbins, William G. *Hard Times in Paradise: Coos Bay, Oregon, 1850-1986.* Seattle: University of Washington, 1988.

Robertson, Daniel C. "The Awakening of Conservation: The Oregon Land Fraud Trials." *Umpqua Trapper* 20 (Summer 1984): 27-34.

Rockwood, E. Ruth, ed. "Diary of Rev. George H. Atkinson, 1847-1858." *OHQ* 40, No. 4 (December 1939): 345-362.

Schmidt, Martin, ed. *Inventory of the Papers of Senator Wayne L. Morse.* Eugene: University of Oregon Press, 1974.

Scofield, John. *Hail, Columbia! Robert Gray, John Kendrick, and the Pacific Fur Trade.* Portland: Oregon Historical Society Press, 1993.

Seiber, Richard, ed. *The Journal of Brewer & Clarke.* Fairfield, WA: Ye Galleon Press, 1984.

Sengstaken, Agnes Ruth. *Destination West!* Portland: Binfords & Mort, 1942.

Skinner, Eugene. "Letters." *Lane County Historian* 21, No. 2 (1976): 18-20.

Smith, Elizabeth. Diary, September 15, 1847. *See* Kenneth Holmes in Section I.

Stampfer, Rabbi Joshua. *Pioneer Rabbi of the West: The Life and Times of Julius Eckman.* Portland: J. Stampfer, 1988.

Stuart, Reginald R. & Grace Stuart. *Calvin B. West: An Obscure Chapter in the History of Southern Oregon.* Stockton, CA: California History Association, 1961.

Sullivan, William L. *Listening for Coyote: A Walk across Oregon's Wilderness.* New York: William Morrow & Co. Publishers, 1988.

Talbot, Theodore. *The Journals of Theodore Talbot, 1843 and 1849-52.* Ed. Charles H. Carey. Portland: Metropolitan Press, 1931.

Telfer, George F. *Manila Envelopes: Oregon Volunteer Lt. George F. Telfer's Spanish-American War Letters.* Ed. Sara Burnett. Portland: Oregon Historical Society Press, 1987.

Thacher, William Franklin Godwin. *Dear W.F.G.* Boston, MA: Little, Brown & Co., 1951.

Thomas, Edward Harper. *Chinook: A History and Dictionary.* Portland: Binfords & Mort, 1935, 1954, 1970.

Tomita, Saku. "Portland Assembly Center: The Diary of Saku Tomita." Trans. Zuigaku Kodachi and Jan Heikkala, ed. Janet Cormack. *OHQ* 81, No. 2 (Summer 1980): 149-171.

Tyack, David. "The Tribe and the Common School." University of Oregon Library, *Call Number* 27 (Spring 1966): 13-17.

Vaughn, Thomas. *Soft Gold: The Fur Trade & Cultural Exchange on the Northwest Coast of America.* Portland: Oregon Historical Society Press, 1990.

Wagner, Henry M., ed. *Spanish Voyages to the Northwest Coast of America.* San Francisco: California Historical Society, 1929.

Waldo, John B. *See* Jeff La Lande.

Walling, Albert G. *History of Southern Oregon . . . .* Portland: Printing House of A.G. Walling, 1884.

Walters, Betty Lawson. "The Lean Years: John L. Casteel's Diaries, 1931-1942." *OHQ* 89, No.3 (Fall 1988): 229-302.

Walton, Pauline. "Letters." *Lane County Historian* 30, No. 2 (1985): 37-42.

West, Calvin B. *See* Reginald R. & Grace Stuart.

Whiteley, Opal. *The Singing Creek where the Willows Grow: The Rediscovered Diaries of Opal Whiteley.* Ed. Benjamin Hoff. New York: Ticknor & Fields, 1986.

Wilkins, Lee. *Wayne Morse: A Bio-Bibliography.* Westport, CT: Greenwood Press, 1985.

Williams, Lucia Lorraine. Letter 1851. *See* Kenneth L. Holmes in Section I.

Wilson, Adrian. *Two against the Tide: A Conscientious Objector in W.W. II.* Ed. Joyce Lancaster Wilson. Austin, TX: W. Thomas Taylor, 1990.

Winther, Oscar Osburn, and Rose Dodge Galey, eds. "Mrs. Butler's 1853 Diary of Rogue River Valley." *OHQ* 41, No. 4 (December 1940): 337-366.

Wood, Elizabeth. "Journal of a Trip to Oregon 1851." *OHQ* 27, No. 1 (March 1926): 192-203.
Wood (aka Word), Tallmadge B. "Letters of Tallmadge B. Wood." *OHQ* 3, No. 4 (December 1902): 394-398 and 4, No. 1 (March 1903): 80-85.

III. Westside: Unpublished Sources

Ainsworth, John C. Diaries & Personal Correspondence. MS, AX 11, KL/UO.
Allen, Eric William. Correspondence. MS, 1917-1934. AX 182, KL/UO.
Anonymous Prisoner. Letter. TS, 1930. Private collection of Eileen Cook.
Applegate, Oliver Cromwell. Papers. MS, 1842-1938, AX 5, KL/UO.
Bancroft, Hubert Howe. "Correspondence Relating to the History of Oregon." MS, 1863-1889. HHB [P-A 169], BL. *See also* Willard H. Rees.
Bannard, Margaret. Letters. MS, 1903-1904, CB B226, KL/UO.
Barclay, William. Diary. MS, 1856. MSS# 236. OHS/MS.
Barette, Leonore Gale. Diary. MS, 1895, 93, LCHM.
Barlow, John L. Letter. MS 1875, A265, KL/UO.
Bates, Kate Stevens. Diaries. MS, 1880-1936. AX 202, KL/UO.
Baugh, Raymond C. Diaries. MS, 1902-1928. 160, LCHM.
Bensell, Royal Augustus. Diary. MS, 1862-1864. AX 118, KL/UO.
Birchman, Anna. Letter. TS, n.d. MSS# 2035B. OHS/MS.
Booth, Georgia Belle, collector. Letters. MS. A170, KL/UO.
Borthwick, Alexander. Letters and Diaries. MS, 1870-1905. In Borthwick Family Papers, AX 16, KL/UO.
Brenne, Fred. Letter to "Doug and Hec." MS, 1934. A262, KL/UO.
Bristol, Elijah. Letters and Miscellaneous Papers. MS. 3, LCHM.
Brooks, Quincy Adams. Letters and Miscellaneous Papers. MS. 51, LCHM.
Brown, Joseph Henry. Letter to Nettie Spencer. MS. CA 1895, Apr. 27. KL/UO.
Burbank, Augustus R. Diary. 12 Ap 1849-7 May 1898, 3 vols. MS. A13, KL/UO.
Bushnell, James A. Letters. MS, 1852. LCHM.
Bybee, Minnie Ida. Diaries 1890-1893. MS, 40. SOHS.
Caddick, Helen. Diary. MF, 1891. MF# 2. OHS/MS.
Campbell, Florence. Journal. TS, 10 Jun 1909 - 30 Jun 1910. MSS# 1509. OHS/MS.
Case, Victoria. Letters. MS 1940s [173]. KL/UO.
Casteel, John L. Diaries. MS, 1931 -1942. MSS# 2804. OHS/MS.
Castor, Laura Rice. Diary. MS, 1884 - 1889. MSS# 154B. OHS/MS.
Chamberlin, Norman Henry. Diary. MS, 1861 - 1884. MSS# 428B. OHS/MS.
Cleator, Frederick W. Diaries. MS, 1944-1954. AX 13, KL/UO.
Colver Family Letters. MS, 1861-1870. AX 126, KL/UO.
Colver, Rachel. Letter, "third day of August, 1864." T.S. Sisley Family File, Baker County Library, Baker City.
Colvig, Vance DeBar. Letter. MS 9, Folder #1. March 10, 1948. SOHS.
Couch-Glisan. Journal and Correspondence. MS, 1911 - 1912. MSS# 952-1. Nan Robertson Papers. OHS/MS.
Cridge, Edward. Diary. MF, 1854. MF# 76. OHS/MS.
Croke, James Fr. Letters to Francis N. Blanchet concerning the State of the Catholic Church in Oregon, 1853-54. MS & T.S. A23, A22.26, KL/UO.
Cummins, Henry. Diaries, 1857-1863. Western Americana Collection, Yale University, New Haven, CT. [Microfilm of Diaries], KL/UO.
Davenport, Homer. Letters. MS, 1891-1912, in Timothy Davenport Coll. AX 242, KL/UO.
Davidson, Albert Franklin. Journal. MS, 1846. MSS# 386. OHS/MS.

Davis, Harold Lenoir. Letters to M. P. Ingram. MS, 1945-1955. A228, KL/UO.
———. Letter. TS, 5 Dec 1937. MSS# 1621. Howard Corning Papers. OHS/MS.
Dease, John Warren. Diary. MS, 1829. MSS# 560. OHS/MS.
deFremery, H.S. Letter. T.S, 1856. Curry County Historical Society, Wederburn.
Donaldson, Amanda Smith. Collections. Tillamook Co. Museum, Tillamook.
Dowell, Benjamin Franklin. Correspondence 1855-1886. MS. HHB [P-A 133-140], BL.
Downs, Warren. Waldport, Camp Angel Diary. T.S. 1944 SFM. 239, KL/UO.
Dunagan, Willis. Diaries. MS, 1865-1872, 1875, 1879-1884, 1886-1891, 1894-1897. AX 133, KL/UO.
Duniway, Abigail Scott. Letter to Barbara M. Booth. MS, 11 Ap., 1914. "Women Miscellany," Folder CA 1914, KL/UO.
Dyson, George Allan. Diaries. MS, 1908, 1919 and 1931. AX 244, KL/UO.
Ellsworth, Harris. Letters. MS, 1943-1957. AX 33, KL/UO.
Evans, Elwood. Letters. MS, 1859-1882 from Frances Fuller Victor and Jesse Applegate. A 36, KL/UO.
Failing, Henry. Diary. MS, 1851. MSS# 650. OHS/MS.
Faubion, Nina Lane. Letters from Harry Lane, MS, 1906-1908. A 185, KL/UO.
Fenton, L.R. Diary. MS, 1890 - 1905. MSS# 818B. OHS/MS.
Fisher, Guy. Diary and Correspondence. MS, 1945 - 1963. MSS# 1627. OHS/MS.
Forrest, Bernice. Handwritten Journal. MS, 2 Oct 1916-10 Sep 1917.#983-84-5. Horner Museum, Oregon State University, Corvallis.
Fort Langley, BC / Hudson's Bay Co. Journal. MF, 1827 - 1830. MF# 46. OHS/MS.
Fox, Douglas H. Letters to Oregon Literary Figures. MS, 1920s. A 262, KL/UO.
Geiger, William. Letter to Brother and Sister. MS, 1849. A 41, KL/UO.
Gillihan, Sara. Letter. TS, 10 July 1879. Columbia C. Museum, Vernonia.
Gillespie, Agnes L. Diary. MS, 1852. 168, LCHM.
Gillette, Preston W. MS 86:56. Collections, Clatsop Co. Historical Society, Astoria.
Green, Beryl A. Letters to Wayne Morse. MS (1942-1953). AX 559, KL/UO.
Gregor, Elsie Allen. Child's Diary. MS 1917, LCHM.
Griffin, Myron. Letters to Douglas H. Fox, 1930s. MS. A 262, KL/UO.
Hall, Lindlsey F. Diary. MS, MSS# 1653. OHS/MS.
Hallock, A.B. "Journal of Daily Transactions, MS, Dec. 15, 1880-July 6, 1882." A 35, KL/UO.
Hamilton, James W. Diary, MS, Jan. 7, 1878-Sept.11, 1879. A 45, KL/UO.
Hanzen, Henry M. Correspondence with Charles L. McNary MS, (1917-1944) and Wayne Morse (1946-1959). AX 507, KL/UO.
Harlow, Mahlon H. Diary, 1851-1854. MS. 108, LCHM.
Haycox, Ernest James. Correspondence of Ernest Haycox and W.F.G. Thacher, MS, 1930-1947. A 47, KL/UO. *See also* W.F.G. Thacher.
Hemenway, Ansel. Diaries. MS, 1866, 1868-1871, 1876-1878, 1881-1889. AH 49, KL/UO.
Hermann, Binger. Letters. MS, 1888-1920. AH 426, KL/UO.
Hilleary, William M. Diary. MS, 1865 - 1866. MSS# 919. OHS/MS.
Hills, Florence Neet. Diaries. MS, 1907-1928. 167, LCHM.
Hirsh, Harold. Letter. TS, 1960. MSS# 1819. OHS/MS.
Historic Record Survey. Foreign Language Press in Oregon. MS. BX 66, 39, 40, 80, KL/UO.
Historical Records Survey, Oregon. Bx 66.73. (2) Individual manuscript file. (8) Transcripts of county commissioner's journals, Baker, Benton, Clatsop, Columbia, Coos, et al. Manuscripts file, published and unpublished. KL/UO.

Hofer, Florence. Florence Hofer Material. Lincoln Co. Historical Society, Newport.

Holaday, Joseph. Journal and Miscellaneous Family Papers. MS. 120, LCHM.

Horning, Cynthia. Letters to Ann Foster. MS. Foster Family Papers, Schminck House Museum, Lakeview.

Ireland, Asher. U.S. Forest Service Field Diaries. MS, 1914-1920. A 60, KL/UO.

Jacoby, Gainey. Diary. MS, 1911, 1912. 39, LCHM.

John, David. Diary of Life on a Farm. MS, 1864-1879. AX 180, KL/UO.

Kambouris, Haralambos. Diary, "Pages of My Life." MS, 1912- 1914. MS 530, Manuscript Division, Marriott Library, University of Utah, Salt Lake City, UT.

Kimmel, Martin Luther. Diary. MS, 1917 - 1919. MSS# 2201. OHS/MS.

Kraemer, Otto Julius. Letters Re. Oregon Jews, MS, 1987-1939. A 161, KL/UO.

Lampman, Ben Hur. "Letters to My Sonne Herbert." MS, 1925. AX 426, KL/UO.

Lane, Joseph. Letters & Diary. MS, 1872-1881. AX 183, KL/UO.

Lawrence, E.F. Correspondence with Louis Conrad Rosenberg and H.W. Gardner. MS, 1912-1914. AX 56, BX 12, KL/UO.

Leonard, Herman Camp. Diary. MS, 1850 - 1851. MSS# 2259. OHS/MS.

"Letters Written by Members of the Holt Family." TMs [photocopy], OHS.

Lewelling, Seth. Diary. MS, 1860 - 1877. MSS# 23. OHS/MS.

Lewis, Charles C. Letter to Mother. MS, CA 1895 Ag 18, KL/UO.

Lockley, Fred. Letters Received 1915-1933. [See MS Catalogue]. KL/UO.

Lofton, Blanche De Good. Correspondence with Oregon Poet, Ethel Romig Fuller. MS. AX 282, KL/UO.

Marble, Amy E. Diary. MS, 1942 - 1983. MSS# 2809. OHS/MS.

Marks, Saul & Co., Roseburg, Ore. Letters. MS, 1871-1885. B 45, KL/UO.

Marshall, Charles Louis. "Diary Jan. 1907 to June 1908 in the R & S Goldmine, Curry Co., Oregon." MS. AX 408, KL/UO.

Matthews, Rufus B. Letters of R.B. and Grace Matthews. MS. D-3 to D-70, Matthews Family. Douglas County Museum, Roseburg.

McCall, Thomas. Assorted Correspondence. MS. MSS# 625. OHS/MS.

McDowall, Bruce Campbell. Diaries. MS, 1907-1916. 110, LCHM.

McKay, James. Diary. MS, 1879 - 1891. MSS# 1145. OHS/MS.

McNary, Charles Linza. Office Papers Relating to Oregon Affairs. MS, 1921-1941. AX 49, KL/UO. *See also* Henry M. Hanzen; Steve Neal in Section II.

Merritt, Melvin Leroy. "Field Diaries of Regional Forester, Region 6, 1909-1920." MS. AX 66, KL/UO.

Millard, Bailey. Letters from Joaquin Miller. MS. AX 431, KL/UO.

Miller, Henry. Diaries (German). MS, 1851 - 1893. MSS# 24. OHS/MS.

Miller, Robert Aubrey. "Journal of a Trip to the Cave in Josephine County, August 13-19, 1878." MS. AX 70, KL/UO.

Millican, Robert. Diary. MS, 1900. 9, LCHM.

Mills, W.P. Diary. MS, 1876. Polk Co. Hist. Society/Brunk House Museum, Monmouth.

Minto, John. Letter to William P. Lord. MS. CA 1892, Jan. 15, KL/UO.

Moore, Harry De Witt. Letter to Unnamed Woman. MS, Ap 29, 1873. File # M-28, Order of Indian Wars Collection, U.S. Army Military History Research Collection, National Archives, Washington, D.C.

Morse, Wayne Lyman. General Correspondence on Labor Arbitration Cases. MS, 1938-1942. Coll. 1, KL/UO. *See also* Beryl A. Green, Henry M. Hanzen.

Murphy, Sr. Miriam. Intensive Journal, Excerpts. Courtesy of an Anonymous Donor. Marylhurst College, Portland, OR.

Neuberger, Maurine Brown. Correspondence and Documents, 1960 Campaign. MS. AX 78, KL/UO.

Neuberger, Richard Lewis. Personal Files, 1931-1960, including Original Letters by Senator Harry Lane. MS. AX 78, KL/UO.

Nighswander, Frances Marion. Journals, MS, 1864-1867. A 91, KL/UO.

Noble, John F. Diary. MS, 1849-1898. MSS# 1000. OHS/MS.

Nunn, William. Manuscripts. MSS 485. OHS/MS.

Onthank, Karl William. Conservation Correspondence MS, 1950-1967. AX 356 (1) through (12), KL/UO.

Oregon Pioneer Records. Overland Diaries: T.S.: Soloman Tetherow, Lester Hulin, John Joseph Callison, Basil Nelson Longworth. Elliott Cut-Off 1853 Diaries: T.S.: Benjamin Franklin Owen, Agnes Stewart Warner; Charlotte E. Stearns Pengra, John Corydon Bushnell. [P.A. 337], BL.

Parker, Inez Adams. Letter. MS, 13 Dec 1927. MSS# 1089.OHS/MS.

Pauling, Linus Carl. Ava Helen and Linus Pauling Papers, Kerr Library Special Collections, Oregon State University.

Porter, William. Diary. MS, 1848. MSS# 1508. OHS/MS.

Puter, S.A.D. Letter. TS, 19 Nov 1906. MSS# 1500. OHS/MS.

Ramp, Floyd Cleveland. Diaries. MS, 1904-1910, Feb.-April 1914, May-June 1922. Coll. 189, KL/UO.

Raymond, Almira A. Letters from Oregon. MS, 1849-1870. A 104, KL/UO.

Reber, Kenneth. Vietnam Letters. Courtesy of Reber Family, Roseburg.

Rees, Willard H. Letters to H. H. Bancroft. MS, 1879. HHB [p-a 115], BL.

Renshaw, Maria Jane. Diary. MS, 1858. MSS# 418. OHS/MS.

Roberts, George B. Diary. MS, 1847 - 1848. MSS# 1001. OHS/MS.

Roche, Fr. Fintan. Letter T.S. 1950. Courtesy Files of St. Benedict Lodge, McKenzie Bridge.

Rostel, Carl Gotthilf Berthold. Letters. MS. AX 86, KL/UO.

Royal Family. Diaries and Papers. MS, 1849-1912. MSS# 1628. OHS/MS.

Seely, Alvane Cary. Diary. MS, 1883-1905. AX 266, KL/UO.

Seitz, Corwin V. Diaries, 1917, 1942, 1949-52. MS. AX 677, KL/UO.

Shepherd Family Letters. MS Copies, 1930s. Courtesy Jane Applegate, Yoncalla.

Skaggs, Lucinda. Letters. MS, 1883-1884. 35, LCHM.

Skinner, Eugene F. Letters. MS, 1860. 63, LCHM.

Smith, Alvin Thompson. Letters Received. MS, 1843-1852. A 111, KL/UO.

Smith, Delazon. Letters to William Smith. MS, 1857-1859. A 112, KL/UO.

Spencer, Israel. Letter. TS, n.d. Columbia County Historical Museum, Vernonia.

Stark, James. Diary. MS, 1861. MSS# 479B. OHS/MS.

Stone, Lee Owen. MSS 2423. OHS/MS.

Taylor, D.H. Diary. TS, 1 Jan 1862. MSS# 1541. OHS/MS.

Taylor, Elsie. Handwritten Journal. MS, 28 Jun 1933 - 27 Dec 1936. Yamhill County Historical Society & Museum, Lafayette.

Taylor, George. Diary. MS, 1859. MSS# 748B. OHS/MS.

Teal, Joseph Nathan. Correspondence. MS, 1916-1925. MSS# 1381. OHS/MS.

Thacher, William Franklin Godwin. Letters. MS. 48, LCHM.

Thornton-Hayes Family. Diary. MS, 1883 - 1884. MSS# 2755. OHS/MS.

Tittinger, A. J. Letter to Paul E. Hartmus re: Tillamook Rock. MS, 1978-40. Tinkham Collection, Columbia River Maritime Museum, Astoria.

Trevett, Emily. MSS 854. OHS/MS.

Trimberger, Elizabeth. Diary. T.S. Courtesy of Spackman Family, Roseburg.

Waldo, Clara. "Clara Humason Waldo: Her Life & Letters." T.S. Ed. Brian Waldo Johnson. Polk Co. Hist. Society/Brunk House Museum, Monmouth.

Walrad, Jane. Diary, 1861-1867. MS. 48 T.S. and Calendar, SOHS.

Walton, Ellen Pauline. Diaries. MS, 1911-1933 and Miscellaneous Letters. 44, LCHM.

Warrack, Robert. Letter concerning Lighthouse Keeper, Roberg Gerlof. MS, 20 Aug. 1930. Tinkham Collection, 1978-40, coll., Columbia River Maritime Museum, Astoria.

Weiss, Michael, ed. "Henry Cummins: A Youth on the Urban Rural Frontier, Eugene City and Salem, 1857-1863." (Paper prepared for American West course for Richard Maxwell Brown, History Department, UO, March 7, 1986.)

Wells, William B. Diary. MS, 1888 - 1894. MSS# 894-1. OHS/MS.

West, Calvin B. Letter 23 Jan, 1854. T.S. BX 149, KL/UO.

Wetjen, Albert R. Letters to Douglas H. Fox, MS, 1930s. A 262, KL/UO.

Williams, Gerald W. Umpqua National Forest Report: "Background of the Umpqua National Forest 1898-1986." MG 162, Douglas County Museum, Roseburg.

Williams, L.L. Journal, 1851. (Henry Baldwin Collection, CB B193), KL/UO.

Wood, Charles Erskine Scott. Diary. MS, 1878. MSS# 800. OHS/MS. *See* Part V.

Yasui Family. Assorted Correspondences. MSS# 2949. OHS/MS.

Young, Calvin M. Letters. MS, 1926-1950. 109, LCHM.

V. Eastside: Published Sources

Allen, Barbara. *Homesteading the High Desert.* Salt Lake City: U. Utah Press, 1987.

Applegate, Jesse. "Letter to Bethenia Owens Adair."

Applegate, Oliver Cromwell. "Letter to A.B. Meacham."

Barklow, Irene. *From Trails to Rails: The Post Offices, Stage Stops & Wagon Roads of Union County, Oregon.* Enterprise: Enchantments Press of Oregon, 1987.

Barlow, Jeffrey and Christine Richardson. *Gum Sam: Land of the Golden Mountain.* Bend: High Desert Museum, 1991.

Bartlett, Grace. *From the Wallowas.* Enterprise: Pika Press, 1992.

Brimlow, George Francis. *Harney County, Oregon, and Its Range Land.* Portland: Binfords & Mort, 1951.

Brooks-Scanlon Lumber Co. *Deschutes Pine Echoes.* Ed. Paul Hosmer. Bend: 1925.

Clark, Keith. *Redmond: Where the Desert Blooms.* Portland: Western Imprints of the Oregon Historical Society, 1985.

Clegg, Edith. "Rattlesnakes and Rapids: A Woman's Journey against the Current in 1939." Ed. Cort Conley. *Idaho Yesterdays* (Fall 1984): 1-27.

Cressman, Luther S., and Anthony Yturrri. "The Basques in Oregon." *Commonwealth Review,* March 1938.

Dodd, Lawrence, ed. *Narcissa Whitman on the Oregon Trail.* Fairfield, WA: Ye Galleon Press, 1985.

Eakin Family. *A Long and Wearisome Journey: The Eakin Family Diaries.* Ed. Shirley Ewart, Jane and John Anderson. Enterprise: Pika Press, 1993.

Evans, John W. *Powerful Rockey: The Blue Mountains and the Oregon Trail 1811-1883.* La Grande: Eastern Oregon State College, 1990.

Fairchild, Cindy Donnelly. Diary. "Mt. Emily Lookout Summer 1974." *Underpass* V. 1974-1975. La Grande: Eastern Oregon State College, pp. 11-16.

Farnham, Thomas J. *Travels in the Great Western Prairies. . . .* Ed. Reuben Gold Thwaites. Cleveland: 1906. Reprint, AMS Press, New York, 1966.

Ferguson, Denzel and Nancy. *Oregon's Great Basin Country.* Burns: Gail Graphics, 1978.

Findley, Sarah Jane. Letter in "Memoirs of Alexander B. & Sarah Jane Findley." *Chief Joseph Herald,* May 29, 1958.

Fort Rock Valley Historical Society. *Portraits: Fort Rock Valley Homestead Years.* Ed. Helen Parks. Bend: Maverick Publications, 1990.

Franchere, Hoyt C. *The Overland Diary of Wilson Price Hunt 1811.* Portland: The Oregon Book Society, 1973.

Frees, Jane A. *Dear Dad, Love, Jane.* Portland: Binfords & Mort, 1980.

French, Giles. *These Things We Note.* Portland: Binfords & Mort, 1966.

Fretwell-Johnson, Hazel R. *In Times Past: A History of the Lower Jordan Creek Communities.* Filer, ID: The Print Shoppe, 1990.

Gildemeister, Jerry, ed. *A Letter Home: Lucia William's Letter.* Union: Bear Wallow Press, 1987.

Gilliss, Julia. *So Far from Home: An Army Bride on the Western Frontier 1865-1869.* Ed. Priscilla Knuth. Portland: Oregon Historical Society Press, 1993.

Good, Rachel Applegate. *History of Klamath County, Oregon: Its Resources and People.* Ed. Linsy Sisemore. Klamath Falls: 1941.

Gray, William H. *William H. Gray: Journal of His Journey East, 1836-1837.* Ed. Donald R. Johnson. Fairfield, WA: Ye Galleon Press, 1980.

Hanley, Mike. *Tales of the I.O.N. Country.* Jordan Valley: Mike Hanley IV, 1988.

Hawley, Brooks. *Gold Dredging in the Sumpter Valley.* Baker: Baker Printing and Lithography, 1977.

Hazeltine, George Irving. *Whiskey Gulch: The Letters of George Irving Hazeltine Written from the Goldmines, 1862-1863.* Ed. Helen B. Rand. Baker: The Record-Courier Printers, 1981.

Hopkins, Sarah Winnemucca. *Life among the Piutes: Their Wrongs and Claims.* Ed. Mrs. Horace Mann. Boston, MA: Cupples, Upham, 1883.

Jackson, William E. *William Emsley Jackson's Diary of a Cattle Drive from La Grande, Oregon, to Cheyenne, Wyoming, in 1876.* Ed. J. Orin Oliphant. Fairfield, WA: Ye Galleon Press, 1983.

Johnson, Don. *The Journals of Captain Nathaniel J. Wyeth Expeditions to the Oregon Country 1831-1836.* Fairfield, WA: Ye Galleon Press, 1984.

Jordan, Michael Ignatius. "The Diary of Michael Ignatius Jordan, Jan. 1, 1863 to May 30, 1863." Ed. Jerry E. Stanke. *The Owyhee Outpost* 5 (1974): 1-30.

Keyes, (John) Robert. "Robert Keyes' Youthful Diary." *Deschutes Pioneers' Gazette* (1990-91) 47: 6-8; 48: 7.

Lees, William. Letter to Jennie F. Lyford. Malheur *County Review* 8, No. 10, 1987.

Lorenz, Claudia Spink. "Letter to the Editor. Klamath County: False Armistice Day, Nov. 9, 1918." *Oregon Historical Society Quarterly* 71, No. 3 (September 1970): 274-276 .

McComas, E.S. *A Journal of Travel.* Beaverton: Champoeg Press, 1954.

McGuire, Essie. "The Potato Show Letter." *Redmond: Where the Desert Blooms.* Ed. Keith Clark. Portland: Western Imprints of the Oregon Historical Society, 1985.

McKinley, Mary. *See* Helen Guyton Rees.

Metschan, Phil, Jr. "Little Boy's Letter, 1888, Canyon City." *Blue Mountain Eagle* Sept. 18, 1942: 5. Oliver Museum, Canyon City.

Miller, Henry. "Letters from the Upper Columbia." *Idaho Yesterdays* 4 (Winter 60-61).

Miller, Loye. "Journal of First Trip of University of California to John Day Beds of Eastern Oregon." Ed. J. Arnold Shotwell. *Bulletin* 19, Museum of Natural History, University of Oregon, 1972.

Oliphant, J. Orin. *On the Cattle Ranges of the Oregon Country.* Seattle: University of Washington Press, 1968.

O'Neil, Bill. *Cattlemen vs. Sheepherders: Five Decades of Violence in the West.* Austin, TX: Eakin Press, 1989.

Pratt, Alice Day. *A Homesteader's Portfolio.* New York: Macmillan, 1922. Repr. Corvallis: Oregon State University Press, 1993.

Rees, Helen Guyton. *Shaniko People.* Portland: Binfords & Mort, 1983.

Rich, E.E., ed. *Peter Skene Ogden's Snake Country Journals.* London: The Hudson's Bay Record Society, 1950.

Seufert, Francis. *Wheels of Fortune.* Portland: Oregon Historical Society Press, 1980.

Shirk, David. *The Cattle Drives of David Shirk.* Portland: Champoeg Press, 1956.

Smith, Elizabeth Dixon. *See* Kenneth L. Holmes in Section I.

Stearns, Orson A. Letters in "Pioneer Klamath Homesteader." *Klamath Echoes* 15, 1977: 1-7.

Stephens, Louise G. *Letters from an Oregon Ranch by "Katherine."* Chicago: A.C. McClurg & Co., 1905.

Sutton, James McCall. "Letters to Ashland Tidings, August 10, 1876." *Klamath Echoes* 1, 1964: 42-43.

Treadwell, Edward F. *The Cattle King: A Dramatized Biography of Henry Miller, Founder of Miller & Lux Cattle Empire.* Santa Cruz: Western Tanager, 1981.

Urizar, Felix. "Letter to Editor." Burns, OR *Burns Time Herald* 17 Nov. 1937: 4, col. 1 and 2.

Wasson, Caroline. *In the Wallowas.* New York: Exposition Press, 1954.

Watson, Wm. J. *Journal of an Overland Journey to Oregon Made in the Year 1849.* Fairfield, WA: Ye Galleon Press, 1985.

Whitman, Narcissa Prentis. *The Letters of Narcissa Whitman.* Fairfield, WA: Ye Galleon Press, 1986.

Wolverton, Beverly A. *A Hundred and Sixty Acres in the Sage: Homestead History of the Immediate Post Area.* Post: B.A. Wolverton, 1984.

Wood, Charles Erskine Scott. "Private Journal, 1878 and 1879." *OHQ* 70, No.1 (March 1969): 5-38 and No. 2 (June 1969): 139-170.

Wood, Erskine. "Days with Chief Joseph." *OHQ* 51, No. 2 (June 1950).

Wyeth, Nathaniel Jarvis. *The Correspondence and Journals of Captain Nathaniel J. Wyeth, 1831-6: A Record of Two Expeditions for the Occupation of the Oregon Country . . .* Ed. Frederick George Young. Eugene: University Press, 1899.

Zieter, Patrick. "Owyhee County and the Basques." *Owyhee Outpost* 21.

Zumfe, Frank, and Vlasta Petrik. "Settling of Southern Klamath County by the Czech Colonization Club." *The Journal of the Shaw Historical Library* 1 (Fall 1986): 33-45.

VI. Eastside: Unpublished Sources

Abrahms, Mrs. S.L. Diary. MS, 1868-1908. MSS# 2817. OHS/MS.

Anonymous Blacksmith. "A Journal, 1865-69." MS. Oliver Museum, Canyon City.

Anonymous Chinese Miner. Letter to His Wife (unfinished), 1904(?). Kam Wah Chung Archive, OHS/MS.

Anonymous Tong Yick Chuen Co. Employee. Letter to Long On, May 18, 1904. Trans. Jodi Varon and Ying-Ju Chen. Kam Wah Chung Collection, OHS/MS.

Applegate, Lindsay. Letters. MS, 1863-1897. AX 4, KL/UO.

Applegate, Moray. Letters to Herb. C. Thompson, 1924-1956. MS. A 5, KL/UO.

Bancroft-Trevett Families. Correspondence and Diaries. MS, 1835-1918. MSS# 854. OHS/MS.

Bautelle, Frazier Augustus. Letters to and from His Wife, 1870-1888. MS. AX 12, KL/UO.

Brown, Joseph H. Diary of a Trip over Minto Pass in 1875. MS. HHB [P-A 9], BL.

Bush, E.R. Letter. MS, 1953, Ag 24. Files of Crater Lake National Park. Steve Marks, Park Historian.

Cayuse, Yakima, and Rogue River Wars. Letters. MS, 1847-1858. BX 47, KL/UO.

Chi-Kwang, Lao. Letter to Ing Hay, June 6, 1905. Trans. Jodi Varon and Ying-Ju Chen. Kam Wah Chung Archive, OHS/MS.

Congleton, Charles S. Diary. MS, 1907-1927. MSS# 2706. OHS/MS.

Condon, Thomas. Diary 1852. Voyage to Oregon. MS. Museum of Natural History, University of Oregon, Eugene.

Condon, Thomas. Letters. MS, 1870-1900. A 22, KL/UO.

Cornelius, Thomas R. Letters to Mrs. Cornelius 1855 and 1856. KL/UO.

Darling, Linus W. Diary. MS, 1883-1890. MSS# 129. OHS/MS.

Davis, Gilbert F. Diary. MS, 1873. MSS# 868. OHS/MS.

Drake, Lee D. Letters. MS, 1922-1934. AX 27, KL/UO.

Ducey, Brant E. "John Watermelon Redington—Hell on Hogthieves and Hypocrites." MA Thesis, 1963, School of Jour., University of Oregon, Eugene.

Edgington, Ellen Crawford. Letter. MS, Copy to Author. Courtesy of Georgia Gallagher, Sisters.

Garatea, Paquita Lucia. "*Burns Eko Etxekoandreak*: Basque Women Boarding Housekeepers of Burns, OR." MA Thesis, 1990, Dept. of History, PSU.

Goltra, Elizabeth J. Journal of Travels across the Plains to Oregon, April 29 to September 29, 1853. MS. A 34, KL/UO.

Griffin, B.W. "Letter from the Past: Granite Creek, 1862." T.S. Leah Menefree to Pearl Jones, 1982. Baker County Library, Baker City.

Haines, Ida Marie. Diary. MS, 1889-1891. MSS# 1509. OHS/MS.

Hanna, Esther Belle. Overland Diary 1852. T.S. [P-A 313], BL.

Hawley, Brooks. Annual Letters to Masonic Lodge Brothers. Copies to Author, 1991. Courtesy of Brooks Hawley, Sumpter.

Higginson, Ella. Letter to Kate Hanley. MS. CB EA 85, KL/UO.

Holstrom, Haldane. Diaries. MS, 1936-1939. A 492, KL/UO.

Howard, Charles. "Diary of a Trip from Clackamas County to Goldfields of Eastern Oregon. April to September 1862." MS. A 54 (Stor.)

Indian Wars Miscellany. Letters. See MS Catalogue, KL/UO.

Jackson, Charles S. Letters of Charles S. Jackson to Fred Lockley, 1902-1906. MS. A 62, KL/UO.

Kelly, James Kerr. Assorted Papers. MS, 1855-1856. MSS# 1514. OHS/MS.

Kam Wah Chung. Correspondence 1892. Anon: T.S. Courtesy of Carolyn Micnhimer, Kam Wah Chung Museum, John Day.

Kwang-Chi. Letter to Lung On from His Cousin and Others, February 4, (18??). Trans. Jodi Varon and Ying-Ju Chen. Kam Wah Chung Archive, OHS/MS.

Longoria, Nora. Diary. MS Copy to Author. Courtesy of the Longoria Family, Nyssa.

McComas, Evans S. Diary. MS, 1862-1867. AX 181, KL/UO.

McCrary, Grace. Diary. MS Copy. Courtesy of Shirley Goodwin, Baker City.

Meacham, Walter E. Letters Relating to American Pioneer Trails Association and with Oregon Pioneers. MS. AX 65, KL/UO.

Meldrum, John Williams. Journals. MS, 1889-1911. MSS# 1293. OHS/MS.

Menefee, Leah C. Papers. MS, 1940-1976. 118, Lane Co. Hist. Society, Eugene.

Miller, Henry. Letters to Henry N. Fulgham. MS, 1891-1894. A 80, KL/UO.

Moore, Jonathan Limerick. Overland Diary, Mar. 3 to Sept. 6, 1852. MS. A 153, KL/UO.

Mote, Daniel. Diaries. MS. Courtesy of Lucille Briggs, Enterprise.

Munro, Sarah Baker. "Basque Folklore in Southeastern Oregon." Master's Thesis, 1972, Folklore Program, University of California, Berkeley.

Oliver, Herman. "Cattleman's Viewpoint on Conservation." T.S. 1967. Courtesy of Mildred Jones, Ontario.

Page, Margaret. "My Diary, 1897." Typescript MS. Oliver Museum, Canyon City.

Palmer, Almira E. States. "Honeymoon Trip across the Plains to Oregon in 1866: A Diary." T.S. Baker County Library, Baker City.

Piper, Alexander. Diary. MS, Jul.-Oct 1860. MSS# 2332B. OHS/MS.

Redington, John W. Letters, 1880-1935. AX 93, KL/UO. *See also* Brant E. Ducey.

Robbins, Kate L. Letters of Kate and Eunice Robbins to Family Members. MS, 1869-1886. AX 105, KL/UO.

Roberts, Albert S. Diary. MS, 1885-1933. MSS# 1828. OHS/MS.

Scharff, John. Letter to Kenneth Porter. MS 1970. Historical Files, Misc. Correspondence, Malheur National Wildlife Refuge, Headquarters, Burns.

Shirk, David Lawson. Diary. MS and T.S. 1873. A 116, KL/UO.

Springer, Viola. Diary, Harney Valley, 1885. T.S. A 116, KL/UO.

Steinhoff, Anna. Diary. MS. Courtesy of Richard Anderson, Portland.

Stevens, Millie. "A Record of My Trip to Eastern Oregon in October 1904." T.S. Deschutes County Historical Society, Bend.

Stewart, Agnes. "A Pioneer Girl's Diary 1853." T.S. by Kenneth Holmes, 11/85. Baker County Library, Baker City.

Stewart, Helen Love. "Diary 1853." T.S. Baker County Library, Baker City.

Stirewalt, Dave. Letter. MS. Courtesy of Nellie Zook, Sisters, and Dave Stirewalt, Spray.

Stratton, Vivian. "Letters of a Forest Service Wife." T.S. Courtesy of Vivian Stratton, Fort Rock.

Thomas, Jack Ward. Diary. MS Copy to Author. Courtesy of Jack Ward Thomas, Washington, D.C.

Tippett, Jane Bachman. "Brown Paperbag Notes, 1975." T.S. to Author. Courtesy of Jane Bachman Tippett, Joseph.

Trenkel Family Papers. Letters. MS Copies. Courtesy of Mr. and Mrs. Harold Trenkel, Ontario.

Tubbs, R. U.S.F.S. Daily Diary, Mule Peak Lookout, 1980. Photocopy, Union County Museum, Union.

Vincent, Dr. L.H. Diary. Courtesy of Helen Gillard, Palo Alto, CA. MS Housed in Deschutes County Library, Sisters.

Wasson, Caroline. Child's Diary, Wallowa Co., 1895. MS Copied. Courtesy of Its Owner, Mrs. Ray Hughes, Joseph.

Watson, Cornelia Bernard Knox. Diary. MS Copy & T.S. 1899-1900. Schmink House Museum, Lakeview.

Wen-teh, Ing. Letter to Ing Pang-chi, June 16, 1897. Trans. Jodi Varon and Ying-Ju Chen. Kam Wah Chung Archive, OHS/MS.

Wilson, Julia. May Be Letter. MS. 2nd Card, Carroll Family Records, Bowman Museum, Crook County Historical Society, Prineville.

Zook, Nellie. "Cattle Drive Diary, 1981." T.S. by Author. Sisters.

Copyright Acknowledgments

TEXTS

Anonymous miner. Letter from the Kam Wah Chung Collection, letters translated by Dr. Chia-Lin Chen, held in the Manuscript Department, Oregon Historical Society. Reproduced courtesy of the Oregon Historical Society.

Anonymous soldier. Letter from *An Arrow in the Earth* by Terence O'Donnell. Portland: Oregon Historical Society Press, 1991. Reproduced courtesy of the Oregon Historical Society Press.

Applegate, Gertrude and Harriette. Letters courtesy of Shannon Applegate.

Bensell, Royal. Diary excerpt courtesy of the Department of Special Collections, Knight Library, University of Oregon.

Brenne, Fred. Letter courtesy of the Department of Special Collections, Knight Library, University of Oregon.

Burnett, Peter. Letters from *The Quarterly of the Oregon Historical Society*, 24, No. 1 (March 1923): 105-108. Reproduced courtesy of the Oregon Historical Society.

Bush, Dr. E.R. Letter courtesy of Crater Lake National Park.

Casteel, John. Diary excerpts from Betty Lawson Walters, "The Lean Years: John L. Casteel's Diaries, 1931-1942," *Oregon Historical Quarterly*, 89, No. 3 (Fall 1988): 229-302. Reproduced courtesy of the Oregon Historical Society.

Chinook, Billy. Letter from *An Arrow in the Earth* by Terence O'Donnell. Portland: Oregon Historical Society Press, 1991. Reproduced courtesy of the Oregon Historical Society Press.

Colver, Rachel. Letter courtesy of Baker County Library. From Sisley family file, Special Collections.

Colvig, Vance DeBar. Letter courtesy of the Southern Oregon Historical Society.

Cummins, Henry. Diary excerpt courtesy of Yale Collection of Western Americana, Beinecke Rare Book and Manuscript Library.

Deady, Matthew P. Diary excerpt from *Pharisee Among Philistines: The Diary of Judge Matthew P. Deady 1871-1892*. 2 vols. Ed. Malcolm Clark, Jr. Portland: Oregon Historical Society Press, 1975. Reproduced courtesy of the Oregon Historical Society Press.

Donaldson, Amanda Smith. Letter courtesy of the Tillamook County Pioneer Museum.

Duniway, Abigail Scott. Letter courtesy of the Department of Special Collections, Knight Library, University of Oregon.

Fairchild, Cindy Donnelly. Diary excerpt courtesy of Cindy Donnelly Fairchild.

Findley, Sara Jane. Letter courtesy of Diane Bradshaw.

French, Giles. Letters from *Dear Dad, Love, Jane*. Portland: Binfords & Mort, 1980. Reproduced courtesy of Jane Frees and Patricia Moore.

Gillette, Preston W. Diary excerpt courtesy of the Clatsop County Historical Society, CCHS Archives 86.56.

Gilliss, Julia. Letters from *So Far From Home: An Army Bride on the Western Frontier 1865-1869*. Ed. Priscilla Knuth. Portland: Oregon Historical Society Press, 1993. Reproduced courtesy of the Oregon Historical Society Press.

Iwatsuki, Shizue. Letter from *Issei: A History of Japanese Immigrants in North America*. Trans. Shinichiro Nakamura and Jean S. Gerard. Seattle: Japanese Community Service, 1973.

Haswell, Robert. Diary excerpt from "Haswell's Log of a Voyage Round the World on the Ship *Columbia Rediviva* and the Sloop *Washington*." Intro. and notes by T.G. Elliott. *Oregon Historical Quarterly* 29, No. 2 (June 1928): 162-188. Reproduced courtesy of the Oregon Historical Society.

Hawley, Brooks. Letters courtesy of Brooks Hawley.

Haycox, Ernest. Letter courtesy of the Department of Special Collections, Knight Library, University of Oregon.

Hazeltine, George Irving. Letter from "Whiskey Gulch," copyright © 1981, Helen Rand. Reproduced courtesy of Helen Rand.

Higginson, Ella. Letter courtesy of the Department of Special Collections, Knight Library, University of Oregon.

Hofer, Florence. Diary excerpt courtesy of the Lincoln County Historical Society.

Hopkins, Sarah Winnemucca. Letter from *Life Among the Piutes: Their Wrongs and Claims* by Sarah Winnemucca Hopkins. Reproduced courtesy of Chalfant Press.

Horning, Cynthia. Letters courtesy of Schminck Memorial Museum.

Hull, Robert. Letter from *An Arrow in the Earth* by Terence O'Donnell. Portland: Oregon Historical Society Press, 1991. Reproduced courtesy of the Oregon Historical Society Press.

Humphrey, Ellen Hemenway. Diary excerpt from *Diary of Ellen Hemenway Humphrey*. Ed. Edwin A. Simpson. Saratoga, CA: Edwin A. Simpson, 1973. Reproduced courtesy of John Simpson.

Judson, Nancy. Letter from *Echoes of Oregon 1837-1859*. Salem: Oregon State Archives, 1987. Reproduced courtesy of Oregon State Archives.

Kambouris, Haralambos. Diary excerpt courtesy of the Special Collections Department, University of Utah Library.

Keyes, John Robert. Letter courtesy of Deschutes Pioneers Association.

Kwang-chi. Letter from the Kam Wah Chung Collection, letters translated by Dr. Chia-Lin Chen, held in the Manuscript Department, Oregon Historical Society. Reproduced courtesy of the Oregon Historical Society.

Lao Chi-Kwang. Letter from the Kam Wah Chung Collection, letters translated by Dr. Chia-Lin Chen, held in the Manuscript Department, Oregon Historical Society. Reproduced courtesy of the Oregon Historical Society.

Lees, William. Letter from *Malheur Country Review* 8, No. 10, 1987. Reproduced courtesy of *Malheur Country Review*.

Lewis, Charles C. Letter courtesy of the Department of Special Collections, Knight Library, University of Oregon.

Longoria, Nora. Diary excerpts courtesy of the Longoria family.

Lorenz, Claudia Spink. Letter courtesy of the Oregon Historical Society Press.

McArthur, Polly Hewitt. Letter from *Letters to a Doll* by Polly Hewitt McArthur. Portland: By the author, 1928. Used by permission.

McCrary, Grace. Diary excerpt courtesy of Grace Elizabeth Goodwin Sullivan.

McGuire, Essie. Letter courtesy of Descutes Pioneers Association.

McKinley, Mary. Diary excerpt from *Shaniko People*. Ed. Helen Guyton Rees. Portland: Binfords & Mort, 1982. Reproduced courtesy Helen Guyton Rees.

McNary, Charles. Letter courtesy of the Department of Special Collections, Knight Library, University of Oregon.

Marshall, Charles. Diary excerpt courtesy of the Department of Special Collections, Knight Library, University of Oregon.

Matthews, Rufus B. and Grace Smith. Letters courtesy of the Douglas County Museum of History and Natural History.

Miller, Henry K. Letter from *Idaho Yesterdays* 4 (Winter 60-61). Reproduced courtesy of the Idaho State Historical Society.

Miller, Loye. Diary excerpt from "Journal of First Trip of University of California to John Day Beds," University of Oregon Museum of Natural History *Bulletin* 19, 1972. Used by permission.

Mote, Daniel. Diary excerpt courtesy of Lucille Briggs.

Murphy, Sr. Miriam. Diary excerpts courtesy of an anonymous donor.

Nunn, William. Letter courtesy of Terence O'Donnell.

Palmer, Joel. Letter from *An Arrow in the Earth* by Terence O'Donnell. Portland: Oregon Historical Society Press, 1991. Reproduced courtesy of the Oregon Historical Society Press.

Pauling, Linus Carl. Diary excerpt from Ava and Linus Pauling Papers, Box 137, Folder 1, Kerr Library Special Collections, Oregon State University.

Reber, Kenneth. Letters courtesy of the Reber family.

Robbins, Eunice. Letter courtesy of the Department of Special Collections, Knight Library, University of Oregon.

Robbins, Kate. Letter courtesy of the Department of Special Collections, Knight Library, University of Oregon.

Scharff, John. Letter courtesy of Mr. and Mrs. John Scharff.

Skinner, Eugene. Letter courtesy of the Lane County Historical Society.

Smith, Elizabeth. Diary excerpt from *Covered Wagon Women: Diaries and Letters from the Western Trails 1840-1890*, edited by Kenneth L. Holmes. Glendale, CA: The Arthur Clark Co., 1983. Reproduced courtesy of Kenneth L. Holmes.

Stearns, Orson A. Letter courtesy of Klamath County Historical Society.

Steinhoff, Anna. Diary excerpt courtesy of Richard E. Anderson.

Stirewalt, Dave. Letter courtesy of Nellie Lines Zook and Dave Stirewalt.

Stone, Rev. Lee Owen. Letter courtesy of the Oregon Historical Society. From Lee Owen Stone papers, Oregon Historical Society, Mss. 2423.

Sullivan, William L. Diary excerpt from *Listening for Coyote: A Walk Across Oregon's Wilderness* by William L. Sullivan, © 1988 by William L. Sullivan, by permission of William Morrow and Company, Inc.

Thomas, Jack Ward. Diary excerpts courtesy of Jack Ward Thomas.

Tippett, Jane Bachman. Letter courtesy of Jane Bachman Tippett.

Tittinger, A.J. Letter courtesy of Columbia River Maritime Museum, Tinkham Collection (1978.40).

Tong Yick Chuen Co. Letter from the Kam Wah Chung Collection, letters translated by Dr. Chia-Lin Chen, held in the Manuscript Department, Oregon Historical Society. Reproduced courtesy of the Oregon Historical Society.

Trevett, Emily. Diary excerpt courtesy of the Oregon Historical Society. Bancroft-Trevett families, papers. Oregon Historical Society, Mss. 854.

Trimberger, Elizabeth. Diary excerpt courtesy of Rosemary Spires.

Urizar, Felix. Letter from Burns *Times Herald*, 17 November, 1934.

Vincent, Dr. L.H. Diary excerpt courtesy of Helen Gillard.

Waldo, Judge John. Letter from Jeff La Lande, "A Wilderness Journey with Judge John B. Waldo, Oregon's First Preservationist." *Oregon Historical Quarterly* 90, No. 2 (Summer 1989): 116-166. Reproduced courtesy of the Oregon Historical Society.

Watson, Cornelia Bernard Knox. Diary excerpt courtesy of Schminck Memorial Museum, Lakeview.

West, Calvin B. Letter courtesy of the Department of Special Collections, Knight Library, University of Oregon.

Whiteley, Opal. Diary excerpt from *The Story of Opal: The Story of an Understanding Heart*. New York: Atlantic Monthly Press, 1920.

Wilson, Adrian. Letters from *Two Against the Tide: A Conscientious Objector in WWII*. Ed. Joyce Lancaster Wilson. Austin, TX: W. Thomas Taylor, 1990. Reproduced courtesy of Joyce Lancaster Wilson.

Wilson, Julia. Letter courtesy of the Crook County Historical Society.

Wood, Charles Erskine Scott. Diary excerpt courtesy of the Oregon Historical Society Press.

Wood, Elizabeth. From "Journal of a Trip to Oregon 1851," *The Quarterly of the Oregon Historical Society*, 27, No. 1 (March 1926): 192-203. Reproduced courtesy of the Oregon Historical Society.

Word Talmadge. Letter from *The Quarterly of the Oregon Historical Society*, 3, No. 4 (December 1902): 394-398 and 4, No. 1 (March 1903): 80-85. Reproduced courtesy of the Oregon Historical Society.

ART

Cover of paperback edition: Detail of Quilt, ca. 1876. More information on page xvi. Courtesy of Benton County Historical Society and Museum. Photograph by Oscar Palmquist.

"Bone carvings of Cascade Indians," (detail) photographer Edward Curtis, 1910, on page 4. Courtesy of the Oregon Historical Society, negative no. Or Hi 67528.

"Yamhill Bunk House" by Constance Fowler on page 18. Woodcut, ca. 1940. Courtesy of the artist.

"Crossing the Umpqua Mountains, Oregon, 1841" by Henry Eld on page 36. From the Stephen Dow Beckham Collection. Courtesy of Stephen Dow Beckham.

"Funeral Portrait of Harry Schille Whitehouse," only child of B.G. and Clara Whitehouse (born 10/22/1863; died 10/31/1864), photographer unknown, on page 59. Courtesy of the Oregon Historical Society, negative no. 017589.

"Farmer" by Lloyd Reynolds on page 77. Wood engraving. Courtesy of the Portland Art Museum, Vivian and Gordon Gilkey Collection (G8345).

"Morning Light" by Carl Hall on page 85. Lithograph, 1949. Courtesy of the Portland Art Museum, Vivian and Gordon Gilkey Collection (81.81.146).

"Alley, John Day" by Charles Heaney on page 122. Graphite pencil, gift from Mony Dimitre. Courtesy of the Portland Art Museum, Vivian and Gordon Gilkey Collection (85.87.1).

"SP & S Railroad Radio Lounge Car" (detail) , 1932, photographer unknown, on page 137. Courtesy of the Oregon Historical Society, negative no. Or Hi 73454.

"#6923:470" by Lloyd Reynolds on page 154. Wood engraving. Courtesy of the Portland Art Museum, Vivian and Gordon Gilkey Collection (G8315).

"Snakes Descending the Stairs" by Gordon Gilkey on page 195. Ink-wash. Courtesy of the Portland Art Museum, Vivian and Gordon Gilkey Collection.

"High Desert Valley" by Melville T. Wire on page 228. Etching. Courtesy of the Portland Art Museum, Vivian and Gordon Gilkey Collection (79.50.564).

"Buckaroo Saddle" on page 240 courtesy of The High Desert Museum. Typical buckaroo saddle as ridden in the high desert in the early twentieth century, made by the George Lawrence Co., Portland.

"Plowing" by C.S. Price on page 269. Etching, gift of Anselm Boskowitz. Courtesy of the Portland Art Museum, Vivian and Gordon Gilkey Collection (74.13.8).

"Eastern Oregon" by William Givler on page 284. Lithograph. Courtesy of the Portland Art Museum, Vivian and Gordon Gilkey Collection.

"Pines at the Deschutes River" by Gregory Pfarr on page 299. Lithograph, 1988. Courtesy of the Portland Art Museum, Vivian and Gordon Gilkey Collection (G8803).

AUTHOR PHOTOGRAPHS

The Oregon Council of Teachers of English and the Oregon State University Press would like to thank the following for providing photographs of authors and for permission to reproduce them: Calvin B. West, photo from *Calvin B. West: An Obscure Chapter in the History of Southern Oregon*, California History Foundation; Henry Cummins and Eugene Skinner courtesy of the Lane County Pioneer Museum; Gertrude Applegate, Jesse Applegate (a sketch done by George "Buck" Applegate), and Rufus B. Matthews courtesy of the Douglas County Museum of History and Natural History; Royal Bensell, (no date, Print Collection #A6299) and Charles L. Marshall (May 1913, Charles L. Marshall Collection, PH12) courtesy of Special Collections, University of Oregon Library; Ellen Hemenway Humphrey courtesy of John Simpson; O.C. Applegate courtesy of the Applegate family collection; the opening pages of Haralambos Kambouris's diary courtesy of University of Utah Special Collections; Elizabeth Trimberger courtesy of Rosemary Spackman Spires; Linus Carl Pauling courtesy of OSU Library Special Collections; Vance DeBar Colvig courtesy of the Southern Oregon Historical Society and Capitol Records (negative 11662); Shizue Iwatsuki, photo from *Issei: A History of Japanese Immigrants in North America*, Japanese Community Service, Seattle; Kenneth Reber courtesy of the Reber family; Sr. Miriam Murphy courtesy of the *Catholic Sentinel*, Portland; William Sullivan, photo by J. Wesley Sullivan, courtesy of the author; Orson A. Stearns courtesy of the Klamath County Historical Society; Sara Jane Findley courtesy of Diane Bradshaw; Sarah Winnemucca Hopkins courtesy of the Smithsonian Institution; Henry K. Miller courtesy of Western Tanager Press; Loye Miller courtesy of the University of Oregon Museum of Natural History; Cornelia Knox Watson and photograph by Watson courtesy of Schminck Memorial Museum; Daniel Mote courtesy of Wallowa County Museum; Dave Stirewalt courtesy of Nellie Lines Zook and Dave Stirewalt; Earl Russell Bush and the Lady of the Woods courtesy of U.S. National Parks Service, Crater Lake; Brooks Hawley courtesy of Shannon Applegate; Nora Longoria courtesy of the Longoria family; Jane Bachman Tippett and Jack Ward Thomas courtesy of the subject.

The following photographs of authors were provided courtesy of the Oregon Historical Society: Robert Haswell, negative OrHi 90667; William Clark, negative Or Hi 13082; David Douglas, negative Or Hi 19683; Peter Burnett, negative CN 021773; Preston W. Gillete, negative Or Hi 364; Matthew P. Deady, negative CN 002391; Polly Hewitt McArthur, negative Or Hi 89164; Emily Trevett Nunn, negative Or Hi 83715; Florence Hofer, negative 0086G004; Abigail Scott Duniway, negative Or Hi 37312; Charles McNary, negative Or Hi 4754; John Casteel, negative Or Hi 82643; Ernest Haycox, negative CN022203; Lee Owen Stone, negative Or Hi 66547; William Nunn, negative Or Hi 90668; Joel Palmer, negative Or Hi 362; George Irving Hazeltine, negative Or Hi 90666; Julia Gilliss; C.E.S. Wood, negative Or Hi 56266; Judge John Waldo, negative Or Hi 64412; Ing Hay, negative OrHi26468; Lung On, negative 53840-a; Claudia Spink Lorenz, negative 0045G058; Ella Higginson; Giles French, negative Or Hi 90586.

INDEX